The
Encyclopedia
of Crystals

The
Encyclopedia
of Crystals

Judy Hall

FAIR WINDS

PRESS

BEVERLY, MASSACHUSETTS

First published in Great Britain in 2006 by
Hamlyn, a division of Octopus Publishing Group Ltd
2–4 Heron Quays, London E14 4JP

Text © Octopus Publishing Group Ltd 2006

First published in the USA in 2006 by
Fair Winds Press, a member of
Quayside Publishing Group
100 Cummings Center, Suite 406L
Beverly, MA 01915

10 09   5

ISBN-10: 1-59233-266-8
ISBN-13: 978-1-59233-266-3

A Cataloging-in-Publication Data record for this book
is available from the British Library

Printed and bound in China

Disclaimer
The information given in this book is not intended to
act as a substitute for medical treatment, nor can it be
used for diagnosis. Crystals are powerful and are open
to misunderstanding or abuse. If you are in any doubt
about their use, a qualified practitioner should be
consulted, especially in the crystal-healing field.

Every care has been taken to validate and standardize
chemical formulas but sources disagree as to precise
formulations and crystal names and mineral content.

Contents

Crystal index

Introduction

Crystals are found all over in the world in a rainbow of colors and myriad forms. Many are stunning, but others could easily be overlooked unless you know their true worth. This book will introduce you to their deepest secrets and their mystical powers.

Crystal potency has been recognized for years, and crystals have the ability to adorn, to heal, to divine, to protect, to manifest, and to transmute and transform energy.

The history of crystals

Crystals have been revered for thousands of years for their decorative, healing, and protective properties. Amber beads have been found in graves over 8,000 years old and a calcite mirror was created over 30,000 years ago. One of the earliest written accounts of the use of crystals is in the Bible.

The breastplate of the High Priest

The breastplate of the High Priest is described in Exodus. The Hebrew word for breastplate actually means "pouch," so Aaron would have been wearing a linen bag around his neck and chest, with 12 crystals that represented the 12 tribes of Israel, and two special holy objects, the Urim and Thummin, which some scholars believe to have been meteorites and which, according to the biblical account, were designed by God to be used as an "oracle" to ascertain his will and divine the course the future would take.

Translation problems make it difficult to know exactly which crystals were used, but they included sardius, probably Sardonyx, a stone of authority, strength, and protection; Topaz, one of the ancient stones of abundance; Turquoise, another protective stone that enhances spiritual attunement; and Amethyst, still used today by bishops in the church to show their spiritual authority. The stones were, according to God's instructions, to be set in gold and inscribed with the names of the tribes to show they were under divine protection. In other words, they were creating amulets, something that was extremely popular in Egypt.

Crystals and the Pharaohs

The use of crystals in Egypt goes back to at least 4500 BCE and may also have influenced the Israelites who, at the time of the Exodus, had recently left Egypt to wander in the desert. Crystals in Egypt were valued for decorative, medical, and spiritual purposes.

Tutankhamun's funerary mask has a Lapis Lazuli band around his Snow Quartz and Obsidian eyes. Lapis was one of the most sacred and spiritual stones. An ancient Egyptian text states that "Lapis is the god, Amun, and the god is Lapis." Its function is to open spiritual sight, a useful attribute on the journey to the Otherworld, which Obsidian would facilitate. In the headdress are set Turquoise and Carnelian, both popular for protective amulets. This mask was for more

Tutankhamun's funerary mask is inset with semiprecious stones.

than decoration—it had a magical function to guide and guard the young Pharaoh on his way home to the stars and to ensure a good rebirth.

Crystal traditions

The traditions associated with crystals in Egypt moved into Greece, where Pliny the Elder wrote a treatise on precious stones (based on that of an earlier Greek writer, Theophrastus). These traditions continued to be handed on, along with traditions from countries such as India, to which were added local myths. In Germany, for instance, miners in the Middle Ages called Cobalto-calcite *kobald* because they believed a goblin lived in the stone. Nowadays, Cobalto-calcite is considered a beneficent stone that opens the heart and fills it with love.

Crystals such as Calcite take varied outer form and color.

Traditional wedding anniversary gems and metals

Year	Gem
12th	Agate
13th	Moonstone
14th	Moss Agate
15th	Clear Quartz
16th	Topaz
17th	Amethyst
18th	Garnet
23rd	Sapphire
25th	Silver
26th	Blue Star Sapphire
30th	Pearl
35th	Coral
39th	Cat's Eye
40th	Ruby
45th	Alexandrite
50th	Gold
52nd	Star Ruby
55th	Emerald
60th	Yellow Diamond
65th	Gray Star Sapphire
75th	Diamond

Topaz

Amethyst

Blue Sapphire

Ruby

Crystal chemistry

Crystals are identified by their structure and mineral content. Structure is the basic building block of a crystal, describing the alignment of its inner axes. There are seven crystal systems, based on triangles, squares, rectangles, hexagons, rhomboids, parallelograms, and trapeziums, which are characterized by axis length, angles between axes, and the number of symmetry centers, plus the amorphous noncrystalline form. All crystals are formed from a limited number of minerals that bond differently to create the various types, but it is the internal lattice, rather than the outward form, that determines crystal type and what a crystal is called.

Some crystals take many forms and colors, owing to slight mineral variations (which may vary the formula according to trace elements and where they are found), but will share the same internal structure. Whatever form they take, their crystalline structure can absorb, conserve, focus, and emit energy, especially on the electromagnetic waveband. Knowing the chemistry of a stone means that you know specific attributes. For example, copper-containing crystals are powerful energy conduits that work quickly to heal joint pain and arthritic swelling, lithium-based crystals lift depression, and those with iron can give strength.

The outward shape of a crystal does not necessarily reflect its internal structure.

Crystal formation

Defined as a solid body with a geometrically regular shape, crystals were created as the earth cooled, and continued to metamorphose and reform as the earth underwent eons of geological change. Containing the record of the development of the planet over millions of years, and bearing the indelible imprint of the powerful forces that shaped it, crystals can be regarded as the earth's DNA and, indeed, many native peoples call them the brain cells of Mother Earth.

From a whirling cloud of gas, a dense dust bowl was created that contracted into a white-hot, molten ball. Gradually, over immeasurable time, a thin layer of this molten material, magma, cooled into a crust about as thick as

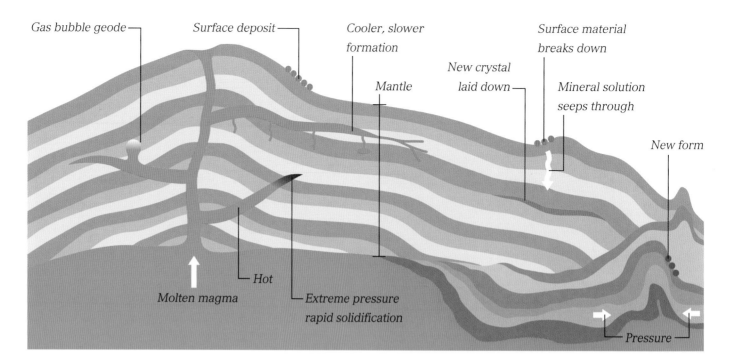

Gas bubble geode — Surface deposit — Cooler, slower formation

Mantle

New crystal laid down —

Surface material breaks down

Mineral solution seeps through

New form

Molten magma — Hot — Extreme pressure rapid solidification

Pressure

the skin on an apple, forming the earth's mantle. Within the crust new crystals continued to form as the hot, mineral-rich, molten magma core boiled and bubbled toward the surface. Carrying a chemical imprint for evolution, some grew in chambers deep underground, some have been subjected to enormous pressure and transformation, others were laid down in layers, some dripped into being. The method of formation affects their appearance, energetic properties, and the way they function.

Igneous and metamorphic crystals

Igneous crystals, such as Quartz, the most common crystal on or under the earth, formed from the fiery gases and minerals in the earth's molten center as, superhot, they rose toward the surface, propelled by irresistible forces from the movement of huge tectonic plates on the earth's surface. Penetrating the mantle, the gases met solid rock, forcing them to cool and solidify. If this process is relatively slow, or if the crystal forms in a gas bubble, large crystals can grow unhindered. If the process is rapid, then the crystals will be small; if the process is exceptionally fast, a glasslike substance, such as Obsidian, is formed rather than crystals. If the process stops and starts, effects such as phantom or self-healed crystals will be seen.

Crystals such as Aventurine or Peridot are created at high temperatures from liquid magma, and others, such as Topaz and Tourmaline, form when gases penetrate into adjoining

rocks. When magma cools sufficiently for water vapor to condense into a liquid, the resulting mineral-rich solution lays down crystals such as Aragonite, which can take several forms and colors.

Metamorphic crystals such as Garnet are formed deep in the earth when, under intense pressure and enormous heat, minerals melt and recrystallize, undergoing a chemical change that reorganizes the original lattice. Calcite and other sedimentary crystals form because of erosion. Rocks at the surface of the crust break down and mineralized water drips through rock, laying down the weathered material as new crystals, or the loose minerals become cemented together into a conglomerate stone. Sedimentary crystals tend to be laid down in layers and are softer in texture. Such crystals are often found still attached to the bedrock on which they formed or as a conglomerate. This bedrock is known as a matrix.

The atom, and its component parts, forms the heart of a crystal. An atom is dynamic—particles rotate around a center that is in constant motion. So, although a crystal may look outwardly serene, it is actually a seething molecular mass vibrating at its own unique frequency. This is what gives a crystal its energy.

Building blocks

Chemical impurities, radiation, earth and solar emissions, and the exact means of their formation, mean that each type of crystal has its own unique signature. Formed out of a variety of minerals, a crystal is defined by its internal structure—an orderly, repeating atomic lattice. Recognizable under a microscope, a large or small version of the same crystal will have exactly the same internal structure as will very different external forms and colors, which at first glance could not possibly be the same crystal. It is this structure, rather than the mineral or minerals out of which it is formed, that is crucial to crystal classification. In some cases the mineral content differs slightly. Several types of crystals may be formed from the same mineral or combination of minerals, but each type will crystallize differently. Some structures, such as Aragonite and Hemimorphite, appear in radically different forms.

Basic crystal shapes and geometric forms

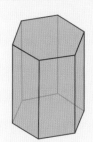

Hexagonal

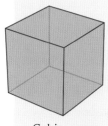

Cubic

Trigonal

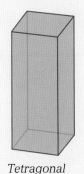

Tetragonal

Crystals are built from one of seven, plus amorphous (without internal structures), possible geometric forms that lock together into a number of potential crystal shapes, which have generic names based on their internal geometry. The outer form of the crystal will not necessarily reflect its inner structure but does affect how energy flows through it.

Hexagonal
Created from hexagons forming a three-dimensional shape, highly energetic hexagonal crystals are particularly useful for energy balancing and for exploring specific issues.

Cubic
Created from squares with their axes at right angles to each other, cubic crystals are extremely stabilizing and grounding. Excellent for structure and reorganization, this is the only crystal form that does not bend light rays as they pass through it.

Trigonal
Created from triangles, trigonal crystals radiate energy and are invigorating and protective, rebalancing the biomagnetic sheath.

Tetragonal
Created from rectangles with long and short axes at right angles to each other, tetragonal crystals absorb and transform energy and are excellent balancers and resolvers.

Orthorhombic
Formed from rhomboids, orthorhombic crystals have unequal axes that encompass energy and are useful cleansers and clearers.

Triclinic
Formed from trapeziums, asymmetric triclinic crystals integrate energy and opposites and assist in exploring other dimensions.

Monoclinic
Formed from parallelograms, monoclinic crystals are useful for purification and perception.

Amorphous
Lacking an inner structure, amorphous crystals allow energy to pass through freely and act rapidly, and may be a catalyst for growth.

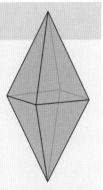

Orthorhombic

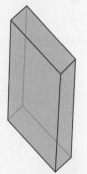

Triclinic

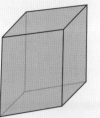

Monoclinic

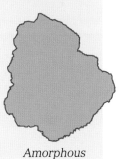

Amorphous

Hardness

Diamond is the hardest crystal.

Hardness is the ability of a crystal to withstand surface scratching and is measured by the Hardness scale invented by Friedrich Mohs in 1822. The scale relates to the strength of the structure in relation to the chemical bonds that cohere it; small, tightly packed atoms with strong bonds make for a hard stone.

The scale progresses from 1, the softest, to 10, the hardest, although the progression is not uniform. Diamond, for instance, the hardest known natural mineral, is a perfect 10 while Sapphire is 9 and Topaz 8, but Sapphire and Topaz are much closer to each other in hardness than Sapphire is to Diamond, which is immensely hard. Gemstones need to be at a minimum of 7 on the scale to withstand constant wear, and soft minerals such as talc are often used as lubricants. Each mineral can scratch itself or something lower in the table, but will not scratch anything higher. Simple equivalents are:

- 2 Marks with a fingernail
- 3 Marks with a copper coin
- 4 Marks easily with a knife blade
- 5 Marks with a knife blade with difficulty
- 6 Marks with a steel file
- 7 Scratches window glass

High-vibration stones

Many of the newly discovered stones carry the generic properties of, say, Amethyst or Quartz, of which they are a

type, but have a very high vibration rate, which means that they are far more effective at subtle energy work than physical work. Selecting the generic crystal will be more effective, therefore, for physical and emotional healing.

To use these stones, your own vibratory rate has to be in harmony. When using them for spiritual or soul work, hold the stone in your hands for a few minutes to align your vibration to the stone.

Vera Cruz Amethyst is a very high-vibration stone that works at a subtle level.

Fluorescence

Many crystals exhibit the fascinating property of fluorescence, sometimes known as "cold light." Fluorescence is the ability to change color under ultraviolet light, or other energetic activation, and to emit electromagnetic radiation that is seen as colored light. Specialized equipment is needed to stimulate the color change, but many mineralogical museums have permanent displays, and hand-held ultraviolet lights are available for viewing specimens in a darkened room or for taking into the field. Old quarries and mine tailings suddenly light up as the abandoned minerals come to life, a truly magical sight.

Fluorescence occurs because the basic building block of the crystal, the atom, has a central nucleus around which electrons travel in a roughly circular orbit, somewhat like the planets circling the sun in our solar system. If the crystal absorbs ultraviolet light, and not all do, then one of the electrons will be excited by the light and will move into a higher energetic state. As it begins to fall back into its normal energetic state it emits the excess energy, which is perceived as light. Fluorescence, therefore, is the result of an energy exchange that, for a short time, changes the vibration of the crystal.

Perhaps not surprisingly, since crystal healing is a result of subtle energetic changes, many of the crystals that fluoresce also make excellent healers. Fluorite and Calcite, which display fluorescent colors ranging through red, green, white, and deep- to violet-blue, are among the most commonly used healing crystals.

Septarian geode fluorescing in ultraviolet light.

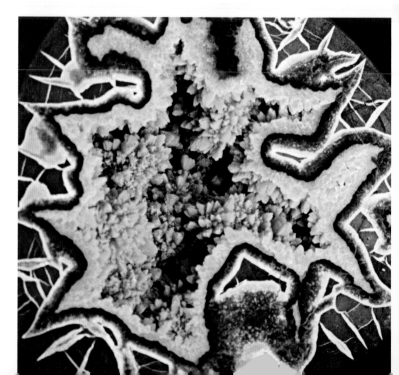

Cleansing, activating, and maintaining your crystals

Wearing a crystal infuses you with its energy.

Dedicate your crystals to the highest good.

Crystals absorb energy, which means that they are very effective at soaking up vibrations—negative and positive—from the air and people around them. When you first buy or are given a crystal, it will carry the energy of everyone who has already handled it and places where it has spent time. So, it needs cleansing, recharging, activating, and dedicating to working for specific needs as soon as possible. Crystals also need cleansing after wearing or healing. Always cleanse jewelry that comes to you from someone else, as it can hold their vibrations and pass them on to you.

Crystal cleansing

Crystals that will not be damaged by water can be held under a tap or immersed in salt water. Friable crystal clusters, those on a matrix, and those that dissolve can be placed in salt or brown rice overnight. If you have a large Quartz cluster or a big Carnelian, these stones will do the cleansing for you but will need cleansing themselves. You can smudge crystals or pass them through the light from a candle or visualize them surrounded by light that purifies and reenergizes them. Placing the crystal in the light of the sun or moon for a few hours recharges its batteries and gets it ready to work. Citrine, Kyanite, and Azeztulite are among the few crystals that never need cleansing.

Activating your crystal

A crystal needs to be activated and programmed to start working. Hold the crystal in your hands. Picture light surrounding it or hold your hands in front of a light source, and then formulate your intention for the stone. Be specific about how you want to use it, because focused intention is part of the process. If you want it to attract love, list exactly what kind of love you are looking for and the timescale. If you are using the crystal for healing, say precisely for which condition and the result you that seek. If you are using your crystal for protection you can be less specific; a generalized "keep my vibrations positive and protect me from anything negative that may harm me" could be suitable. When you have formulated your program, attune to the crystal. Check out that this is exactly the right crystal for the purpose—the crystal will feel lifeless if it is not. When you are totally in tune, say out loud: "I program this crystal for/to ... [state your purpose]." Then wear the crystal, place it on your body as appropriate, put it in a place where you will see it frequently, or keep it in your pocket to remind you. (If you are using it for healing, see pages 18–19.)

Maintaining your crystals

Crystals are delicate and need to be treated with care. Keep colored crystals out of the sun or they will fade. Layered or clustered stones can separate and points may fracture, especially if they have been dyed. Crystals such as Halite and Selenite are water-soluble, and polished surfaces are easily scratched or damaged, although tumbled stones are more durable. When not in use, wrap your crystals in a silk or velvet scarf. This prevents scratching and protects the crystal against absorbing negative emanations.

Healing and energy enhancement

Crystal healing is an excellent way to harness the energy of crystals and is growing in popularity, as is the use of crystals for energy enhancement. All the crystals in this book have healing properties for body, emotions, mind, or spirit, although not all work on every level; many of the newer finds act at a multidimensional cellular and spiritual level, the effect of which filters down to the physical body rather than working directly on it. High-vibration stones only work if your own vibrations are in tune with them, and you may need to work with other stones first. Crystals act differently on every body, so you need to find the most appropriate stone for you—this can easily be accomplished by finger-dowsing (see below).

Healing does not necessarily imply that stones will cure a condition and is the term used for the beneficial effect crystals have. Dealing with subtle disease and emotional imbalances, crystals bring body, mind, emotions, and spirit back into harmony, supporting the organs and process of the body—in other words, providing holistic healing and bringing about increased well-being. Energy enhancement involves the wearing or placing of crystals to support your personal or environmental energy field, keeping it purified and protected—and crystals used in this way need regular cleansing and reenergizing themselves (page 17).

Crystals quickly absorb energy when worn.

Crystals for energy enhancement

Crystals draw off, or block, negative energy and then replace it with positive vibes. You can either place the crystal on your skin over the site of the disease, or blockage, for 15 minutes, or wear it constantly. You can also place in it the environment around you—if you are sensitive to electromagnetic emanations, for instance, you can place a suitable stone on your computer, or put one on your desk to enhance relationships with colleagues, or by your bed to help you sleep, or against a wall to quiet noisy neighbors—Rose Quartz is excellent for this.

Crystals for healing

A crystal can be placed over the site of disease or pain and left in place for 15 minutes once or twice a day, or be worn for long periods of time (unless there is a warning against this in the directory), but remember to cleanse it regularly. The other main system of crystal healing is through the chakras (page 19) with appropriately colored stones or those mentioned in the directory as appropriate to that chakra. The crystal will activate, cleanse, and align the energy center and the organs connected with it, and will connect chakras if appropriate. For past-life healing, place the appropriate crystal on the past-life chakra or the soma chakra and move around the body as required.

To finger-dowse

1. Loop your thumb and finger together as shown above.

2. Slip your other thumb and finger through the loop and close together.

3. Ask your question. Pull steadily. If the loop breaks, the answer to your question is no. If the loop holds, the answer to your question is yes. If you finger-dowse over a crystal, or a photograph of one, it will tell you if it is the right crystal for your purpose.

The chakras

The chakras are energy linkage points between the physical body and the subtle bodies that comprise the biomagnetic sheath around it. Each of these subtle bodies carries imprinted patterns and subtle DNA, and each has its own "blueprint" that energetically affects the physical body and the energy meridians that run through it. If a blockage occurs in the chakra or the subtle body, then the physical body or the emotions go out of balance. To correct a specific condition, an appropriate crystal can be placed on the corresponding chakra.

Chakra balance

Each chakra has a color associated with it, although crystals connected to chakras are not limited to those colors. The simplest way to experience a crystal healing is to place a stone of the appropriate color, or one recommended in the directory, on each chakra for 20 minutes. This balances the chakras and recharges the bodies. It works best if you are in a quiet, receptive frame of mind, so choose a time when you can relax and will not be disturbed. Talking on the phone is definitely counterproductive.

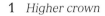

1 *Higher crown*
2 *Crown*
3 *Soma*
4 *Third eye*
5 *Past life*
6 *Throat*
7 *Higher heart*
8 *Heart*
9 *Spleen*
10 *Solar plexus*
11 *Sacral*
12 *Base*
13 *Earth*

How this book works

The word "crystal" has been adopted to cover all stones and metals that have healing properties, not just gemstones, and this book includes noncrystalline, precious, and semiprecious stones with their attributes and story. The book has been arranged by color, although, since many stones occur in myriad hues, and certain colors, varieties, or combinations have specific properties, a crystal may belong in two or more sections. Each color, or variety, of a crystal shares generic properties, and stones that combine different crystals are cross-referenced since you will need to read both generic and specific entries. Crystals are sold under a multitude of names and look different when tumbled and raw, so stones are illustrated for ease of identification.

To use the book, look up your crystal in the index at the front of the book to find its page number, or identify it from the illustrations (bearing in mind that stones may take different colors and forms). If you need a crystal for a specific purpose, the detailed index at the back of the book will assist you. Finger-dowsing will help you refine your selection to exactly the right stone for you.

The properties

For each stone, you will find the crystal system; the chemistry, the minerals from which it formed; its hardness, which tells you how easily energy passes through; and its source. The related chakra, number, zodiac sign, and planet are also listed, but in some cases these have yet to be determined or are not relevant.

So, for example, if you have Rose Quartz, an easily obtained crystal, you will see that this is a trigonal crystal, created from triangles, that radiates energy and is invigorating and protective, rebalancing the biomagnetic sheath. Like all quartzes, it is formed from silicon dioxide, the most common mineral on the planet. It is a hard crystal, 7 on the Mohs scale, which allows energy to pass through it relatively slowly. Its sources are South Africa, the USA, Brazil, Japan, India, Madagascar, and Germany, and it resonates to the heart and higher heart chakras, the number 7, the zodiac signs Taurus and Libra and the planet Venus. Its generic properties include promoting unconditional love and peace, and it is an excellent heart-healer. Lavender Quartz, related to Rose Quartz, has a higher, more refined energy.

Pink and peach crystals

Pink stones carry the essence of unconditional love and resonate with the heart and higher heart chakras and the planet Venus. These comforting stones alleviate anxiety. Excellent emotional healers, they overcome loss, dispel trauma, and promote forgiveness and attunement to universal love. Peach stones are gently energizing, uniting the heart and sacral chakras and combining love with action. Pink and peach stones are ideal for wearing for long periods of time.

Rose Quartz

Crystal system	Trigonal
Chemistry	SiO_2 Silicon dioxide with impurities
Hardness	7
Source	South Africa, USA, Brazil, Japan, India, Madagascar, Germany
Chakra	Heart, higher heart
Number	7
Zodiac sign	Taurus, Libra
Planet	Venus
Beneficial for	Inducing love, reducing tension, overcoming trauma, sexual imbalances, grief, addiction, overcoming rape, heart and circulatory system, chest, lungs, kidneys, adrenals, vertigo, fertility, burns, blistering, Alzheimer's, Parkinson's, senile dementia.

Tumbled Rose Quartz

Raw Rose Quartz

A stone of unconditional love and infinite peace, Rose Quartz is the most important crystal for healing the heart and the heart chakra. This beautiful stone promotes receptivity to beauty of all kinds. Romantic Rose Quartz attracts love. Placed by your bed or in the relationship corner of your home, it draws love toward you or supports an existing partnership, restoring trust and harmony.

Rose Quartz is the finest emotional healer. Releasing unexpressed emotions and heartache and transmuting emotional conditioning that no longer serves, it soothes internalized pain and heals deprivation, opening your heart so that you become receptive. If you have loved and lost, it comforts your grief. Rose Quartz teaches how to love yourself and encourages self-forgiveness and acceptance, invoking self-trust and self-worth. Excellent for trauma or crisis, Rose Quartz acts as a rescue remedy, providing reassurance and calm. This stone draws off negative energy and replaces it with loving vibes. Strengthening empathy and sensitivity and aiding the acceptance of necessary change, it is an excellent stone for midlife crisis. Holding Rose Quartz enhances positive affirmations, the stone then reminding you of your intention.

Note: Rose Quartz is a high-vibration stone.

Shaped Rose Quartz

Section of raw Rose Quartz showing its characteristic texture.

Rose Quartz Wand

Crystal system	Trigonal
Chemistry	SiO_2 Silicon dioxide with impurities
Hardness	7
Source	Specially shaped
Chakra	Heart, higher heart
Zodiac sign	Taurus, Libra
Planet	Venus
Beneficial for	Inducing love, reducing tension, overcoming trauma, sexual imbalances, grief, addiction, overcoming rape, heart and circulatory system, chest, lungs, kidneys, adrenals, vertigo, fertility, burns, blistering, Alzheimer's, Parkinson's, senile dementia.

In addition to carrying the generic properties of Wands (page 279) and Rose Quartz (left), a Rose Quartz wand is an excellent tool for drawing out emotional distress and for healing a broken heart. It works equally well for agitation or anxiety. Raised blood pressure is lowered and a racing pulse normalizes under this stone's calming influence. If the chakras are spinning erratically, a Rose Quartz wand applied at the heart chakra stabilizes and brings them into harmony.

Rose Quartz wand

Smoky Rose Quartz

Crystal system	Trigonal
Chemistry	Complex
Hardness	7
Source	South America
Chakra	Heart, higher heart, base, earth
Number	2, 7, 8
Zodiac sign	Scorpio, Capricorn, Taurus, Libra
Planet	Pluto, Venus
Beneficial for	Inducing love, reducing tension, overcoming trauma, sexual imbalances, libido, grief, addiction, overcoming rape, concentration, nightmares, stress, geopathic stress, X-ray exposure, pain relief, fear, depression, heart, circulatory and reproductive system, chest, lungs, kidneys, adrenals, abdomen, hips, legs, the back, muscle, nerve tissue, headaches, cramp, nerves, assimilation of minerals, fluid regulation, vertigo, burns, blistering, Alzheimer's, Parkinson's, senile dementia.

Bringing together the cleansing and restorative qualities of Smoky Quartz (see page 186 for generic properties) and the loving energy of Rose Quartz (left), Smoky Rose Quartz dissolves resentment and draws out abuse. Filling the heart with unconditional love, it provides a protective shield. This beautiful stone keeps your environment pure and loving, and accompanies anyone who is frightened of death or dying through the process, healing the fear.

Smoky crystals on Rose Quartz base

Strawberry Quartz

Crystal system	Hexagonal
Chemistry	Complex
Hardness	7
Source	Russia. May be manufactured
Chakra	Heart
Zodiac sign	Libra
Beneficial for	Anxiety, heart, dreams, auric healing, energy enhancement.

Tumbled Strawberry Quartz

In addition to carrying the generic properties of Quartz (page 230), Strawberry Quartz, a rare crystal, makes a potent elixir for bringing love into the heart. It has an intense energy that assists in remembering your dreams. This stone creates a loving environment and facilitates living consciously and joyfully in the moment, seeing the humor in all situations. Stabilizing connections between the physical body and the aura, it brings to light the hidden causes of current situations, especially when these are being self-created. It can lessen the restrictions you place upon yourself and reprogram false beliefs.

Raw Strawberry Quartz

Pink Crackle Quartz

Crystal system	Hexagonal
Chemistry	Complex amendment
Hardness	7 (may be affected by manufacture)
Source	Artificially amended
Chakra	Heart
Zodiac sign	Taurus, Libra
Beneficial for	Pancreas, diabetes, cellular memory, brittle bones, compound fractures, anxiety, earwax, ear pain caused by pressure, energy enhancement.

Crackle Quartz is natural Quartz that has been superheated and dipped into a dye bath. It retains some underlying Quartz properties (page 230), which are enhanced by the color vibration. Flirty Pink Crackle Quartz is a party animal that promotes fun and joy in life. This lively stone is an excellent companion for life-enhancing, joyful pursuits that help you relax and recharge. A useful adjunct to Reiki healing, it provides contact with your own higher self and heals abused or emotionally damaged children. It is very good at helping you love your body, no matter what size, shape, or age it is, and is excellent for accepting who you are in your entirety.

Note: Pink Crackle Quartz is a high-vibration stone.

Pink Crackle Quartz pillar

Pink Phantom Quartz

Crystal system	Hexagonal
Chemistry	SiO_2 Silicon dioxide plus inclusions
Hardness	7
Source	Worldwide
Chakra	Heart
Zodiac sign	Taurus, Libra
Beneficial for	Restriction, abandonment, betrayal, alienation, the heart, lupus and other autoimmune diseases, cellular healing, energy enhancement, multidimensional cellular memory healing, efficient receptor for programming, cleans and enhances the organs, protects against radiation, immune system, brings the body into balance, soothes burns, old patterns, hearing disorders, clairaudience.

Pink Phantom within Quartz point

In addition to carrying the generic properties of Quartz (page 230) and Phantom Quartz (page 239), gentle pacifist Pink Phantom Quartz provides empathetic communication between friends or lovers; or between yourself and a spirit guide or higher self. It assists in accepting life as it is—and making changes that enable you to find fulfillment. If two healers are working at a distance, this crystal provides a strong link, stimulating telepathy and providing spiritual protection.

Rose Aura Quartz

Crystal system	Hexagonal
Chemistry	Complex amendment
Hardness	Brittle
Source	Manufactured
Chakra	Heart, third eye, base, sacral
Planet	Sun, Moon
Beneficial for	Emotional healing, ameliorating anger, cellular healing, multidimensional cellular memory healing, efficient receptor for programming, brings the body into balance, soothes burns, energy enhancement.

Rose Aura Quartz is formed through bonding Quartz (page 230) and platinum, producing a dynamic energy that works on the pineal gland and the heart chakra to transmute deeply held doubts about self-worth, bestowing the gift of unconditional love of yourself and making a powerful connection to universal love. This form of Aura Quartz imbues the whole body with love, restoring the cells to perfect balance.

Note: Rose Aura Quartz is a high-vibration stone.

Rose Aura Quartz

Danburite

Crystal system	Orthorhombic
Chemistry	$CaB_2SiO_2O_8$ Calcium borosilicate
Hardness	7–7.5
Source	USA, Mexico, Bolivia, Russia, Japan, Germany, Czech Republic, Myanmar, Switzerland
Chakra	Heart, higher heart, crown, higher crown, third eye
Number	4
Zodiac sign	Leo
Beneficial for	Allergies, chronic conditions, detoxifying, liver, gallbladder, weight gain, muscular and motor function.

Danburite was named after Danbury, Connecticut, where it was first found, and is a highly spiritual stone carrying a pure vibration that promotes lucid dreaming. A powerful healer for the heart, it activates intellect and higher consciousness, linking into angelic realms and to serenity and eternal wisdom. Excellent for facilitating deep change and leaving the past behind, Danburite changes recalcitrant attitudes, inducing patience and peace of mind. Acting as a karmic cleanser, it releases miasms and mental imperatives and encourages conscious spiritual transition.

Note: Danburite is a high-vibration stone.

Natural Danburite wand

Pink Danburite

Crystal system	Orthorhombic
Chemistry	Complex
Hardness	7–7.5
Source	USA, Mexico, Bolivia, Russia, Japan, Germany, Czech Republic, Myanmar, Switzerland
Chakra	Heart, higher heart, crown, higher crown, third eye
Number	4
Zodiac sign	Leo
Beneficial for	Heart, allergies, chronic conditions, detoxifying, liver, gallbladder, weight gain, muscular and motor function.

In addition to carrying the generic properties of Danburite (above), Pink Danburite opens the heart and encourages you to love yourself unconditionally. It is particularly supportive during a ritual to claim back your heart, assisting in cleansing and integrating the returning energy and healing the emotional blueprint.

Note: Pink Danburite is a high-vibration stone.

Pink Danburite

Eudialyte

Crystal system	Trigonal
Chemistry	Complex
Hardness	5.5–5
Source	Russia, Greenland, Canada, Madagascar, USA
Chakra	Heart, links base and heart, opens and aligns all
Number	3
Zodiac sign	Virgo
Beneficial for	Energy depletion, forgiveness, jealousy, anger, guilt, resentment, animosity, confidence, brain waves, multidimensional cellular healing, optic nerve damage.

Tumbled Eudialyte

Eudialyte was discovered in 1819 in Greenland and named from the Greek *eu*, well, and *dialytos*, decomposable, because it rapidly dissolves in acid. This stone draws together former soul-companions and throws light into the reason for meeting. Meditating or sleeping with Eudialyte under the pillow will reveal the reason if you have met a "soulmate" who, seemingly, rejects you, or someone to whom you are strongly attracted but it is unclear whether you are destined for a sexual relationship or whether there is spiritual work to do. Strongly imbued with life force and a personal-power stone, Eudialyte heals depression and dissatisfaction with yourself, releasing negative emotions that lie beneath. Promoting self-forgiveness and healthy self-love, it assists in learning from your "mistakes." Useful at a turning point and connecting the mind with the emotional body, Eudialyte brings about profound changes in your inner being.

Pink Topaz

Crystal system	Orthorhombic
Chemistry	Complex
Hardness	8
Source	USA, Russia, Mexico, India, Australia, South Africa, Sri Lanka, Pakistan, Myanmar, Germany
Chakra	Heart, higher heart
Number	3
Zodiac sign	Libra, Sagittarius
Planet	Venus, Jupiter
Beneficial for	Hope, astuteness, problem-solving, honesty, forgiveness, self-realization, emotional support, manifesting health, digestion, anorexia, sense of taste, nerves, metabolism, skin, vision.

In addition to carrying the generic properties of Topaz (page 87), Pink Topaz is a stone of hope. Gently easing out old patterns of disease, it dissolves resistance and opens the way to radiant health. This stone shows you the face of the divine.

Pink Fluorite

Crystal system	Cubic
Chemistry	Complex
Hardness	4
Source	USA, England, Mexico, Canada, Australia, Germany, Norway, China, Peru, Brazil
Chakra	Heart
Number	9
Zodiac sign	Pisces
Planet	Mercury
Beneficial for	Heartache, migraine, soul retrieval, emotional healing, balance, coordination, self-confidence, shyness, worry, centering, concentration, psychosomatic disease, absorption of nutrients, bronchitis, emphysema, pleurisy, pneumonia, antiviral, infections, disorders, teeth, cells, bones, DNA damage, skin and mucus membranes, respiratory tract, colds, flu, sinusitis, ulcers, wounds, adhesions, mobilizing joints, arthritis, rheumatism, spinal injuries, pain relief, shingles, nerve-related pain, blemishes, wrinkles, dental work.

Pink Fluorite on matrix

In addition to carrying the generic properties of Fluorite (page 177), Pink Fluorite is a useful adjunct to soul retrieval because it encourages soul fragments to reintegrate and provides a safe home for a lost soul until it is ready to return. As with all pink stones, Pink Fluorite facilitates deep emotional healing and soothes despair.

Pink Carnelian

Crystal system	Trigonal
Chemistry	SiO_2 + (Fe, O, OH)
Hardness	7
Source	Brazil, Russia, India, Australia, Madagascar, South Africa, Uruguay, USA, UK, Czech Republic, Slovakia, Peru, Iceland, Romania
Chakra	Heart, lower chakras
Number	5, 6
Zodiac sign	Taurus, Scorpio
Beneficial for	Trust, analytic ability, dramatic pursuits, courage, vitality, metabolism, concentration, envy, anger, emotional negativity, nosebleeds, infertility, frigidity, impotence, increasing potency, food assimilation, absorption of vitamins and minerals, heart, circulation, female reproductive organs, arthritis, neuralgia, depression in advanced years, rebalances bodily fluids, kidneys, accelerates healing in bones and ligaments, headaches.

Tumbled Pink Carnelian

In addition to carrying the generic properties of Carnelian (page 44), Pink Carnelian improves the parent–child relationship and restores love and trust after abuse or manipulation. It is said to protect against envious people.

Bustamite

Crystal system	Triclinic
Chemistry	$(CaMnSi_2)_6$ Manganese calcium silicate
Hardness	5.5–6.5
Source	South Africa, Sweden, Russia, Peru, Argentina, Austria, Bulgaria, Germany, Honduras, Italy, Japan, New Zealand, Norway, UK, Brazil
Chakra	Base, sacral, heart, third eye, aligns all
Number	2
Zodiac sign	Libra
Beneficial for	Stress-related illness, fluid retention, legs and feet, circulation, headaches, heart, skin, nails, hair, motor nerves, muscle strength, spleen, lungs, prostate, pancreas, calcium deficiencies.

Bustamite is the pinky-red portion of this tumbled stone.

Named after a Mexican general, Anastasio Bustamente, Bustamite is a rare but powerful energy worker that provides deep connection to the earth and facilitates earth healing. Said to lose its luster in the presence of danger, Bustamite realigns the meridians of earth's etheric body and can be gridded to create safe space for ritual work, initiation, or meditation. Stimulating conscious dreaming and intuition, it enhances channeling and accesses angelic realms.

Bustamite realigns energy meridians in the physical and subtle bodies, removing blockages and emotional pain. A stone of composure bringing about inner congruency, it assists you in removing yourself mentally from disharmonious situations while remaining physically present, or in removing yourself physically from detrimental situations. Turning ideals and ideas into positive action, Bustamite insists that you follow your life path with vigor.

Bustamite with Sugilite

Crystal system	Complex combination
Chemistry	Complex combination
Hardness	Complex combination
Source	South Africa, Sweden, Russia, Peru, Argentina, Austria, Bulgaria, Germany, Honduras, Italy, Japan, New Zealand, Norway, UK, Brazil
Chakra	Soma, third eye, past life
Beneficial for	Migraine, stress-related illness, fluid retention, legs and feet, circulation, headaches, heart, skin, nails, hair, motor nerves, muscle strength, spleen, lungs, prostate, pancreas, calcium deficiencies, self-forgiveness, learning difficulties, Asperger's autism, accelerating body's natural healing ability, spirituality, addiction, eating disorders, dyslexia, mental fatigue, despair, hostility, paranoia, schizophrenia, pain relief, headaches, epilepsy, motor disturbances, nerves, brain alignment.

Excellent for relieving migraine and headaches, this combination of Bustamite (see above for generic properties) and Sugilite (page 183) increases spiritual and metaphysical awareness while remaining grounded. Opening intuition, it improves your ability to listen to the voice of your Self. The stone can be programmed to draw like-minded souls together.

Tumbled Bustamite with Sugilite

Kunzite

Crystal system	Monoclinic
Chemistry	$LiAl(SiO_6)_2$ with impurities (contains lithium)
Hardness	6.5–7
Source	USA, Madagascar, Brazil, Myanmar, Afghanistan
Chakra	Heart, higher heart, aligns heart chakra with throat and third eye
Number	7
Zodiac sign	Taurus, Leo, Scorpio
Planet	Venus, Pluto
Beneficial for	Combining intellect, intuition, and inspiration; humility; service; tolerance; self-expression; creativity; stress-related anxiety; bipolar disorder; psychiatric disorders and depression; geopathic stress; introspection; immune system; witness for radionic practitioners; anesthetic; circulatory system; heart muscle; neuralgia; epilepsy; joint pain.

Natural Kunzite

An extremely high-vibration stone, Kunzite offers unconditional love to awaken the heart. Inducing a deep and centered meditative state, it is beneficial for those who find meditation challenging. With the power to dispel negativity, it provides a protective sheath around the aura that dispels attached entities and mental influences. Kunzite imparts the ability to be self-contained even within a crowd. Removing obstacles to your path, it helps you adjust to the pressure of life. A useful healer for anyone who grew up too fast, Kunzite assists in recovering blocked memories and, placed on the heart, brings back lost trust and innocence. Clearing emotional debris and freeing up emotions, it heals heartache, especially that carried forward from other lives. Dissolving resistance, it effects compromises between personal needs and those of others, and stimulates acting on constructive criticism.

Note: Kunzite is a high-vibration stone.

Pink Petalite

Crystal system	Monoclinic
Chemistry	Complex
Hardness	6–6.5
Source	Brazil, Madagascar, Namibia
Chakra	Heart, higher heart, higher crown
Number	7
Zodiac sign	Pisces
Beneficial for	Fear, worry, flexibility, stress relief, stabilizing the pulse, depression, endocrine system, triple heater meridian, AIDS, cancer, cells, eyes, lungs, muscular spasm, intestines.

Raw Pink Petalite

In addition to carrying the generic properties of Petalite (page 255), Pink Petalite is a stone of compassion. It strengthens the emotional body, clears the heart meridian, and encourages letting go of emotional baggage, opening the way for love to flourish.

Note: Pink Petalite is a high-vibration stone.

Natural Pink Petalite

Muscovite

Crystal system	Monoclinic
Chemistry	$KAl_2(AlSi_3O_{10})(F,OH)_2$
Hardness	2–3.5
Source	Switzerland, Russia, Austria, Czech Republic, Brazil, USA (New Mexico), Canada, India, Italy, Scotland, Germany, Austria, Finland, Madagascar, Afghanistan, Dominican Republic
Chakra	Heart
Number	1
Zodiac sign	Aquarius
Planet	Mercury
Beneficial for	Dyspraxia and left–right confusion, problem-solving, quick-wittedness, insomnia, allergies, anger, insecurity, self-doubt, nervous stress, hair, eyes, weight, blood sugar, pancreatic secretions, dehydration, fasting, kidneys, repetitive strain injury, tendonitis.

Natural Muscovite

Muscovite, named for Muscovy in Russia, where it was used instead of glass in buildings, is the commonest form of mica. A mystical stone with strong angelic contact, it stimulates awareness of the higher self, facilitating astral journeying and opening metaphysical vision. Mirroring back projections and facilitating seeing ourselves as others see us, Muscovite assists in changing the image presented to the world and supports during exploration, release, and integration of painful feelings. Bringing flexibility at all levels of being, it assists in looking forward joyfully to the future and back to the past to appreciate lessons that have been learned and put them into practice.

Gridded in earthquake areas, Muscovite relieves tensions within the earth. It also releases tension within the physical body and aligns it with the aura and meridians. Use as a wrist support when typing.

Pink Agate

Crystal system	Trigonal
Chemistry	Complex
Hardness	6
Source	USA, India, Morocco, Czech Republic, Brazil, Africa
Chakra	Heart
Number	7
Zodiac sign	Libra, Capricorn
Beneficial for	Unconditional love, emotional trauma, self-confidence, concentration, perception, analytical abilities, aura stabilization, negative-energy transformation, emotional disease, digestive process, gastritis, eyes, stomach, uterus, lymphatic system, pancreas, blood vessels, skin disorders.

Tumbled Pink Agate

In addition to carrying the generic properties of Agate (page 190), Pink Agate promotes unconditional love between parent and child and assists in the acceptance of individual difference.

Rhodochrosite

Crystal system	Hexagonal
Chemistry	$MnCO_3$ Manganese carbonate
Hardness	3.5–4
Source	USA, South Africa, Russia, Argentina, Uruguay, Peru, Romania
Chakra	Heart, higher heart, clears solar plexus and base
Number	4
Zodiac sign	Leo, Scorpio
Planet	Mars
Beneficial for	Emotional release, mental stress, self-worth, denial, instilling positive attitude, overcoming chronic self-blame, irrational fears, memory, intellect, anorexia, migraine, asthma, respiratory problems, circulatory system, kidneys, eyesight, depression, low blood pressure, herpes, cancer of the ovaries, bladder, colon and prostate gland, sexual organs, infections, thyroid.

Polished Rhodochrosite

Polished Rhodochrosite

Representing selfless love and compassion, Rhodochrosite expands consciousness and integrates spiritual with material energies. Excellent for the heart and relationships, this stone heals sexual abuse. Attracting a soulmate who helps you learn lessons for your higher good, it teaches the heart to assimilate painful feelings without shutting down. This stone insists that you face the truth, about yourself and others, without excuses or evasion but with loving awareness.

Rhodochrosite links to the higher mind and aids in integrating new information, encouraging a positive attitude and enhancing dream states and creativity. Encouraging spontaneous expression of feelings, including passionate and erotic urges, it lifts a depressed mood, bringing lightness into life.

Gem Rhodochrosite

Crystal system	Hexagonal
Chemistry	$MnCO_3$ Manganese carbonate
Hardness	3.5–4
Source	USA, South Africa, Russia, Argentina, Uruguay, Peru, Romania
Chakra	Heart, higher heart, clears solar plexus and base
Number	4
Zodiac sign	Leo, Scorpio
Planet	Mars
Beneficial for	Psychosomatic disease, emotional release, mental stress, self-worth, denial, instilling positive attitude, overcoming chronic self-blame, irrational fears, memory, intellect, anorexia, migraine, asthma, respiratory problems, circulatory system, low blood pressure, cancer of the ovaries, sexual organs.

Natural Rhodochrosite crystals on matrix

In addition to carrying the generic properties of Rhodochrosite (above), Gem Rhodochrosite links you into the karmic purpose for your present incarnation, enabling you to see prior soul contracts and to renegotiate these if necessary. Healing disconnection from the spiritual realms and encouraging you to open your heart to universal love, this stone has been used to ameliorate the psychosomatic causes of cancer and to reprogram the emotional blueprint to prevent recurrence.

Note: Gem Rhodochrosite is a high-vibration stone.

Pink Sapphire

Crystal system	Hexagonal
Chemistry	Complex
Hardness	9
Source	Myanmar, Czech Republic, Brazil, Kenya, India, Australia, Sri Lanka, Canada, Thailand, Madagascar
Chakra	Heart
Zodiac sign	Libra
Beneficial for	Emotional blockages, serenity, peace of mind, concentration, multidimensional cellular healing, overactive body systems, glands, eyes, stress, blood disorders, excessive bleeding, veins, elasticity.

Raw Pink Sapphire (gem quality)

In addition to carrying the generic properties of Sapphire (page 160), Pink Sapphire acts as a magnet to draw into your life all that you need in order to evolve. Teaching how to master emotions, it dissolves emotional blockages and integrates transmuted energies.

Faceted Pink Sapphire

Rhodonite

Crystal system	Triclinic
Chemistry	$(MnFeMgCa)SiO_3$
Hardness	5.5–6.5
Source	Spain, Russia, Sweden, Germany, Mexico, Brazil
Chakra	Heart, solar plexus
Number	9
Zodiac sign	Taurus
Planet	Mars
Beneficial for	Mantra-based meditation, closing metaphysical gates, confusion, doubt, confidence, excellent wound healer, insect bites, scarring, bone growth, hearing organs, fertility, emphysema, inflammation of joints, arthritis, autoimmune diseases, stomach ulcer, multiple sclerosis.

An emotional balancer that nurtures love and encourages the brotherhood of humanity, Rhodonite stimulates and heals the heart. It grounds energy, balances yin–yang, and aids in achieving one's highest potential. This stone has a strong resonance with forgiveness, assists in reconciliation after long-term pain and abuse, and is beneficial in emotional self-destruction and codependency. In past-life healing it deals with betrayal and abandonment, clearing away emotional wounds and scars from the past—whenever that might be—and bringing up painful emotions for transmutation. Promoting unselfish self-love and forgiveness, Rhodonite helps in taking back projections that blame a partner for what is really inside oneself. A useful "first-aid stone," Rhodonite heals emotional shock and panic, supporting the soul during the process. Rhodonite turns back insults and prevents retaliation. It recognizes that revenge is self-destructive and assists in remaining calm in dangerous or upsetting situations.

Tumbled Rhodonite

Pyrophyllite

Crystal system	Monoclinic
Chemistry	$Al_2Si_4(OH_2)$ Aluminum silicate hydroxide
Hardness	2.5
Source	USA, Canada, Russia, Australia
Chakra	Sacral, solar plexus
Number	1
Zodiac sign	Pisces
Beneficial for	Autonomy, indigestion, heartburn, overacidity, diarrhea.

Natural Pyrophyllite

Pyrophyllite, a form of kaolin, is useful for people whose boundaries can be easily breached or are too diffuse. If you are easily swayed, hold Pyrophyllite in front of your solar plexus to strengthen your boundaries and learn how to say "no" to those who try to control you, or when renegotiating promises or obligations that keep you attached to another person.

Cobalto-calcite (Cobaltite)

Crystal system	Hexagonal
Chemistry	$CaCO_3$ Calcium carbonate
Hardness	3
Source	USA, UK, Belgium, Czech Republic, Slovakia, Peru, Iceland, Germany, Romania, Brazil
Chakra	Heart
Zodiac sign	Cancer
Beneficial for	Emotional healing, self-discovery, emotional maturation, nurturing, scars, broken heart, loneliness, grief, study, motivation, laziness, revitalization, emotional stress, organs of elimination, calcium uptake in bones, tissue healing, immune system, growth in small children.

Cobalto-calcite was named, *kobald*, or "goblin" by German miners because they believed it to be a mischievous and malicious stone. Crystal healers see it as symbolizing unconditional love and forgiveness. In addition to carrying the generic properties of Calcite (page 245), it soothes intense feelings and assists you in loving yourself and others. Harmonizing intellect and emotion, it transfers ideas into action and facilitates finding your innate talents and life purpose. This stone supports those who carry pain for other people or the planet and those who have given up hope. Place Cobalto-calcite on a photograph for distance healing and use to send pink light to support someone else in becoming all that they might be, or to overcome an emotional block.

Cobalto-calcite crystals on matrix

Mangano Calcite

Crystal system	Hexagonal
Chemistry	Complex
Hardness	3
Source	USA, UK, Belgium, Czech Republic, Slovakia, Peru, Iceland, Romania, Brazil
Chakra	Heart, higher heart
Zodiac sign	Libra
Planet	Venus
Beneficial for	Trauma, pain, self-worth, self-acceptance, nervous conditions, tension, anxiety, nightmares, study, motivation, laziness, revitalization, emotional stress, organs of elimination, calcium uptake in bones, dissolving calcification, skeleton, joints, intestinal conditions, skin, tissue healing, immune system, growth in small children.

Tumbled Mangano Calcite

In addition to carrying the generic properties of Calcite (page 245), Mangano Calcite facilitates contact with the angelic realm. A stone of forgiveness, it brings unconditional love, releasing fear and grief that keep the heart trapped in the past.

Morganite (Pink Beryl)

Crystal system	Hexagonal
Chemistry	Complex
Hardness	7.5–8
Source	USA, Brazil, China, Ireland, Switzerland, Australia, Czech Republic, France, Norway
Chakra	Heart, higher heart
Number	1
Zodiac sign	Libra
Planet	Venus
Beneficial for	Soul retrieval, realigning body and soul, stress and stress-related illness, TB, asthma, emphysema, heart problems, vertigo, impotence, lungs, nervous system, oxygenating cells, courage, stress, overanalysis, elimination, pulmonary and circulatory systems, sedation, resistance to toxins and pollutants, liver, heart, stomach, spine, concussion, throat infections.

Tumbled Morganite

In addition to carrying the generic properties of Beryl (page 81), Morganite is a love attractor that encourages loving thoughts and actions and creates space to enjoy life. Recognizing the escape tactics, closed-mindedness, or egotism that blocks spiritual advancement, it releases karmic emotional pain. Bringing into awareness unfulfilled emotional and soul needs and unexpressed feelings, Morganite holds the emotional body stable during psychosomatic change. Dissolving resistance to healing and transformation, this stone clears victim mentality and opens the heart to receive unconditional love.

Thulite (Pink Zoisite)

Tumbled Thulite

Crystal system	Orthorhombic
Chemistry	$Ca_2Al_3Si_3O_{12}$ (OH) Hydrous calcium aluminum silica
Hardness	6–6.5
Source	Norway
Number	5
Zodiac sign	Taurus, Gemini
Beneficial for	Extreme weakness, nervous exhaustion, calcium deficiencies, gastric upsets, fertility, PMS, reproductive organs, lethargy, detoxification, neutralizing overacidification, reducing inflammation, immune system, cell regeneration, heart, spleen, pancreas, lungs, fertility, ovaries, testicles. Place on pubic bone to stimulate the reproductive system.

Raw Thulite

The name Thulite derives from *Thule*, the ancient name for Norway. In addition to carrying the generic properties of Zoisite (page 56), this dramatic stone has a powerful link with the life force, stimulating healing and regeneration. Helpful when resistance has to be overcome, it encourages curiosity and inventiveness. Thulite explores the dualities of the human condition, combining love with logic, and teaches that lust, sensuality, and sexuality are a natural part of life. Facilitating expression of passion and sexual feelings, it brings out the extrovert in you, promoting eloquence and showmanship.

Unakite (Epidote)

Crystal system	Monoclinic
Chemistry	Complex
Hardness	6–7
Source	USA, South Africa
Chakra	Third eye
Number	9
Zodiac sign	Scorpio
Beneficial for	Electromagnetic smog, recovery from major illness, reproductive system, weight gain, pregnancy, skin, tissue, hair.

A stone of vision, Unakite balances emotions with spirituality and opens the third eye, providing grounding after meditation or metaphysical work. This stone facilitates rebirthing, bringing to light and integrating insights from the past about the cause of blockages, and gently releasing conditions that inhibit spiritual and psychological growth. It is also helpful in past-life healing for going back to the source of a problem and reframing it, clearing a need for vengeance if required. Whether it arises in the far or near past, Unakite reaches the root cause of emotional disease at whatever level it occurs, bringing it to the surface for transformation.

Raw Unakite

Pink Halite

Crystal system	Cubic
Chemistry	NaCl Sodium chloride with burkeite
Hardness	2
Source	USA
Chakra	Crown, heart
Number	1
Zodiac sign	Cancer, Pisces
Beneficial for	Dispelling oppression, diuretic, anxiety, detoxification, metabolism, water retention, intestinal problems, bipolar disorders, respiratory disorders, skin.

Pink Halite is found in California, the color being created by the mineral burkeite. In addition to carrying the generic properties of Halite (page 250), Pink Halite is a useful tool for detaching entities and spirit possessions and prevents reattachment, especially when someone is under the influence of alcohol or drugs. Encouraging spiritual development, Pink Halite opens metaphysical abilities and removes negativity. Placed in the environment, it facilitates well-being and a sense of being loved.

Natural Pink Halite

Pink Chalcedony

Crystal system	Trigonal
Chemistry	SiO$_2$ Silicon dioxide with impurities
Hardness	7
Source	USA, Austria, Czech Republic, Slovakia, Iceland, England, Mexico, New Zealand, Turkey, Russia, Brazil, Morocco
Number	9
Zodiac sign	Cancer, Sagittarius
Planet	Moon
Beneficial for	Empathy, inner peace, trust, psychosomatic disease, heart, immune system, breastfeeding, lymphatic fluids, generosity, hostility, lawsuits, nightmares, fear of the dark, hysteria, depression, negative thoughts, turbulent emotions, bad dreams, cleansing, maternal instinct, lactation, mineral assimilation, mineral build-up in veins, dementia, senility, physical energy, holistic healing, eyes, gallbladder, bones, spleen, blood, circulatory system.

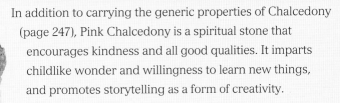

In addition to carrying the generic properties of Chalcedony (page 247), Pink Chalcedony is a spiritual stone that encourages kindness and all good qualities. It imparts childlike wonder and willingness to learn new things, and promotes storytelling as a form of creativity.

Raw Pink Chalcedony

Cherry Opal

Crystal system	Amorphous
Chemistry	$SiO_2\ nH_2O$ Hydrated silica
Hardness	5.5–6.5
Source	Australia, Brazil, USA, Tanzania, Iceland, Mexico, Peru, UK, Canada, Honduras, Slovakia
Chakra	Base, sacral, third eye
Number	4
Zodiac sign	Gemini
Beneficial for	Clairvoyance, clairsentience, headaches arising from a blocked third eye, tissue regeneration, blood disorders, muscle tension, spinal disorders, menopausal symptoms, self-worth, strengthening the will to live, intuition, fear, loyalty, spontaneity, female hormones, Parkinson's, infections, fevers, memory, purifying blood and kidneys, regulating insulin, childbirth, PMS, eyes, ears.

In addition to carrying the generic properties of Opal (page 254), Cherry Opal activates the lower chakras and promotes a feeling of centeredness while opening the third eye and metaphysical abilities.

Natural Cherry Opal

Tumbled Cherry Opal

Heulandite

Crystal system	Monoclinic
Chemistry	$(Na,K,Ca,Sr,Ba)_5(Al_9Si_{27})O_{72}\ 26H_2O$
Hardness	3.5–4
Source	India
Number	9
Zodiac sign	Sagittarius
Beneficial for	Recovering from loss, mobility, weight reduction, growths, lower limbs, blood flow, kidneys, liver, detoxification, goiter, addictions, bloating, agriculture, gardening, Reiki.

Heulandite assists in traversing interdimensional spaces and facilitates reading, and understanding, the Akashic Record. An excellent stone for moving on, it takes you back into the past to release negative emotions and change ingrained habits or behavior, replacing these with openness to new ways and exciting possibilities. This stone can also take you back to regain ancient knowledge and skills from Lemuria and Atlantis and your own past lives. See also Zeolite (page 261).

Natural Heulandite

Peach Selenite

Crystal system	Monoclinic
Chemistry	$CaSO_4\text{-}2\,(H_2O)$ Hydrated calcium sulfate with impurities
Hardness	2
Source	England, USA, Mexico, Russia, Austria, Greece, Poland, Germany, France, Sicily
Chakra	All, especially solar plexus and sacral
Planet	Pluto
Beneficial for	Emotional healing, judgment, insight, aligning the spinal column, flexibility, epilepsy, mercury poisoning from dental amalgam, free radicals, breastfeeding. Its finest healing occurs at the energetic levels.

Shaped Peach Selenite cube

In addition to carrying the generic properties of Selenite (page 257), Peach Selenite is a stone of emotional transformation. It is a powerful healer and is the perfect accompaniment for those who are immersed in old trauma and who need to review their past lives in the context of their present life. Drawing out issues of abandonment, rejection, alienation, and betrayal, Peach Selenite transmutes the energy into healing, forgiveness, and acceptance. This is the perfect accompaniment for an evolutionary jump into self-awareness and new life.

Note: Peach Selenite is a high-vibration stone.

Peach Aventurine

Crystal system	Trigonal
Chemistry	Complex
Hardness	7
Source	Italy, Brazil, China, India, Russia, Tibet, Nepal
Chakra	Heart, sacral
Number	3
Zodiac sign	Aries
Planet	Mercury
Beneficial for	Excessive shyness, excessive worry, emotional stress, heart, lungs, adrenals, urogenital system, balancing male–female energy, prosperity, leadership, decisiveness, compassion, empathy, irritation, creativity, stuttering, severe neurosis, thymus gland, connective tissue, nervous system, blood pressure, metabolism, cholesterol, arteriosclerosis, heart attacks, anti-inflammatory, skin eruptions, allergies, migraines, sinuses.

Natural Peach Aventurine

In addition to carrying the generic properties of Aventurine (page 97), Peach Aventurine is a lucky stone that opens the door to new possibilities and promotes making the most of opportunities, encouraging creativity and well-being. Setting aside anxiety and quieting the inner critical voice, the "whisper stone" creates the right state of mind for meditation. When Peach Aventurine has silver flecks in it, it enhances the flow of healing energy from Mother Earth through the body, balancing yin and yang.

Watermelon Tourmaline

Crystal system	Trigonal
Chemistry	Complex silicate
Hardness	5–7
Source	Sri Lanka, Brazil, Africa, USA, Australia, Afghanistan, Italy, Germany, Madagascar
Chakra	Heart and higher heart
Number	2
Zodiac sign	Gemini, Virgo
Beneficial for	Love, tenderness, friendship, emotional dysfunction, old pain, depression, fear, inner security, regeneration of nerves, paralysis, multiple sclerosis, stress, relaxation, wisdom, compassion, emotional pain, destructive feelings, dysfunctional endocrine system, heart, lungs, skin, compassion, tenderness, patience, sense of belonging, openness, rejuvenation, restful sleep, claustrophobia, panic attacks, hyperactivity, detoxification, constipation, diarrhea, nervous system, eyes, heart, thymus, brain, immune system, weight loss, relieving chronic fatigue and exhaustion, spinal realignment, strained muscles, gallbladder, liver.

Tumbled Watermelon Tourmaline

Carrying the generic properties of Pink Tourmaline (see below) and Verdelite (page 125), Watermelon Tourmaline is beneficial for relationships because it assists you in recognizing soul agreements and life purpose. Helping to find the gift in situations no matter how dire, this pink enfolded in green stone is a superactivator for the heart chakra, healing it and linking it to the higher self. Teaching patience, tact, and diplomacy, it assists in understanding situations and clearly expressing intentions. Extremely beneficial for wounded healers, Watermelon Tourmaline dissolves any resistance there may be to becoming whole once more.

Pink Tourmaline

Crystal system	Trigonal
Chemistry	Complex silicate
Hardness	7–7.5
Source	Sri Lanka, Brazil, Africa, USA, Australia, Afghanistan, Italy, Germany, Madagascar, Tanzania
Chakra	Heart, earth, protects all
Number	9, 99
Zodiac sign	Libra
Beneficial for	Relaxation, wisdom, compassion, emotional pain, destructive feelings, dysfunctional endocrine system, heart, lungs, skin, protection, detoxification, spinal adjustments, balancing male–female energy, paranoia, dyslexia, hand-eye coordination, assimilation and translation of coded information, bronchitis, diabetes, emphysema, pleurisy, pneumonia, energy flow, removal of blockages.

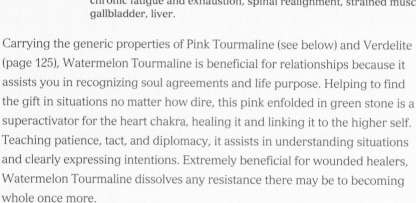

Tumbled Pink Tourmaline

Raw Pink Tourmaline

In addition to carrying the generic properties of Tourmaline (page 210), Pink Tourmaline is an aphrodisiac stone that attracts love in both the material and spiritual world. Placed over the heart, it assures you that it is safe to love. This stone inspires trust in love while pointing out that it is necessary to love oneself before one can hope to be loved by others. It assists in sharing physical pleasure and activates receptivity to healing energies.

Rhodolite Garnet

Crystal system	Cubic
Chemistry	Magnesium aluminum silicate with manganese, chromium, and/or iron silicate
Hardness	6–7.5
Source	Europe, USA (Arizona and New Mexico), South Africa, Australia
Chakra	Base
Number	7
Zodiac sign	Leo
Planet	Mars
Beneficial for	Metabolism, heart, lungs, hips, attracting love, dreaming, blood diseases, regenerating the body, metabolism, spinal and cellular disorders, blood, heart, lungs, regeneration of DNA, assimilation of minerals/vitamins.

Rhodolite Garnet in matrix

In addition to carrying the generic properties of Garnet (page 47), warm, trusting, and sincere Rhodolite Garnet stimulates contemplation, intuition, and inspiration. It enhances healthy sexuality, raising the kundalini and overcoming frigidity.

Grossular Garnet

Crystal system	Cubic
Chemistry	Magnesium aluminum silicate with manganese, chromium, and/or iron silicate
Hardness	6–7.5
Source	Europe, USA (Arizona and New Mexico), South Africa, Australia
Chakra	Base and heart, purifies and energizes all
Number	2, 6
Zodiac sign	Cancer
Planet	Mars
Beneficial for	Stress-related disease, nervous system, mistrust, anorexia, assimilation of vitamins, fertility, attracting love, dreaming, blood diseases, regenerating the body, metabolism, spinal and cellular disorders, blood, heart, lungs, regeneration of DNA, assimilation of minerals/vitamins.

In addition to carrying the generic properties of Garnet (page 47), Grossular Garnet is particularly helpful in lawsuits, inspiring cooperative effort and ingenious solutions.

Grossular Garnet

Additional pink and peach stones

Pink stones: *Amblygonite (page 77), Diamond (page 248), Dumortierite (page 150), Lepidolite (page 181), Phenacite (page 256), Smithsonite (page 138), Stichtite (page 178), Stilbite (page 260), Tiger's Eye (page 206), Zircon (page 261).* **Peach stones:** *Apophyllite (page 242), Zeolite (page 261).*

Red and orange crystals

Red stones resonate with the base and sacral chakras and the planet Mars, energizing and initiating action. These crystals heighten libido and stimulate creativity. Traditionally, red stones are used to treat hemorrhages and inflammation. Their effect is extremely stimulating and for short-term use. The color of vitality, orange stones resonate with the sacral chakra and the sun. Excellent for stimulating creativity and assertiveness, they have a vibrant yet grounding energy that gets things done.

Carnelian

Crystal system	Trigonal
Chemistry	SiO_2 + (Fe, O, OH)
Hardness	7
Source	Brazil, Russia, India, Australia, Madagascar, South Africa, Uruguay, USA, UK, Czech Republic, Slovakia, Peru, Iceland, Romania
Chakra	Base, sacral
Number	6
Zodiac sign	Taurus, Cancer, Leo, Scorpio
Planet	Sun
Beneficial for	Analytic ability, dramatic pursuits, courage, vitality, metabolism, concentration, envy, weak memory, anger, emotional negativity, nosebleeds, infertility, frigidity, impotence, increasing potency, physical wounds, blood disorders, food assimilation, absorption of vitamins and minerals, heart, circulation, blood purification, female reproductive organs, lower-back disorders, rheumatism, arthritis, neuralgia, depression in advanced years, bodily fluids, kidneys, accelerates healing in bones and ligaments, stanches blood, headaches.

Tumbled Carnelian

The name Carnelian is derived from the Latin *carnis*, flesh. Deep red Carnelian may be heat-treated and, held against light, shows stripes, while natural Carnelian shows a cloudy color. Carnelian was beloved of the Egyptians, who believed that it assisted the soul on its journey and had great protective powers in the afterlife. They wore it to calm anger, jealousy, and envy. A stabilizing stone with high energy, Carnelian anchors into the present reality, and is excellent for restoring vitality. Carnelian has the ability to cleanse other stones.

Imparting acceptance of the cycle of life, Carnelian removes fear of death and assists positive life choices. Useful for overcoming abuse, it helps you trust yourself and your perceptions, overcoming negative conditioning. Removing extraneous thoughts when meditating, it tunes daydreamers into everyday reality. A stone of abundance, it motivates for success in business and other matters.

Large tumbled Carnelian

Tumbled Carnelian geode

Jasper

Crystal system	Trigonal
Chemistry	SiO_2 Silicon dioxide
Hardness	7
Source	Worldwide
Chakra	Aligns all (varies according to color)
Number	6 (varies according to type)
Zodiac sign	Leo (varies according to type)
Beneficial for	Electromagnetic and environmental pollution, radiation, stress, prolonging sexual pleasure, prolonged illness or hospitalization, circulation, digestive and sexual organs, balancing mineral content of the body.

Raw Red Jasper

Known as the "Supreme Nurturer," Jasper sustains and supports during times of stress and unifies all aspects of life. This stone facilitates shamanic journeys, dowsing, and dream recall. Providing protection, it absorbs negative energy, balances yin and yang, and aligns the physical, emotional, and mental bodies with the etheric realm.

Bringing the courage to get to grips with problems assertively, and encouraging honesty with oneself, Jasper imparts determination to all pursuits and supports during necessary conflict. This stone aids quick thinking, promotes organizational abilities and seeing projects through, and stimulates imagination, transforming ideas into action.

Red and Brecciated Jasper

Crystal system	Trigonal
Chemistry	SiO_2 + Fe, O
Hardness	7
Source	Worldwide
Chakra	Base, sacral
Number	6
Zodiac sign	Aries, Scorpio
Planet	Mars
Beneficial for	Libido, rebirthing, boundaries, circulatory system, fevers, blood, liver, blockages in the liver or bile ducts, electromagnetic and environmental pollution, radiation, stress, prolonging sexual pleasure, prolonged illness or hospitalization, circulation, digestive and sexual organs, balancing mineral content of the body.

Tumbled Red Jasper

In addition to carrying the generic properties of Jasper (above), Red and Brecciated Jasper provide gentle stimulation, grounding energy and rectifying unjust situations. Bringing problems to light before they escalate, Red Jasper makes an excellent "worry bead" for calming emotion. Placed under the pillow, it promotes dream recall. Stimulating the base chakras, cleansing and stabilizing the aura, Red Jasper returns negativity to its source. It calms sexual aggressiveness, promotes sexual compatibility, and enhances tantric sex.

Cuprite

Crystal system	Cubic
Chemistry	Cu_2O Copper oxide
Hardness	3.5–4
Source	USA, UK, Australia, Bolivia, Japan, Mexico, Russia, Germany, France, Namibia, Peru
Chakra	Base
Number	3
Zodiac sign	Aquarius
Planet	Venus
Beneficial for	Rejuvenation, vitality, libido, sexual function, metabolic imbalances, heart, blood, muscle tissue, skeletal system, AIDS, cancer, blood disorders, water retention, bladder and kidney malfunction, vertigo, altitude sickness. Helpful to smokers and to lungs in a polluted atmosphere.

Cuprite on matrix

The name Cuprite comes from the Latin *cuprum*, meaning copper. This stone teaches humanitarian principles and how to help others. It assists in exploring past lives and learning from experiences the soul has undergone. Cuprite overcomes difficulties with father, guru, teacher, or other authoritarian figures, present or past, releasing rigid control. Strengthening the will and assisting in taking responsibility for one's own life, Cuprite attracts a mentor where required. A powerful energy conduit, this stone gives great vitality and strength, providing support if there is fear of a terminal condition or when you are determined to overcome a potentially fatal illness. It attracts what you need to survive and helps the body take in vital life force. Through the blood, life force passes to the cells of the body, which it invigorates and rejuvenates, restoring normal functioning. Cuprite eases the mind with regard to worries and situations over which one has no control.

Red Jade

Crystal system	Monoclinic
Chemistry	Complex
Hardness	6
Source	USA, China, Italy, Myanmar, Russia, Middle East
Chakra	Base, sacral
Zodiac sign	Aries
Planet	Venus
Beneficial for	Anger, longevity, self-sufficiency, detoxification, filtration, elimination, kidneys, suprarenal glands, cellular and skeletal systems, stitches, fertility, childbirth, hips, spleen, water–salt–acid–alkaline ratio.

Red is the most passionate and stimulating Jade, associated with love and letting off steam constructively. In addition to carrying the generic properties of Jade (page 120), it accesses anger, releasing tension so that it can be harnessed creatively and can enhance assertion in timid people.

Shaped Jade amulet

Garnet

Crystal system	Cubic
Chemistry	Magnesium aluminum silicate with manganese, chromium, and/or iron silicate
Hardness	6–7.5
Source	Europe, USA (Arizona and New Mexico), South Africa, Australia
Chakra	Base, heart, purifies and energizes all
Number	2 (varies according to type)
Zodiac sign	Leo, Virgo, Capricorn, Aquarius (varies according to type)
Planet	Mars
Beneficial for	Attracting love, dreaming, blood diseases, regenerating the body, metabolism, spinal and cellular disorders, blood, heart, lungs, regeneration of DNA, assimilation of minerals/vitamins.

Tumbled Garnet

Named for the seed of the pomegranate, *granatum*, it is said to be good luck to be given a Garnet but bad luck to steal one. Five hundred years ago it was used to drive off phantoms and demons. Garnet is a powerfully energizing stone that protects you, and is said to warn of approaching danger, but draws harm to enemies. Traditionally used for engagement rings, Garnet inspires love and devotion and removes inhibitions and taboos. Opening the heart, it bestows self-confidence. This stone balances the sex drive and alleviates emotional disharmony. Red Garnet stimulates controlled rise of kundalini energy and adds potency, heightening the effect of tantric sex, and attracting a compatible partner for sexual healing.

Useful in a crisis, Garnet is helpful in situations where there seems to be no way out or where life has fragmented or is traumatic. It fortifies the survival instinct, bringing courage and hope. Crisis becomes challenge under Garnet's influence, and it promotes mutual assistance. Dissolving ingrained behavior patterns and outworn ideas that no longer serve, it bypasses resistance or self-induced unconscious sabotage. With strong links to the pituitary gland, Garnet stimulates expanded awareness, past-life recall, and out-of-body experiences. Garnet activates other crystals, amplifying their effect. Square-cut garnets bring success in business matters.

Note: Garnet takes many forms; see individual entries.

Raw Garnet

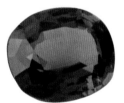

Faceted Garnet

Almandine Garnet

Crystal system	Cubic
Chemistry	Complex
Hardness	6–7.5
Source	Europe, USA (Arizona and New Mexico), South Africa, Australia
Chakra	Base, sacral, heart, crown
Number	1
Zodiac sign	Virgo, Scorpio
Planet	Mars
Beneficial for	Eyes, liver, pancreas, absorption of iron, attracting love, dreaming, blood diseases, regenerating the body, metabolism, spinal and cellular disorders, heart, lungs, regeneration of DNA, assimilation of minerals/vitamins.

Orangey-red Almandine Garnet is strongly regenerative, offering strength that supports taking time for yourself. In addition to carrying the generic properties of Garnet (page 47), this stone brings deep love, and assists in integrating truth and an affinity with the higher self. Opening the higher mind, it initiates charity and compassion. Almandine opens the pathway between the base and crown chakras, grounding spiritual energies into the body and the body into incarnation.

Pyrope Garnet

Crystal system	Cubic
Chemistry	Complex
Hardness	6–7.5
Source	Europe, USA (Arizona and New Mexico), South Africa, Australia
Chakra	Base, crown
Number	5
Zodiac sign	Cancer, Leo
Planet	Mars
Beneficial for	Circulation, digestive tract, heartburn, sore throat, attracting love, dreaming, blood diseases, regenerating the body, metabolism, spinal and cellular disorders, heart, lungs, regeneration of DNA, assimilation of minerals/vitamins.

In addition to carrying the generic properties of Garnet (page 47), blood-red Pyrope Garnet is a stabilizing stone, bestowing vitality and charisma and promoting an excellent quality of life. Uniting the creative forces within oneself, this stone protects the base and crown chakras, aligning them with the aura, and linking groundedness with wisdom.

Tumbled Pyrope Garnet beads

Red Garnet

Crystal system	Cubic
Chemistry	Magnesium aluminum silicate with manganese, chromium, and/or iron silicate
Hardness	6–7.5
Source	Europe, USA (Arizona and New Mexico), South Africa, Australia
Chakra	Heart, base
Zodiac sign	Leo, Capricorn, Aquarius
Planet	Mars
Beneficial for	Anger, attracting love, dreaming, blood diseases, regenerating the body, metabolism, spinal and cellular disorders, heart, lungs, regeneration of DNA, assimilation of minerals/vitamins.

In addition to carrying the generic properties of Garnet (page 47), Red Garnet represents love. Attuned to the heart energy, it revitalizes feelings, enhances sexuality, and controls anger, especially toward yourself. Worn during ritual magic, it bestows additional energy.

Tumbled Garnet

Hessonite Garnet

Hessonite Garnet

Crystal system	Cubic
Chemistry	Complex
Hardness	6–7.5
Source	Europe, USA (Arizona and New Mexico), South Africa, Australia
Chakra	Base, heart, purifies and energizes all
Number	6
Zodiac sign	Aries
Planet	Mars
Beneficial for	Regulating hormone production, olfactory system, infertility, impotence, drawing off negative influences responsible for ill health, attracting love, dreaming, blood diseases, regenerating the body, metabolism, spinal and cellular disorders, heart, lungs, regeneration of DNA, assimilation of minerals/vitamins.

Hessonite Garnet is a form of Grossulite Garnet and the lightest of all the Garnets owing to its high calcium content. In addition to carrying the generic properties of Garnet (page 47), Hessonite imparts self-respect, eliminating feelings of guilt and inferiority and encouraging service to others. It provides support to seek out new challenges and opens intuition and metaphysical abilities. During out-of-body journeys, Hessonite carries you to your destination.

Raw Hessonite Garnet

Melanite Garnet

Crystal system	Cubic
Chemistry	Complex
Hardness	6–7.5
Source	Europe, USA (Arizona and New Mexico), South Africa, Australia
Chakra	Base, heart, throat, purifies and energizes all
Number	7
Zodiac sign	Gemini
Planet	Mars
Beneficial for	Dispels anger, envy, jealousy, and mistrust; bones; cancer; strokes; rheumatism; arthritis; assists the body in adjusting to medication; attracting love; dreaming; blood diseases; regenerating the body; metabolism; spinal and cellular disorders; heart; lungs; regeneration of DNA; assimilation of minerals/vitamins.

In addition to carrying the generic properties of Garnet (page 47), Melanite Garnet strengthens resistance and promotes honesty. It releases blockages from the heart and throat chakras, enabling you to speak your truth. Overcoming lack of love in any situation, this stone moves a partnership on to the next stage, no matter what that might be.

Cinnabar

Crystal system	Hexagonal
Chemistry	HgS Mercuric sulfide
Hardness	2–2.5
Source	China, USA, Spain
Number	8
Zodiac sign	Leo
Planet	Mercury
Beneficial for	Blood, strength and flexibility in physical body, stabilizing weight, fertility. *(Cinnabar is toxic.)*

Cinnabar was the alchemists' stone. Because it contains mercury, they believed it could be transmuted into gold. The name originated in ancient Persia from *zinjifrah*, meaning dragon's blood, because of its wonderful vermilion color—which was the pigment used in Stone Age cave art. At a spiritual level, Cinnabar connects to the acceptance of everything being perfect exactly as it is, releasing energy blockages and aligning the energy centers.

One of the stones of abundance, Cinnabar is strongly energetic and was placed in the cash box to increase income and to hold on to wealth. Increasing persuasiveness and assertiveness, it aids in prospering in one's endeavors without inciting aggression, and assists in organization and community work, business and finance. This stone is helpful when you want to enhance your persona or change your image, as it invests you with dignity and power and makes your outward demeanor aesthetically pleasing and elegant. Mentally, Cinnabar imparts fluency to the mind and to speech.

Cinnabar crystals on matrix

Red Chalcedony

Crystal system	Trigonal
Chemistry	Complex
Hardness	7
Source	USA, Austria, Czech Republic, Slovakia, Iceland, England, Mexico, New Zealand, Turkey, Russia, Brazil, Morocco
Number	9
Zodiac sign	Sagittarius
Beneficial for	Circulation, blood pressure, blood clotting, reduces hunger pangs, generosity, hostility, lawsuits, nightmares, fear of the dark, hysteria, depression, negative thoughts, turbulent emotions, bad dreams, cleansing, mineral assimilation, mineral build-up in veins, physical energy, holistic healing, eyes, gallbladder, bones, spleen, circulatory system. *(May inhibit absorption of nutrients and cause temporary nausea.)*

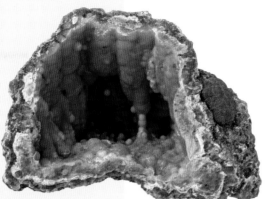

Natural Red Chalcedony geode

In addition to carrying the generic properties of Chalcedony (page 247), Red Chalcedony bestows strength and persistence in reaching goals, advising you when to fight and when to give in gracefully. It manifests dreams, devising strategies to bring these into being in the most positive way.

Red Sardonyx

Crystal system	Trigonal
Chemistry	Complex
Hardness	7
Source	Brazil, India, Russia, Turkey, Middle East
Chakra	Base
Number	3
Zodiac sign	Aries
Planet	Mars
Beneficial for	Depleted energy, tinnitus, lungs, bones, spleen, sensory organs, fluid regulation, cell metabolism, immune system, absorption of nutrients, elimination of waste products.

In addition to carrying the generic properties of Sardonyx (page 204), Red Sardonyx stimulates and energizes the wearer.

Polished Red Sardonyx

Lepidocrosite

Crystal system	Orthorhombic
Chemistry	$Fe_2O_3H_2O$
Hardness	5.5
Source	Spain, India
Chakra	Aligns and stimulates all
Number	8
Zodiac sign	Sagittarius
Beneficial for	Enhancing the healing energy of other stones, appetite suppression, liver, iris, reproductive organs, tumors, cellular regeneration.

Lepidocrosite acts as a bridge between matter and consciousness, encouraging practical application of spiritual insights. Cleansing the aura, it dissolves mental confusion, negativity, aloofness, and disparity, replacing these with love for oneself, the environment, and humanity. Heightening intuition, Lepidocrosite enables you to observe without judgment and to teach without dogma, strengthening the ability to empower others without entering into power issues yourself. It gives you the strength to stay the course and to make commitments to your life journey and the work you must do. Stimulating the mind and grounding your Self in everyday reality, Lepidocrosite recognizes your strengths at whatever level these occur. See also Super 7 (page 266).

Natural formation coated in Lepidocrosite

Lepidocrosite included in Quartz or Amethyst

Crystal system	Complex
Chemistry	Complex
Hardness	Variable
Source	Spain, India
Beneficial for	Reiki, empowerment, enhancing the healing energy of other stones, cellular regeneration, tumors, multidimensional cellular memory healer, efficient receptor for programming, enhances muscle testing, cleanses and enhances the organs, brings the body into balance.

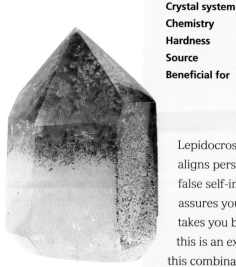

Lepidocrosite in Quartz point

Lepidocrosite (see above) included in Quartz (page 230) or Amethyst (page 168) aligns personal vision with the highest good to manifest dreams. Dissolving a false self-image and delusions, it instills true perception. This combination assures you that everything is in perfect order. An empowerment stone that takes you beyond time and space and communicates with the angelic realms, this is an excellent combination for activating intuition. Used with awareness, this combination can take you into the future to see the effects of present actions or to the highest levels of being to meet your true Self. Maintaining contact, via the silver cord, between the physical and etheric bodies, it protects the soul as it travels and ensures a smooth return, enabling insights to be brought back. Lepidocrosite in Quartz brings together the physical, etheric, and biomagnetic bodies. In healing, it enhances the transfer of Reiki energy or the rebirthing process as it facilitates the release of blockages to progress.

Bushman Red Cascade Quartz

Crystal system	Hexagonal
Chemistry	Complex
Hardness	7
Source	Africa
Chakra	Base, sacral
Number	4
Zodiac sign	Aries, Scorpio
Planet	Mars
Beneficial for	Positive action, vitality, vigor, blood flow, blood vessels, muscles, self-imposed limitations, periodontal disease, lethargy, energy enhancement.

In addition to carrying the generic properties of Drusy Quartz (page 63), Bushman Quartz facilitates drawing on your deepest reserves of energy, physical and emotional. The color comes from iron, which lends a powerful energetic charge to the Quartz. A few minutes with this vigorous stone recharges you, although it may be too powerful if your energies are already high or refined. Bushman Quartz can also take you to a very high level, but needs to be used under supervision as the energies may be too much to handle unless you are skilled in working with crystals.

Natural Bushman Red Cascade Quartz

Bixbite (Red Beryl)

Crystal system	Hexagonal
Chemistry	Complex
Hardness	7.5–8
Source	USA, Brazil, China, Ireland, Switzerland, Australia, Czech Republic, France, Norway
Chakra	Base, sacral
Number	8
Zodiac sign	Aries
Beneficial for	Creative energy, heart, lungs, liver, stomach, spleen, kidneys, pancreas, parathyroid, thyroid, respiratory tract, courage, stress, overanalysis, elimination, pulmonary and circulatory systems, sedation, resistance to toxins and pollutants, liver, heart, spine, concussion, throat infections.

In addition to carrying the generic properties of Beryl (page 81), Bixbite opens and reenergizes the base chakras and harmonizes the heart to universal love, enhancing physical energy and inducing compatibility and harmony in relationships. A stone of right timing, Bixbite enables you to bring things to completion and to commence new projects.

Raw Bixbite

Harlequin Quartz

Crystal system	Complex
Chemistry	Complex
Hardness	Complex
Source	Worldwide
Chakra	Links heart, base, crown
Beneficial for	Anxiety, depression, electrical flow in the brain, veins, memory, thyroid deficiencies, activating the will to recover, relieving despondency after long periods of illness, timid women, self-esteem, willpower, triple heater meridian, compulsions, addictions, overeating, smoking, overindulgence, stress, hysteria, inflammation, courage, hemorrhage, menstrual flooding, drawing heat from the body, formation of red blood cells, regulating blood, iron absorption, circulatory problems, Reynaud's disease, anemia, kidneys, regenerating tissue, leg cramps, nervous disorders, insomnia, spinal alignment, fractures, efficient receptor for programming, immune system, brings the body into balance, energy enhancement.

Harlequin Quartz (Hematite spots in a Quartz point)

More densely included Hematite Harlequin Quartz

In addition to carrying the generic properties of Quartz (page 230) and Hematite (page 222), Harlequin Quartz expresses universal love and acts as a bridge between the spiritual and physical worlds. With strings of red Hematite dots dancing within it, it stimulates healing the heart and draws physical and spiritual vitality into the body, providing inspiration. Balancing the polarities and meridians in the physical body, this crystal anchors them to the etheric to harmonize the subtle and physical nervous systems. Mentally soothing, it is an excellent stone for helping Indigo children adapt to being on earth.

Ruby Aura Quartz

Crystal system	Hexagonal
Chemistry	Complex
Hardness	Brittle
Source	Manufactured
Chakra	Base, heart
Beneficial for	Survival issues, abuse, endocrine system. Natural antibiotic for fungal infections and parasites, efficient receptor for programming, brings the body into balance, energy enhancement.

Ruby Aura is created from Quartz and platinum, bringing in passion and vitality and activating the wisdom of the heart. In addition to carrying the generic properties of Aura Quartz (page 143), it is spiritually uplifting, opening to Christ consciousness. This crystal protects against aggression and violence and is helpful in healing the effects of physical abuse, particularly in children.

Ruby Aura point

Red Phantom Quartz

Crystal system	Trigonal
Chemistry	Complex
Hardness	7
Source	Worldwide
Chakra	Base, sacral, solar plexus
Beneficial for	Inner child, timid women, self-esteem, willpower, old patterns, triple heater meridian, study of mathematics and technical subjects, legal situations, compulsions, addictions, overeating, smoking, overindulgence, stress, hysteria, inflammation, courage, hemorrhage, menstrual flooding, drawing heat from the body, formation of red blood cells, iron absorption, circulatory problems, Reynaud's disease, anemia, energy enhancement.

Red Phantom Quartz

Formed from included Limonite (page 83), Hematite (page 222) and/or Kaolinite, Red Phantom (page 239) removes energy implants and heals the aura. Releasing emotional pain or past-life trauma, this stone imparts tranquillity to your mind and energizes the physical body. Healing your inner child, it facilitates feeling what had to be blocked out and repressed in childhood in order to survive. Chinese Red Phantom, formed from Hematite, is a great stone to help overcome existential despair, and restore life force and vitality to the body. Helpful in business and enhancing financial security, it induces perseverance and helps overcome frustration. Used by knowledgeable earth-healers, it stabilizes the planet.

Ruby

Crystal system	Trigonal
Chemistry	Al_2O_3
Hardness	9
Source	India, Madagascar, Russia, Sri Lanka, Cambodia, Kenya, Mexico, Zimbabwe, Tanzania
Chakra	Heart, base
Number	3
Zodiac sign	Aries, Cancer, Leo, Scorpio, Sagittarius
Planet	Mars
Beneficial for	Dynamic leadership, courage, selflessness, heightened awareness, concentration, anger, enhanced immunity, sexual activity, exhaustion, lethargy, potency, vigor, hyperactivity, detoxification, blood and lymph, fevers, infectious disease, restricted blood flow, heart, spleen, circulatory system, adrenals, kidneys, reproductive organs.

Raw Ruby

Faceted Ruby

Named from the Latin *ruber*, meaning "red," Ruby is one of the Vedic healing gems and a major protector for family and possessions, being a powerful shield against psychic attack and vampirism of heart energy. In years gone by it was fashioned into a specific shape, a cabochon or carbuncle, and Ruby is often referred to by this name in ancient lapidaries. Ruby is one of the warning stones, said to darken when danger or illness threatens. It imparts vigor to life but may overstimulate irritable people. Ruby encourages passion for life, improving motivation and setting realistic goals. This stone wants you to "follow your bliss," promoting positive dreams and clear visualization. One of the stones of abundance, it aids in retaining wealth and passion.

Zincite

Crystal system	Hexagonal
Chemistry	(ZnMn)O
Hardness	4
Source	Italy, USA, Poland (crystalline Zincite is heat-amended or artificially manufactured)
Chakra	Varies according to color, but especially base and sacral
Number	5
Zodiac sign	Taurus, Libra
Beneficial for	Necessary change, lethargy, procrastination, confidence, phobias, hypnotic commands, mental imprints, empty-nest syndrome, creativity, hair, skin, prostate gland, menopausal symptoms, immune system, meridians, ME, AIDS, autoimmune diseases, candida, mucous conditions, bronchitis, epilepsy, organs of elimination and assimilation, infertility.

Born in fiery flames, crystalline Zincite is an excellent stone for transformation and alchemicalizing your life. It anchors the light body into the physical realm, assists in fulfilling karmic agreements and soul evolution, and synthesizes physical energy and personal power. Assisting the manifestation process and reenergizing depleted systems, Zincite removes hypnotic commands and energy blocks and encourages free flow of life force.

This stone attracts abundance at a physical and spiritual level, assists with the rise of the kundalini energy, and enhances gut instincts and intuition. Zincite heals shock and trauma and instills the courage to deal with traumatic situations. It ameliorates depression and releases painful memories so that these can be laid to rest. Zincite may stimulate a healing crisis.

Zoisite

Crystal system	Orthorhombic
Chemistry	$Ca_2Al_3Si_3O_{12}$ (OH) Hydrous calcium aluminum silica
Hardness	6–6.5
Source	Austria, Tanzania, India, Madagascar, Russia, Sri Lanka, Cambodia, Kenya, Italy, Switzerland
Number	4
Zodiac sign	Gemini
Beneficial for	Lethargy, detoxification, neutralizing overacidification, reducing inflammation, immune system, cell regeneration, heart, spleen, pancreas, lungs, fertility, ovaries, testicles.

Named for Baron S. Zois van Edelstein, Zoisite is excellent for transmuting negative energies into positive ones. It assists in manifesting your own truth rather than being influenced by others or trying to conform to the norm, and transforms destructive urges into constructive ones. This stone brings to the surface repressed feelings and emotions so that they can be expressed, and refocuses the mind. It encourages recovery from severe illnesses or stress.

See also Thulite (page 36) and Tanzanite (page 179).

Raw Zoisite

Red (Blood) Agate

Crystal system	Trigonal
Chemistry	Complex
Hardness	6
Source	USA, India, Morocco, Czech Republic, Brazil, Africa
Chakra	Base
Zodiac sign	Aries, Scorpio
Beneficial for	Insect bites, emotional trauma, self-confidence, concentration, analytical abilities, perception, aura stabilization, negative-energy transformation, emotional disease, digestive process, blood vessels, skin disorders.

Tumbled Red Agate

In ancient Rome, Blood Agate was worn to guard against insect bites and to heal the blood. For the generic properties of Agate, see page 190.

Red-brown Agate

Crystal system	Trigonal
Chemistry	Complex
Hardness	6
Source	USA, India, Morocco, Czech Republic, Brazil, Africa
Chakra	Earth, base, sacral
Zodiac sign	Scorpio, Capricorn
Beneficial for	PMS, menstrual cramps, delayed ovulation or menstruation, emotional trauma, aura stabilization, negative-energy transformation, emotional disease, digestive process.

Red-brown Agate is helpful for those who are consumed by the desire for a child, especially if driven by the biological clock, as it disengages the urge to procreate and calms the sacral chakra. It can also quiet overwhelming sexual desire.

Rubellite (Red Tourmaline)

Crystal system	Trigonal
Chemistry	Complex silicate
Hardness	7–7.5
Source	Sri Lanka, Brazil, Africa, USA, Australia, Afghanistan, Italy, Germany, Madagascar
Chakra	Sacral
Zodiac sign	Scorpio, Sagittarius
Beneficial for	Vitality, detoxification, heart, digestive system, blood vessels, reproductive system, circulation, spleen and liver function, veins, muscle spasm, chills, protection, detoxification, spinal adjustments, balancing male–female energy, paranoia, dyslexia, hand-eye coordination, assimilation and translation of coded information, energy flow and removal of blockages.

Raw Rubellite

Raw Rubellite

In addition to carrying the generic properties of Tourmaline (page 210), Rubellite enhances your ability to understand love. This stone promotes tactfulness and flexibility, sociability and extroversion, balancing too much aggression or overpassivity. Energizing the sacral chakra, it increases stamina, endurance, and creativity on all levels.

Red Calcite

Crystal system	Hexagonal
Chemistry	$CaCO_3$ Calcium carbonate with impurities
Hardness	3
Source	USA, UK, Belgium, Czech Republic, Slovakia, Peru, Iceland, Romania, Brazil
Chakra	Base, heart
Number	8
Beneficial for	Constipation, fear, hips, lower limbs, stiff joints, study, motivation, laziness, revitalization, emotional stress, organs of elimination, calcium uptake in bones, dissolving calcification, skeleton, joints, intestinal conditions, skin, blood clotting, tissue healing, immune system.

Raw Red Calcite

In addition to carrying the generic properties of Calcite (page 245), Red Calcite is an energy enhancer that uplifts emotions, strengthens willpower, opens the heart chakra, energizes the base chakra, and overcomes sexual difficulties. This stone removes stagnant energy, dissolves blockages, and, at a subtle level, removes the obstacles that keep you from stepping forward in your life. Red Calcite's vitality makes a party swing.

Hematoid Calcite

Crystal system	Hexagonal
Chemistry	Complex
Hardness	Variable
Source	USA, UK, Belgium, Czech Republic, Slovakia, Peru, Iceland, Romania, Brazil
Beneficial for	Memory, blood cleansing and oxygenation, stress, study, motivation, laziness, revitalization, emotional stress, organs of elimination, calcium uptake in bones, dissolving calcification, skeleton, joints, intestinal conditions, skin, blood clotting, tissue healing, immune system, growth in small children, ulcers, warts, suppurating wounds, timid women, self-esteem, willpower, triple heater meridian, study of mathematics and technical subjects, legal situations, compulsions, addictions, overeating, smoking, overindulgence, stress, hysteria, inflammation, courage, hemorrhage, menstrual flooding, drawing heat from the body, formation of red blood cells, regulating blood, iron absorption, circulatory problems, Reynaud's disease, anemia, kidneys, regenerating tissue, leg cramps, nervous disorders, insomnia, spinal alignment, fractures.

Infusing the staying power of Calcite (see page 245 for generic properties) with the protective and purifying energies of Hematite (page 222), Hematoid Calcite is an excellent stone if you experience an influx of energy that needs grounding. Carry one whenever you are in a strong energy field, particularly if the energies clash. It is a supportive stone for the memory, so if you lose things, or cannot remember birthdays or names, Hematoid Calcite tracks them down.

Natural Hematoid Calcite formation

Red Aventurine

Crystal system	Trigonal
Chemistry	SiO_2 Silicon dioxide with impurities
Hardness	7
Source	Italy, Brazil, China, India, Russia, Tibet, Nepal
Chakra	Base
Number	3
Zodiac sign	Aries
Planet	Mars
Beneficial for	Reproductive system, balancing male–female energy, prosperity, irritation, leadership, decisiveness, creativity, stuttering, severe neurosis, thymus gland, metabolism, cholesterol, arteriosclerosis, allergies, adrenals, muscular system.

Raw Red Aventurine

Red Aventurine (see also page 97) is helpful for genital or reproductive diseases, including cancer. It counterbalances an excess of air in an astrological chart.

Red-black Obsidian

Crystal system	Amorphous
Chemistry	SiO_2 Silicon dioxide with impurities
Hardness	5–5.5
Source	Mexico, volcanic regions
Chakra	Base
Number	1
Zodiac sign	Scorpio, Capricorn
Planet	Saturn
Beneficial for	Fevers, chills, compassion, strength, digestion, detoxification, blockages, hardened arteries, arthritis, joint pain, cramp, injuries, pain, bleeding, circulation, enlarged prostate.

In addition to carrying the generic properties of Obsidian (page 214), Red-black Obsidian raises the kundalini energy. It promotes vitality, virility, and brotherhood.

Polished Red-black Obsidian

Red Serpentine

Crystal system	Monoclinic
Chemistry	$(MgFe)_3Si_2O_5(OH)_4$ Magnesium iron silicate hydroxide with impurities
Hardness	3–4.5
Source	UK, Norway, Russia, Zimbabwe, Italy, USA, Switzerland, Canada
Chakra	Base, spleen
Number	8
Beneficial for	Diabetes, longevity, detoxification, parasite elimination, calcium and magnesium absorption, hypoglycemia.

Water-polished Red Celtic Serpentine

Red Serpentine (see also page 205) is particularly useful for treating diabetes, as it stimulates and regulates the pancreas, and is a strongly grounding stone that is helpful during shamanic work and trance states. Red Serpentine from Cornwall or Ireland is said to be of particular assistance to the Celtic peoples.

Red Spinel

Crystal system	Cubic
Chemistry	$MgAl_2O_4$ Magnesium aluminum oxide with impurities
Hardness	7.5–8
Source	Sri Lanka, Myanmar, Canada, USA, Brazil, Pakistan, Sweden (may be synthetic)
Chakra	Base
Number	3
Zodiac sign	Scorpio
Planet	Pluto
Beneficial for	Vitality, muscular and nerve conditions, blood vessels.

Red Spinel on matrix

In addition to carrying the generic properties of Spinel (page 260), Red Spinel stimulates physical vitality and strength. It arouses the kundalini energy, opening and aligning the base chakra.

Red Tiger's Eye

Crystal system	Trigonal
Chemistry	Complex
Hardness	4–7
Source	USA, Mexico, India, Australia, South Africa
Chakra	Base
Number	4
Zodiac sign	Leo, Scorpio
Planet	Sun
Beneficial for	Libido, brain hemisphere integration, perception, internal conflicts, pride, willfulness, emotional balance, yin–yang, fatigue, hemophilia, hepatitis, mononucleosis, depression, reproductive organs.

Tumbled Red Tiger's Eye

In addition to carrying the generic properties of Tiger's Eye (page 206), Red Tiger's Eye overcomes lethargy and provides motivation. Speeding up a slow metabolism and increasing low libido, Red Tiger's Eye can be used to enhance the flow of Qi.

Red Zircon

Crystal system	Tetragonal
Chemistry	$ZrSiO_3$ Zirconium silicate with impurities
Hardness	6.5–7.5
Source	Australia, USA, Sri Lanka, Ukraine, Canada
Chakra	Base; unites base, solar plexus, and heart
Zodiac sign	Sagittarius
Planet	Sun
Beneficial for	Synergy, constancy, jealousy, possessiveness, victimization, misogyny, homophobia, racism, sciatica, cramp, insomnia, depression, menstrual irregularity, muscles, bones, vertigo, liver. (*Zircon may cause dizziness in those who wear pacemakers or are epileptic—if so, remove immediately.*)

Raw Red Zircon

Red Zircon (see also page 261) lends vitality to the body, particularly during periods of stress. It is reputed to add power to rituals for creating wealth.

Creedite

Crystal system	Monoclinic
Chemistry	$Ca_3 Al_2 (SO_4) (F, OH)_{1}O$
Hardness	4
Source	USA, Mexico
Chakra	Throat, crown
Number	6
Zodiac sign	Virgo
Beneficial for	Fractures, torn muscles and ligaments, stabilizing the pulse, assimilation of A, B, and E vitamins.

Named after Creede, Colorado, where it was first found, Creedite attunes to a high spiritual vibration and can be used to clarify channeled messages and impressions. Said to help attune to the universal wisdom embodied in ancient texts, it enhances spiritual communication at any level. Creedite assists with out-of-body experiences, guiding the soul to its destination and promoting total recall of the experience afterward. Orange Creedite imparts urgency to spiritual evolution, speeding up the ability to move between different levels of consciousness and attuning the physical body to the changing vibration.

Natural Creedite crystal formation

Sunstone

Crystal system	Triclinic
Chemistry	$(NaCa)AlSi_3O_4$
Hardness	5–6
Source	Canada, USA, Norway, Greece, India
Chakra	Base, sacral, solar plexus, cleanses all
Number	1
Zodiac sign	Leo, Libra
Planet	Sun
Beneficial for	Pessimism, self-worth, sexual arousal, codependency, self-empowerment, independence, vitality, procrastination, depression, seasonal affective disorder, self-healing, autonomous nervous system, chronic sore throats, stomach ulcers, cartilage problems, rheumatism, general aches and pains.

Sunstone links to your life plan for the present incarnation and assists in fulfilling karmic contracts or in renegotiating these if no longer appropriate. Said to protect against destructive forces, it instills *joie de vivre* and heightens intuition. If life has lost its sweetness, Sunstone restores it and helps you nurture yourself, allowing the real Self to shine out. Traditionally linked to benevolent gods, luck, and fortune, this alchemical stone connects to the regenerative power of the sun.

Removing energy-drawing "hooks" from other people, whether located in the chakras or the aura, Sunstone returns the contact to the other person and is extremely beneficial for tie-cutting. Keep Sunstone with you at all times if you have difficulty in saying "no" and continually make sacrifices for others. It detaches from feelings of being discriminated against, disadvantaged and abandoned. Removing inhibitions and hang-ups, Sunstone reverses feelings of failure and switches to a positive take on events.

Tumbled Sunstone

Raw Sunstone

Oregon Opal

Crystal system	Amorphous
Chemistry	SiO_2 nH_2O Hydrated silica
Hardness	5.5–6.5
Source	Oregon
Chakra	Throat, solar plexus
Zodiac sign	Cancer, Libra, Scorpio, Pisces
Beneficial for	Mucus, self-worth, strengthening the will to live, intuition, fear, loyalty, spontaneity, female hormones, menopause, Parkinson's, infections, fevers, memory, purifying blood and kidneys, regulating insulin, childbirth, PMS, eyes, ears.

Discovered by a shepherd over a century ago, Oregon Opal is a highly spiritual stone. In addition to carrying the generic properties of Opal (page 254), it assists in past-life exploration and is very effective for releasing old grief, trauma, and disappointment. This stone searches out lies, both those from other people and our own self-deceptions and delusions. It clears the emotional body and amplifies the entire range of positive emotions.

Raw Oregon Opal

Celestobarite

Crystal system	Complex
Chemistry	Complex
Hardness	Variable
Source	England, Poland, Denmark, Australia, USA
Chakra	Solar plexus, base, crown
Number	8
Zodiac sign	Libra
Beneficial for	Nonphysical, multidimensional healing.

A Shamanic Oracle Stone that shows you both sides of the coin (a stone that shows you what can happen in the future), Celestobarite clarifies issues and then lets you decide. It is an excellent journeying stone that holds you suspended between the base and crown chakras and acts as a guardian while you are in the shamanic middle world, wherein reside soul aspects and entities. Celestobarite "cuts through barriers," taking you to the edge and safely beyond. This stone has a "joker" energy that presents the dark side in a joyful way and reminds us that nothing stays the same. Its Janus face (a mythological Greek god) looks to past, present, and future. See also Barite (page 244) and Iron Pyrite (page 91).

Raw Celestobarite

Drusy Quartz

Crystal system	Hexagonal
Chemistry	SiO_2 Silicon dioxide with impurities
Hardness	7
Source	Worldwide
Chakra	Sacral
Number	4
Zodiac sign	All
Planet	Sun and Moon
Beneficial for	Self-imposed limitations, periodontal disease, lethargy, multidimensional cellular memory healer, efficient receptor for programming, cleans and enhances the organs, immune system, brings the body into balance, energy enhancement.

Drusy Quartz on matrix

In addition to carrying the generic properties of Quartz (page 230), Orange Drusy Quartz is the ideal stone for the bedridden and for carers. It fosters harmony, making it easier to accept and give help, and to show thankfulness and appreciation. It increases compassion and instills the ability to laugh at life, even in the most difficult circumstances.

Fire Agate

Crystal system	Trigonal
Chemistry	SiO_2 Silicon dioxide
Hardness	6
Source	USA, India, Morocco, Czech Republic, Brazil, Africa
Chakra	Earth, base, sacral
Number	9
Zodiac sign	Aries
Planet	Mercury
Beneficial for	Fear, insecurity, cravings, destructive desires, addictions, stomach, nervous and endocrine systems, circulation, eyes, night vision, triple heater meridian, hot flushes, energy burnout, emotional trauma, self-confidence, concentration, perception, analytical abilities, aura stabilization, negative-energy transformation, emotional disease, digestive process, gastritis, eyes, stomach, uterus, lymphatic system, pancreas, blood vessels, skin disorders. *(Wear for long periods.)*

Natural Fire Agate

In addition to carrying the generic properties of Agate (page 190), Fire Agate has a deep connection to the earth and its energy is calming, bringing security and safety. With strong grounding powers, it supports during difficult times and has a protective function, especially against ill-wishing. Building a protective shield around the body, it gently returns curses. This stone aids relaxation so that the body "mellows out," enhancing meditation. Said to represent absolute perfection, it instills spiritual fortitude and facilitates the evolution of consciousness. Placed on a "broken" chakra, it gently brings it back online. Fire Agate clears etheric blockages and energizes the aura. Fire Agate links to the fire element, assisting sexual endeavors and stimulating vitality on all levels. Holding a Fire Agate effortlessly brings up inner problems for resolution.

Fire Opal

Crystal system	Amorphous
Chemistry	SiO_2 nH_2O Hydrated silica with impurities
Hardness	5.5–6.5
Source	Australia, Brazil, USA, Tanzania, Iceland, Mexico, Peru, UK, Canada, Honduras, Slovakia
Chakra	Sacral
Number	9
Zodiac sign	Cancer, Leo, Libra, Sagittarius
Beneficial for	Reenergizing and warming, stimulating the sexual organs, preventing burnout, abdomen, lower back, triple heater meridian, intestines, adrenal glands, self-worth, strengthening the will to live, female hormones, menopause, Parkinson's, infections, fevers, memory, purifying blood and kidneys, regulating insulin, PMS.

In addition to carrying the generic properties of Opal (page 254), Fire Opal is an enhancer of personal power and a revitalizer. It awakens your inner fire, and acts as a protector against danger and as an energy amplifier. This symbol of hope is excellent for business, drawing in money, facilitating change, and ushering in progress. It assists in letting go of the past, although it can be explosive in its action. If you are going through injustice and mistreatment, Fire Opal supports the resulting emotional turmoil and helps you find the insights that facilitate an easy transition between your present state and where you need to be. Magnifying thoughts and feelings, this stone releases deep-seated feelings of grief, even when these stem from other lives. It releases anything that blocks your creativity. Fire Opal encourages healthy sexuality and intensifies orgasm. It assists in leaving an abusive relationship and is a useful stone for reestablishing trusting relationships after abuse in this or any other life.

Natural Fire Opal

Orange Grossular Garnet

Crystal system	Cubic
Chemistry	Complex
Hardness	6–7.5
Source	Europe, USA (Arizona and New Mexico), South Africa, Australia
Chakra	Base, sacral, heart, purifies and energizes all
Number	2, 6
Zodiac sign	Cancer
Planet	Mars
Beneficial for	Fertility, assimilation of vitamin A, arthritis, rheumatism, kidneys, mucous membranes, skin, attracting love, dreaming, blood diseases, regenerating the body, metabolism, spinal and cellular disorders, blood, heart, lungs, regeneration of DNA, assimilation of minerals/vitamins.

In addition to carrying the generic properties of Garnet (page 47), Orange Grossular Garnet is a useful stone to have with you during challenges and lawsuits. Igniting your creativity, it also teaches relaxation and going with the flow, and inspires service and cooperation.

Natural Orange Grossular Garnet

Orange Hessonite Garnet

Crystal system	Cubic
Chemistry	Complex
Hardness	6–7.5
Source	Europe, Arizona, New Mexico, South Africa, Australia
Chakra	Base, sacral and heart, purifies and energizes all
Number	7
Zodiac sign	Scorpio
Planet	Mars
Beneficial for	Self-worth, attracting love, dreaming, blood diseases, regenerating the body, metabolism, spinal and cellular disorders, blood, heart, lungs, regeneration of DNA, assimilation of minerals/vitamins.

Orange Hessonite is seen in Vedic astrology as ruling the north node of the moon and is an important remedial gem. When the north node is badly aspected in a birth chart, it is said to bring bad karma, confusion, laziness, offensive speech, and aggressive acts. The mind is dulled, eliminating logic and morality. In addition to carrying the generic properties of Garnet (page 47) and Hessonite Garnet (page 49), Orange Hessonite remedies these qualities as it lessens aggression and encourages self-worth. Acting as a guide during astral journeying, relaxing Orange Hessonite also assists the mind and body in eliminating toxins.

Hessonite crystals on matrix

Spessartite Garnet

Crystal system	Cubic
Chemistry	Complex
Hardness	6–7.5
Source	Europe
Chakra	Base, sacral, heart, purifies and energizes all
Number	1, 7
Zodiac sign	Aquarius
Planet	Mars
Beneficial for	Depression, suppressing nightmares, heart, sexual problems, lactose intolerance, calcium imbalances, attracting love, dreaming, blood diseases, regenerating the body, metabolism, spinal and cellular disorders, blood, heart, lungs, regeneration of DNA, assimilation of minerals/vitamins.

Polished Spessartite Garnet

Named after the Spessarti district of Bavaria in Germany, Spessartite Garnet vibrates at a high rate. In addition to carrying the generic properties of Garnet (page 47), this stone imparts a willingness to help others and enhances analytical processes and the rational mind.

Raw Spessartite Garnet

Orange Calcite

Crystal system	Hexagonal
Chemistry	$CaCO_3$ Calcium carbonate with impurities
Hardness	3
Source	USA, UK, Belgium, Czech Republic, Slovakia, Peru, Iceland, Romania, Brazil
Chakra	Base, sacral
Number	8
Zodiac sign	Cancer
Planet	Sun
Beneficial for	Reproductive system, sexual abuse, gallbladder, intestinal disorders, irritable bowel, mucus, study, motivation, laziness, revitalization, emotional stress, organs of elimination, calcium uptake in bones, dissolving calcification, skeleton, joints, intestinal conditions, skin, blood clotting, tissue healing, immune system, growth in small children.

In addition to carrying the generic properties of Calcite (page 245), Orange Calcite is a highly energizing and cleansing stone. Balancing the emotions, it removes fear and overcomes depression, dissolving problems and maximizing potential. This stone removes karmic hooks and memories of old abuse held in the sacral chakra, facilitating healing on all levels. It assists in integrating new insights and creativity into everyday life.

Natural Orange Calcite (acid-enhanced)

Icicle Calcite

Crystal system	Hexagonal
Chemistry	$CaCO_3$ Calcium carbonate with impurities
Hardness	3
Source	USA, UK, Belgium, Czech Republic, Slovakia, Peru, Iceland, Romania, Brazil
Chakra	Sacral, solar plexus
Number	8
Zodiac sign	Cancer
Beneficial for	Study, motivation, laziness, revitalization, emotional stress, organs of elimination, calcium uptake in bones, dissolving calcification, skeleton, joints, intestinal conditions, skin, blood clotting, tissue healing.

A mix of orange and white Calcite (see page 245 for generic properties), Icicle Calcite is a guidance crystal that increases creativity and the ability to see things in a new way. Releasing fear, it assists in stepping forward into the future to live out your purpose. Use the white section to pull out disease and the orange to recharge and heal.

Natural Icicle Calcite wand

Orange Jade

Crystal system	Monoclinic
Chemistry	$Na(AlFe)Si_2O_6$ with impurities
Hardness	6
Source	USA, China, Italy, Myanmar, Russia, Middle East
Chakra	Sacral
Number	11
Zodiac sign	Aries
Beneficial for	Longevity, self-sufficiency, detoxification, filtration, elimination, kidneys, suprarenal glands, cellular and skeletal systems, stitches, fertility, childbirth, hips, spleen, water–salt–acid–alkaline ratio.

Orange Jade within Yellow Jade

In addition to carrying the generic properties of Jade (page 120), Orange Jade is energetic and quietly stimulating. It brings joy and teaches the interconnectedness of all beings.

Orange-brown Selenite

Crystal system	Monoclinic
Chemistry	$CaSo_{4-2}$ (H_2O) Hydrated calcium sulphate
Hardness	2
Source	England, USA, Mexico, Russia, Austria, Greece, Poland, Germany, France, Sicily
Chakra	Earth, sacral
Zodiac sign	Taurus
Beneficial for	Geopathic stress, judgment, insight, aligning the spinal column, flexibility, epilepsy, mercury poisoning from dental amalgam, free radicals. Its finest healing occurs at the energetic levels.

Raw Orange-brown Selenite

In addition to carrying the generic properties of Selenite (page 257), Orange-brown Selenite grounds angelic energies and aids earth healing. It is particularly useful for houses suffering from geopathic or electromagnetic stress.

Orange Spinel

Crystal system	Cubic
Chemistry	$MgAl_2O_4$ Magnesium aluminum oxide with impurities
Hardness	7.5–8
Source	Sri Lanka, Myanmar, Canada, USA, Brazil, Pakistan, Sweden (may be synthetic)
Chakra	Sacral
Number	9
Zodiac sign	Aries
Planet	Pluto
Beneficial for	Infertility, muscular and nerve conditions, blood vessels.

In addition to carrying the generic properties of Spinel (page 260), Orange Spinel opens and aligns the sacral chakra. It stimulates creativity and intuition, balances emotions, and treats infertility.

Orange Phantom Quartz

Crystal system	Trigonal
Chemistry	SiO_2 Silicon dioxide with inclusions
Hardness	7
Source	Brazil, Russia, India, Australia, Madagascar, South Africa, Uruguay, USA, UK, Czech Republic, Slovakia, Peru, Iceland, Romania
Chakra	Solar plexus, third eye, heart, sacral
Number	5, 6
Zodiac sign	Taurus, Cancer, Leo, Scorpio
Planet	Sun
Beneficial for	Addictions, analytic ability, dramatic pursuits, courage, vitality, metabolism, concentration, envy, weak memory, anger, emotional negativity, nosebleeds, infertility, frigidity, impotence, increasing potency, physical wounds, blood disorders, absorption of vitamins and minerals, heart, circulation, blood purification, female reproductive organs, lower-back disorders, rheumatism, arthritis, neuralgia, depression in advanced years, bodily fluids, accelerates healing in bones and ligaments, stanches blood, headaches, old patterns, hearing disorders, clairaudience.

Orange Phantom Quartz

A strongly energizing and rejuvenating crystal, as the inclusion is Carnelian (for generic properties, see page 44), Orange Phantom Quartz is helpful in overcoming an addictive personality, ending the constant search for "more," and focusing on recovery. Orange Phantoms, especially the paler crystals, enable you to journey to contact your higher self and to access who you really are. Once reconnected to this vital sense of Self, you put your insights to work in everyday life. For the generic properties of Phantoms, see page 239.

Reversed Orange Phantom Quartz

Crystal system	Trigonal
Chemistry	Complex combination
Hardness	Complex
Source	Brazil, Russia, India, Australia, Madagascar, South Africa, Uruguay, USA, UK, Czech Republic, Slovakia, Peru, Iceland, Romania
Chakra	Sacral
Beneficial for	Analytic ability, dramatic pursuits, courage, vitality, metabolism, concentration, envy, weak memory, anger, emotional negativity, nosebleeds, infertility, frigidity, impotence, increasing potency, physical wounds, blood disorders, absorption of vitamins and minerals, heart, circulation, blood purification, female reproductive organs, lower-back disorders, depression in advanced years, bodily fluids, accelerates healing in bones and ligaments, stanches blood, headaches, old patterns, hearing disorders, clairaudience.

This unusual phantom forms when Carnelian (see page 44 for generic properties) fuses around Quartz (page 230), giving clarity of insight into one's own inner workings and into the true meaning of the universe. This stone is helpful in diagnosis as it takes you into the physical body to the site and subtle cause of disease and pinpoints underlying causes. It is a useful stone when you wish to take control of your life or when you are in need of long-term sustenance and vitality. For the generic properties of Phantoms, see page 239.

Reversed Orange Phantom Quartz

Tangerine Quartz

Crystal system	Hexagonal
Chemistry	SiO_2 Silicon dioxide with inclusions and impurities
Hardness	7
Source	Africa
Chakra	Base, sacral
Beneficial for	Infertility, frigidity, reproductive system, intestines, assimilation of vitamins and iron, balancing acidity–alkalinity, removing free radicals, a master healer for any condition, multidimensional cellular memory healer, efficient receptor for programming, brings the body into balance, energy enhancement.

Tangerine Quartz points

Tangerine Quartz (see also page 230) is used for soul retrieval, integration, and to heal after psychic attack. It takes you beyond a limited belief system and into a more positive vibration. It demonstrates that like attracts like and teaches how to both give and receive. Tangerine Quartz is helpful in past-life healing and is beneficial where the soul feels it has made a mistake for which it must pay, as it releases feelings of guilt and the need to make reparation. It is an excellent stone to use after shock or trauma, especially at the soul level; it realigns the aura and the etheric blueprints.

Natural Tangerine Quartz wand with double-terminated points

Orange Zircon

Crystal system	Tetragonal
Chemistry	$ZrSiO_3$ Zirconium silicate with impurities
Hardness	6.5–7.5
Source	Australia, USA, Sri Lanka, Ukraine, Canada (may be heat-treated)
Chakra	Sacral
Number	4
Zodiac sign	Leo
Planet	Sun
Beneficial for	Synergy, constancy, jealousy, possessiveness, victimization, homophobia, misogyny, racism, sciatica, cramp, insomnia, depression, bones, muscles, vertigo, liver, menstrual irregularity. *(Zircon may cause dizziness in those who wear pacemakers or are epileptic—if so, remove immediately.)*

Raw Orange Zircon

Orange Zircon (see also page 261) makes an excellent talisman for use during traveling, as it protects against injury. This stone is reputed to increase beauty and to guard against jealousy.

Additional red and orange stones

Red: *Aventurine (page 97), Cassiterite (page 139), Grossular Garnet (page 41), Hematite (page 222), Idocrase (page 116), Moss Agate (page 101), Muscovite (page 31), Onyx (page 219), Opal (page 254), Phenacite (page 256), Rhodonite (page 33), Stilbite (page 260), Thulite (page 36), Vanadinite (page 203).* **Orange:** *Carnelian (page 44), Idocrase (page 116), Iolite (page 150), Stilbite (page 260), Vanadinite (page 203), Wulfenite (page 207), Zincite (page 56).*

Yellow, cream, and gold crystals

Yellow crystals work with the solar plexus and the mind, balancing emotion and intellect. Traditionally they were used to cure biliousness, jaundice, and other diseases of the liver, and are excellent for reducing seasonal depression, bringing the warmth of the sun into winter. Gold stones have long been associated with wealth and abundance. Yellow crystals resonate with the intellectual planet Mercury, and both yellow and gold crystals resonate with the sun.

Citrine

Crystal system	Trigonal
Chemistry	SiO_2 Silicon dioxide
Hardness	7
Source	Brazil, Russia, France, Madagascar, UK, USA (may be heat-treated amethyst)
Chakra	Cleanses and reenergizes all
Number	6
Zodiac sign	Aries, Gemini, Leo, Libra
Planet	Sun
Beneficial for	Sensitivity to environmental influences, optimism, letting go of the past, self-esteem, self-confidence, concentration, depression, fears, phobias, individuality, motivation, creativity, self-expression, nightmares, Alzheimer's, itching, male hormones, detoxification, elimination, energizing, recharging, ME, degenerative disease, digestion, spleen, pancreas, kidney and bladder infections, eye problems, blood circulation, thymus, thyroid, nerves, constipation, cellulite. As an elixir: menstrual problems, menopause, hot flushes, balancing hormones, alleviating fatigue.

Citrine geode

Large Citrine point

Deriving from the French *citron*, or lemon, lighter shades of Citrine are said to govern the physical body and its functions, and darker shades the spiritual aspects of life. A powerful cleanser and regenerator that carries the power of the sun, this is an exceedingly beneficial stone. Energizing and highly creative, it never needs cleansing. It absorbs, transmutes, and grounds negative energy and protects the environment. It is particularly beneficial for attracting abundance and should be placed in a cashbox and the wealth corner of the house. Encouraging sharing what one has, it imparts joy to all who behold it.

A useful stone for smoothing group or family discord, Citrine reverses self-destructive behavior and assists in acting on constructive criticism. It promotes inner calm, allowing your natural wisdom to emerge, and helps you move into the flow of feelings and become emotionally balanced.

Note: Wear in contact with skin.

This large piece of Citrine may well be heat-amended Amethyst.

Smoky Citrine and Smoky Citrine Herkimer

Crystal system	Trigonal
Chemistry	SiO_2 Silicon dioxide with impurities
Hardness	7
Source	Worldwide
Chakra	Earth, solar plexus
Zodiac sign	Sagittarius
Number	2, 6, 8
Planet	Pluto, Sun
Beneficial for	Sensitivity to environmental influences, energy clearing, optimism, letting go of the past, self-esteem, self-confidence, concentration, depression, fears, phobias, individuality, motivation, creativity, self-expression, nightmares, Alzheimer's, itching, male hormones, detoxification, elimination, energizing, recharging, ME, degenerative disease, digestion, spleen, pancreas, kidney and bladder infections, eye problems, blood circulation, thymus, thyroid, nerves, constipation, cellulite, corrects DNA, cellular disorders, metabolic imbalances, recall of past-life injuries and disease that affect the present, geopathic stress, X-ray exposure, libido, pain relief, fear, reproductive system, muscle, nerve tissue, inner vision, telepathy, multidimensional cellular healing, protection against radioactivity and disease caused by contact, insomnia from geopathic stress or electromagnetic pollution.

Natural Smoky Citrine Cathedral Quartz

Smoky Citrine never needs cleansing and does not accept negative energy. Excellent for enhancing metaphysical abilities and grounding them in everyday reality, it removes blockages from your spiritual path and purifies the etheric blueprint. A Smoky Citrine Herkimer clears away old beliefs and thought forms that keep you mired in poverty, opening the way to abundance. Both stones are excellent for removing vows taken in other lives, especially those of poverty and chastity, and assisting you to move out of present circumstances or an environment that precludes expansion. For the generic properties of Citrine, see left; for Herkimer Diamond, see page 241; and for Smoky Quartz, see page 186.

Smoky Citrine Herkimer

"Citrine" Herkimer

Crystal system	Trigonal
Chemistry	SiO_2 Silicon dioxide with impurities
Hardness	7
Source	North and South America, India
Chakra	Earth, third eye, cleanses and reenergizes all
Number	3, 6
Zodiac sign	Aries, Gemini, Leo, Libra, Sagittarius
Planet	Sun
Beneficial for	Sensitivity to environmental influences, optimism, letting go of the past, self-esteem, self-confidence, concentration, depression, fears, phobias, individuality, motivation, creativity, self-expression, nightmares, Alzheimer's, elimination, energizing, recharging, ME, degenerative disease, cellulite, inner vision, telepathy, stress, detoxification, multidimensional cellular healing, protection against radioactivity and disease caused by contact, insomnia from geopathic stress or electromagnetic pollution, corrects DNA, cellular disorders, metabolic imbalances, recall of past-life injuries and disease that affect the present.

"Citrine" Herkimer— the yellow oily swirls are often confused with Citrine.

The yellow color in a "Citrine" Herkimer usually arises from oil within the crystal. In addition to carrying the generic properties of Citrine (page 72) and Herkimer (page 241), "Citrine" Herkimer clears away poverty consciousness and ingrained programs that trap you in poverty, opening the way to abundance. It is an excellent stone for enhancing earth energies, making them sparkle, and for ethically harvesting the riches and resources of the environment.

Note: "Citrine" Herkimer is a high-vibration stone.

Yellow Kunzite

Crystal system	Monoclinic
Chemistry	$LiAl(SiO_2)_2$ (contains lithium)
Hardness	6.5–7
Source	USA, Madagascar, Brazil, Myanmar, Afghanistan
Chakra	All
Zodiac sign	Taurus, Leo, Scorpio
Planet	Venus, Pluto
Beneficial for	Radiation; DNA; combining intellect, intuition, and inspiration; humility; service; tolerance; self-expression; creativity; stress-related anxiety; bipolar disorder; psychiatric disorders and depression; geopathic stress; introspection; immune system; witness for radionic practitioners; anesthetic; circulatory system; heart muscle; neuralgia; epilepsy; joint pain.

In addition to carrying the generic properties of Kunzite (page 30), Yellow Kunzite clears environmental smog and deflects radiation and microwaves from the auric field. It aligns the chakras, restructures DNA, and stabilizes the cellular blueprint and the calcium-magnesium balance in the body.

Natural Yellow Kunzite

Note: Yellow Kunzite is a high-vibration stone.

Golden Enhydro Herkimer

Crystal system	Trigonal
Chemistry	SiO_2 Silicon dioxide with impurities
Hardness	7
Source	Himalayas
Chakra	Solar plexus, third eye, crown, higher crown
Number	3
Zodiac sign	Sagittarius
Beneficial for	Emotional clearing, gender confusion, inner vision, telepathy, stress, detoxification, multidimensional cellular healing, protection against radioactivity and disease caused by contact, insomnia from geopathic stress or electromagnetic pollution, corrects DNA, cellular disorders, metabolic imbalances, recall of past-life injuries and disease that affect the present, influenza, throat, bronchitis.

Golden Enhydro Herkimer showing oily bubbles.

A rare stone found in the Himalayas, Golden Enhydros are strongly energetic double-terminated crystals with small, clearly visible bubbles or veins of yellow oil floating within them. In addition to carrying the generic properties of Herkimer (page 241), Golden Enhydros are excellent for developing spiritual gifts and stimulating the third eye, taking you straight to the ages-old spiritual wisdom in the sacred mountains. Powerful healers for the solar plexus and for clearing emotional disturbances that have been carried over many lifetimes, Golden Enhydros cleanse the emotional body and blueprint, creating emotional well-being. Eliminating gender confusion or ambivalence in those who have changed sex from one incarnation to another, Golden Enhydros clear implants from the third eye and restrictions placed on it in this or any other life.

Note: Golden Enhydro Herkimer is a high-vibration stone.

Yellow Phenacite

Crystal system	Trigonal
Chemistry	Be_2SiO_4
Hardness	7.5–8
Source	Madagascar, Russia, Zimbabwe, Colorado, Brazil
Chakra	Higher crown
Zodiac sign	Gemini
Beneficial for	Manifestation, multidimensional healing. *(Phenacite works beyond the physical plane.)*

Raw Yellow Phenacite

In addition to carrying the generic properties of Phenacite (page 256), Yellow Phenacite is a stone of manifestation, bringing what is desired into being on the physical plane, providing it is for the highest good of all. It has a particular aptitude for extraterrestrial contact.

Note: Yellow Phenacite is a high-vibration stone.

Citrine Spirit Quartz

Crystal system	Hexagonal
Chemistry	SiO_2 Silicon dioxide with impurities
Hardness	7
Source	Magaliesberg, South Africa
Chakra	Earth, solar plexus
Number	4
Zodiac sign	All
Planet	Sun, Moon
Beneficial for	Abundance, geopathic stress, ascension, rebirthing, self-forgiveness, patience, purifying and stimulating the auric bodies, insightful dreams, reframing the past, blending male and female, yin and yang, healing discord, astral projection, detoxification, obsessive behavior, fertility, skin eruptions, sensitivity to environmental influences, optimism, letting go of the past, self-esteem, self-confidence, concentration, depression, fears, phobias, energizing, recharging, ME, degenerative disease.

Citrine Spirit Quartz

In addition to carrying the generic properties of Spirit Quartz (page 237), Citrine Spirit Quartz promotes self-awareness. It purifies and cleanses the aura, assisting in being centered in your power and directing your life from that place. Bringing about purification of intent, it is particularly useful for accessing abundance while at the same time releasing any dependence on, or attachment to, material things. In business, it focuses goals and plans. Useful in grids to stabilize and protect a house against electromagnetic smog or geopathic stress, it heals disturbed earth energies of any kind. Citrine Spirit Quartz assists in conflict resolution and can be programmed to send forgiveness to those who have wronged you, or to ask for forgiveness for yourself.

Note: Citrine Spirit Quartz is a high-vibration stone.

Lemon Chrysoprase

Crystal system	Trigonal
Chemistry	Complex
Hardness	7
Source	USA, Russia, Brazil, Australia, Poland, Tanzania
Chakra	Heart, sacral
Zodiac sign	Taurus
Planet	Venus
Beneficial for	Depression, detoxification, elimination, liver, heart, hormone imbalances.

Tumbled Lemon Chrysoprase

Deriving its color from nickel, Lemon Chrysoprase is a stone of compassion and loving-kindness. This stone is helpful for childhood night terrors, especially where these arise from a past-life cause. It makes the mind more alert and in contact with inner wisdom, and increases trust in the universe and in others.

Amblygonite

Crystal system	Triclinic
Chemistry	$(Li, Na)Al(PO_4)(F,OH)$
Hardness	5.5–6
Source	USA, Brazil, France, Germany, Sweden, Myanmar, Canada
Chakra	Solar plexus, opens and aligns all
Number	6
Zodiac sign	Taurus
Beneficial for	Stress, genetic disorders, arts, music, poetry, creativity, stomach, digestion, headaches.

Raw Amblygonite

Amblygonite helps you nurture yourself and reconcile dualities, integrating polarities. It awakens your sense of being an immortal soul. A useful stone for gently releasing emotional hooks from the solar plexus, it assists in ending relationships without angry consequences. This stone calms a stomach that is knotted up with anxiety. It can be used to grid areas of discordance or public disorder, especially where young people are involved. In healing, it activates the electrical systems of the body and can be taped over the thymus to protect against computer emanations in those who are sensitive.

Note: Amblygonite is a high-vibration stone.

Astrophyllite

Crystal system	Triclinic
Chemistry	$(KNa)_3 (FeMn)_7 Ti_2 Si_8 (OH)_{31}$
Hardness	3
Source	USA
Chakra	Higher crown
Number	9
Zodiac sign	Scorpio
Beneficial for	Completing projects, epilepsy, reproductive and hormonal systems, PMS and menopausal disturbances, cellular regeneration, large intestine, fatty deposits.

Tumbled Astrophyllite

Meaning "star sheets," Astrophyllite is an excellent stone for promoting out-of-body experiences, acting as guide and protector in other realms, and for standing outside oneself for an objective view. This stone introduces you to your full potential, recognizing that you have no limits. Eliminating without guilt anything outgrown in your life, it teaches that as one door closes another opens, showing you the way forward. Said to increase sensitivity of touch and to improve perception, Astrophyllite is helpful for those undergoing training in massage or acupressure, especially as it makes you aware of other people's needs. This stone activates your dreams and enables you to "dream true" to see the path your soul believes you should tread.

Yellow Zircon

Crystal system	Tetragonal
Chemistry	$ZrSiO_3$ Zirconium silicate
Hardness	6.5–7.5
Source	Australia, USA, Sri Lanka, Ukraine, Canada (may be heat-treated)
Chakra	Solar plexus
Zodiac sign	Sagittarius
Planet	Sun
Beneficial for	Depression, synergy, constancy, jealousy, possessiveness, victimization, homophobia, misogyny, racism, sciatica, cramp, insomnia, depression, bones, muscles, vertigo, liver, menstrual irregularity. *(Zircon may cause dizziness in those who wear pacemakers or are epileptic—if so, remove immediately.)*

Yellow Zircon (see also page 261) assists you in attracting success in business and in love and enhances your sexual energy. It lifts depression and makes you more alert.

Yellow Jade

Crystal system	Complex
Chemistry	$Na(AlFe)Si_2O_6$
Hardness	6
Source	USA, China, Italy, Myanmar, Russia, Middle East
Chakra	Solar plexus
Number	11
Zodiac sign	Gemini
Planet	Venus
Beneficial for	Digestive and elimination systems of the body, self-sufficiency, longevity, detoxification, filtration, elimination, kidneys, suprarenal glands, cellular and skeletal systems, stitches, fertility, hips, water–salt–acid–alkaline ratio.

In addition to carrying the generic properties of Jade (page 120), Yellow Jade is energetic and stimulating, with a mellowness that brings joy and happiness and teaches the interconnectedness of all beings.

Natural Yellow Jade

Yellow Spinel

Crystal system	Cubic
Chemistry	Complex
Hardness	7.5–8
Source	Sri Lanka, Myanmar, Canada, USA, Brazil, Pakistan, Sweden (may be synthetic)
Chakra	Solar plexus
Number	5
Zodiac sign	Leo
Planet	Pluto
Beneficial for	Muscular and nerve conditions, blood vessels.

Yellow Spinel

In addition to carrying the generic properties of Spinel (page 260), Yellow Spinel stimulates the intellect and enhances personal power.

Amber

Crystal system	Noncrystalline
Chemistry	CHO with impurities
Hardness	2–2.5
Source	UK, Poland, Italy, Romania, Russia, Germany, Myanmar, Dominican Republic
Chakra	Throat, cleanses and purifies all
Number	3
Zodiac sign	Leo, Aquarius
Planet	Sun
Beneficial for	Altruism, memory, trust, wisdom, peacefulness, decision-making, depression, vitality, stress, throat, goiter, stomach, spleen, kidneys, bladder, liver, gallbladder, joint problems, mucous membranes, wound healing, natural antibiotic.

Natural Amber

Polished Amber

The most ancient of decorations, Amber beads have been found in graves dating to 8000 BCE. Because of its natural warmth, Amber was regarded as a living being, and the Chinese believed that the souls of tigers metamorphosed into Amber at their death. When Amber is rubbed against wool or silk it becomes electrically charged; its Greek name was *electron*, from which the word "electricity" is derived. Strictly speaking, Amber is not a crystal, being tree resin that solidified and became fossilized. With strong connections to the earth, it is a grounding stone for higher energies. A powerful healer and cleanser that draws disease from the body and assists tissue revitalization, Amber cleans the environment and the chakras. It absorbs negative energies and transmutes them into positive forces that help the body heal itself. This stone provides a protective shield to prevent healers from taking on client's pain and also protects against psychic vampirism.

Adamite

Crystal system	Orthorhombic
Chemistry	$Zn_2AsO_4 (OH)$
Hardness	3.5
Source	Mexico, Greece, USA
Chakra	Solar plexus, heart, throat
Number	8
Zodiac sign	Cancer
Beneficial for	Endocrine system, glands, heart, lungs, throat.

Adamite on matrix

A useful stone for uniting heart and mind, Adamite provides clarity and inner strength when dealing with emotional issues. Helping you move forward confidently into an unknown future, it brings to the fore entrepreneurial skills and the ability to identify new avenues for growth in both business and personal life. It is a stone that can take you back to first principles.

Yellow Apatite

Crystal system	Hexagonal
Chemistry	$Ca_5 (PO_4)_3 (F,CL,OH)$
Hardness	5
Source	Canada, USA, Mexico, Norway, Russia, Brazil
Chakra	Solar plexus
Number	9
Zodiac sign	Gemini
Beneficial for	Toxicity, ME, lethargy, depression, lack of concentration, inefficient learning, poor digestion, cellulite, liver, pancreas, gallbladder, spleen, motivation, nervous exhaustion, irritability, humanitarian attitude, apathy, service, communication, energy depletion, pain, bones, cells, calcium absorption, cartilage, bone, teeth, motor skills, arthritis, joint problems, rickets, appetite suppression, metabolic rate, glands, meridians, organs, hypertension.

Raw Yellow Apatite

In addition to carrying the generic properties of Apatite (page 133), Yellow Apatite is a great eliminator, releasing karmic guilt and victimhood, drawing off stagnant energy, and neutralizing stored anger. This stone balances the mental etheric blueprint, healing blockages and old conditioning and balancing mental over- or underactivity. It is useful for removing ingrained attitudes and faulty assumptions.

Note: Yellow Apatite is a high-vibration stone.

Yellow Sapphire

Crystal system	Hexagonal
Chemistry	Al_2O_3 Aluminum oxide with impurities
Hardness	9
Source	Myanmar, Czech Republic, Brazil, Kenya, India, Australia, Sri Lanka, Canada, Thailand, Madagascar
Chakra	Third eye, crown
Number	4
Zodiac sign	Leo
Planet	Moon, Saturn
Beneficial for	Achieving ambitions, detoxification, protection against snakebite, stomach, gallbladder, liver, spleen, serenity, peace of mind, concentration, multidimensional cellular healing, overactive body systems.

Faceted Yellow Sapphire

One of the Vedic remedial gems linked to the Hindu god Ganesha, Yellow Sapphire attracts wealth to the home and is placed in cashboxes to increase prosperity and income. In addition to carrying the generic properties of Sapphire (page 160), it stimulates the intellect and improves overall focus so that the bigger picture is seen.

Yellow Zincite

Crystal system	Hexagonal
Chemistry	(ZnMn)O
Hardness	4
Source	Italy, USA, Poland (crystalline Zincite is heat-amended or artificially manufactured)
Chakra	Solar plexus
Number	5
Zodiac sign	Taurus, Libra
Beneficial for	Urinary infections, necessary change, lethargy, procrastination, confidence, phobias, hypnotic commands, mental imprints, empty-nest syndrome, creativity, hair, skin, prostate gland, menopausal symptoms, immune system, meridians, ME, AIDS, autoimmune diseases, candida, mucous conditions, epilepsy, organs of elimination and assimilation, infertility.

In addition to carrying the generic properties of Zincite (page 56), Yellow Zincite is particularly efficacious for urinary infections.

Artifically made crystalline Zincite

Beryl

Crystal system	Hexagonal
Chemistry	$Be_3Al_2Si_6O_{18}$
Hardness	7.5–8
Source	USA, Brazil, China, Ireland, Switzerland, Australia, Czech Republic, France, Norway
Chakra	Varies according to color, solar plexus, crown
Number	1
Zodiac sign	Leo (see also specific types of Beryl)
Planet	Moon
Beneficial for	Courage, stress, overanalysis, elimination, pulmonary and circulatory systems, sedation, resistance to toxins and pollutants, liver, heart, stomach, spine, concussion, throat infections.

Raw Beryl

The name Beryl derives from the Greek *beryllos,* meaning a green gemstone, and this stone was traditionally used for rain magic and protection against storms. Dr. Dee, metaphysical adviser to Queen Elizabeth I, had a crystal ball made of Beryl, now in the British Museum. It is a powerful protection against outside influences and manipulation. This stone helps you deal with a stressful life and shed unnecessary baggage. Representing purity of being, Beryl helps actualize potential and reawakens love in those who are married but jaded.

Faceted Beryl

Golden Beryl (Heliodor)

Crystal system	Hexagonal
Chemistry	$Be_3Al_2Si_6O_{18}$
Hardness	7.5–8
Source	USA, Brazil, China, Ireland, Switzerland, Australia, Czech Republic, France, Norway
Chakra	Solar plexus, third eye, crown
Zodiac sign	Leo
Beneficial for	Menopause, burnout, courage, stress, overanalysis, elimination, pulmonary and circulatory systems, sedation, resistance to toxins and pollutants, liver, heart, stomach, spine, concussion, throat infections.

Tumbled Golden Beryl

Golden Beryl ball

Golden Beryl is a seer's stone used over eons for ritual magic and scrying. In addition to carrying the generic properties of Beryl (page 81), this stone promotes purity of being, teaching initiative and independence. It stimulates the will to succeed and the ability to manifest potential into reality. A stone that supports energy expansion, it is said to assist souls who are finding life on earth difficult, and to support anyone who is suffering from healer's burnout or is overtaxed by protracted emotional-release work.

Chrysoberyl

Crystal system	Orthorhombic
Chemistry	$BeAl_2O_4$
Hardness	8.5
Source	Russia, Sweden, Sri Lanka, Myanmar, Brazil, Canada, Ghana, Norway, Zimbabwe, China, Australia, Canada
Chakra	Opens crown and aligns to solar plexus
Number	6
Zodiac sign	Leo
Beneficial for	Creativity, strategic planning, compassion, forgiveness, generosity, confidence, self-healing, adrenaline, cholesterol, chest, liver.

Chrysoberyl combines the Greek words *chrysos* and *beryllos*, indicating its golden yellow color. No longer considered a type of Beryl, Chrysoberyl is a stone of new beginnings that releases outworn energy patterns and helps to see both sides of a problem, encouraging forgiveness of family or friends who have perpetrated injustices. Used with other crystals, this stone highlights the cause of disease and is excellent for promoting creativity.

Raw Chrysoberyl

Cacoxenite

Crystal system	Hexagonal
Chemistry	$Fe_4 (PO_4)_{3-12}H_2O$ Hydrated iron aluminum phosphate oxide hydroxide
Hardness	3–4
Source	England, Sweden, France, Germany, Holland, USA
Chakra	Third eye, crown
Number	9
Zodiac sign	Sagittarius
Beneficial for	Stress, holistic healing and psychosomatic awareness, fear, hormonal and cellular disorders, heart, lungs, cold, flu, respiratory ailments.

Raw Cacoxenite in Quartz matrix

A stone of ascension, Cacoxenite heightens spiritual awareness and assists in using planetary alignments to stimulate evolution of the earth, and takes you to core soul memories that assist your spiritual evolution. Accentuating the positive, Cacoxenite releases restrictions and inhibitions. If you have seemingly insurmountable problems, meditate with Cacoxenite. Included within Amethyst, Cacoxenite opens the mind to receive new ideas, and harmonizes personal will with the higher self. This stone amplifies the power of full- or new-moon rituals, especially when set in silver.

Limonite

Crystal system	Amorphous
Chemistry	$2FE_3O_3\ 3H_2O$
Hardness	4–5.5
Source	Brazil, France, Germany, Luxembourg, Italy, Russia, Cuba, Zaire, India, Namibia, USA
Number	7
Zodiac sign	Virgo
Beneficial for	Dehydration, cleansing, musculoskeletal system, iron and calcium assimilation, jaundice, fevers, liver, digestion.

Limonite is the generic name for iron oxide, and the name derives from the Greek *leimons*, meaning "boggy meadow." Its association with water led to its being a treatment for dehydration, but it is excellent for removing oneself from the mire. A grounding and protective stone that stabilizes life, Limonite stimulates inner strength, particularly under extreme conditions. It affords the physical body protection during metaphysical activities, defends against mental influence or attack, enhances telepathy, and ameliorates confusion and psychic overwhelm. A powerful mental healer, Limonite restores youthful properties and supports standing firm without needing to fight back. It facilitates inner-child healing with other stones.

Raw Limonite

See also Red (page 55) and Yellow (page 92) Phantom Quartz.

Yellow Jasper

Crystal system	Trigonal
Chemistry	SiO_2 + Fe, O, OH Silicon dioxide
Hardness	7
Source	Worldwide
Chakra	Solar plexus
Zodiac sign	Leo
Beneficial for	Endocrine system, toxicity, electromagnetic and environmental pollution, radiation, stress, prolonged illness or hospitalization, circulation, digestive and sexual organs, balancing mineral content of the body. For pain relief, place Yellow Jasper over site of pain until it eases.

Tumbled Yellow Jasper

Yellow Jasper is an excellent protector during spiritual work and physical travel. In addition to carrying the generic properties of Jasper (page 45), It assists you on your earth journey and keeps you on your life path. This stone clears away outworn emotion. It channels positive energy, making you feel physically better. It is helpful to children who are dyspraxic, clumsy, or accident-prone.

Yellow Labradorite

Crystal system	Triclinic
Chemistry	Complex
Hardness	5–6
Source	Italy, Greenland, Finland, Russia, Canada, Scandinavia
Chakra	Third eye, solar plexus
Number	6, 7
Zodiac sign	Leo, Scorpio, Sagittarius
Beneficial for	Witness during radionic treatment, aligning physical and etheric bodies, vitality, originality, regulating metabolism.

Tumbled Labradorite

In addition to carrying the generic properties of Labradorite (page 227), Yellow Labradorite accesses the highest levels of consciousness, assisting visualization, trance, clairvoyance, and channeling. It expands the mental body, attuning it to higher wisdom. This stone is useful for detaching from undue influence or manipulation by others, and especially for treating codependency or an enabler who is unable to let the person learn their own lessons in life or who unconsciously wants to prolong dependency.

Note: Yellow Labradorite is a high-vibration stone.

Septarian

Crystal system	Trigonal
Chemistry	Complex
Hardness	3
Source	Australia, USA, Canada, Spain, England, New Zealand, Madagascar
Chakra	Base, synthesizes heart, throat, and third eye
Number	66
Zodiac sign	Taurus, Sagittarius
Beneficial for	Seasonal affective disorder, patience, holistic healing, tolerance, endurance, self-healing, metabolism, growths, intestines, kidneys, blood, skin disorders, heart, study, motivation, laziness, revitalization, emotional stress, organs of elimination, calcium uptake in bones, dissolving calcification, skeleton, joints, intestinal conditions, skin, tissue healing, immune system, growth in small children, ulcers, warts, patience, emotional stress, anger, reliability, acceptance, flexibility, grounding, Reynaud's disease, chills, bones, calcium absorption, disc elasticity, night twitches, muscle spasm, regulates processes, generosity, hostility, lawsuits, nightmares, fear of the dark, hysteria, depression, negative thoughts, turbulent emotions, bad dreams, cleansing, open sores, mineral build-up in veins, dementia, senility, physical energy.

Shaped Septarian geode

Septarian is reputedly named from the Latin *septem* or seven, because the mud ball from which it formed on the seabed splits into seven points radiating in every direction. It is also said that it arises from *saeptum*, an enclosure or wall. A combination of Calcite (page 245), Chalcedony (page 247), and Aragonite (page 190), the gray concretions connect to devic energy. Septarian is an excellent support for self-nurturing, caring about others, and caring for the earth. It incubates ideas and assists in bringing them to fruition, and harmonizes emotions and intellect with the higher mind. The NLP stone, it assists in repatterning and reprogramming outgrown behavior and emotions.

A useful tool for public speaking, Septarian makes each individual feel that he or she is being personally addressed and enhances the ability to communicate within a group. This stone coheres spiritual groups, and healers can use it for diagnosis and insight into the cause of disease. It has the ability to focus the body's own healing power.

Snakeskin Agate

Crystal system	Trigonal
Chemistry	SiO_2 Silicon dioxide
Hardness	6
Source	USA, India, Morocco, Czech Republic, Brazil, Africa
Chakra	Base, sacral
Zodiac sign	Gemini
Planet	Mercury
Beneficial for	Wrinkles, hearing disorders, stomach, skin complaints.

Snakeskin Agate (see also page 190) links you to the joy of living, and helps you eliminate worry and depression from everyday life. Placed on the lower chakras, this stone can activate kundalini rise. It can help you blend in and travel without being seen in both the physical and spiritual worlds, and is a useful accompaniment for soul retrieval in the lower realms. Snakeskin Agate is used to smooth the skin.

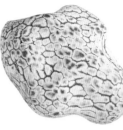

Snakeskin Agate

Golden Calcite

Crystal system	Hexagonal
Chemistry	$CaCO_3$ Calcium carbonate with impurities
Hardness	3
Source	USA, UK, Belgium, Czech Republic, Slovakia, Peru, Iceland, Romania, Brazil
Chakra	Solar plexus, crown
Zodiac sign	Leo
Beneficial for	Elimination, study, motivation, laziness, revitalization, emotional stress, organs of elimination, calcium uptake in bones, dissolving calcification, skeleton, suppurating wounds.

Golden Calcite (see also page 245) is a great eliminator. Its energy, especially as an elixir, is uplifting. Enhancing meditation, it induces a deep state of relaxation and spirituality, and links to the highest source of spiritual guidance. It stimulates the higher mind and the will.

Raw Golden Calcite

Yellow Fluorite

Crystal system	Cubic
Chemistry	CaF_2 Calcium fluoride
Hardness	4
Source	USA, England, Mexico, Canada, Australia, Germany, Norway, China, Peru, Brazil
Chakra	Solar plexus, cleanses all
Zodiac sign	Capricorn, Pisces
Planet	Mercury
Beneficial for	Cooperative endeavors, intellectual activities, toxicity, cholesterol, liver, balance, coordination, self-confidence, shyness, worry, centering, concentration, psychosomatic disease.

In addition to carrying the generic properties of Fluorite (page 177), Yellow Fluorite enhances creativity and stabilizes group energy.

Yellow Fluorite on matrix

Yellow Topaz

Crystal system	Orthorhombic
Chemistry	$Al_2(SiO_4)(F,OH)_2$ Aluminum hydroxyl fluoro
Hardness	8
Source	USA, Russia, Mexico, India, Australia, South Africa, Sri Lanka, Pakistan, Myanmar, Germany
Chakra	Solar plexus
Zodiac sign	Sagittarius, Leo
Planet	Sun, Jupiter
Beneficial for	Astuteness, problem-solving, honesty, forgiveness, self-realization, emotional support, manifesting health, digestion, anorexia, sense of taste, nerves, metabolism, skin, vision.

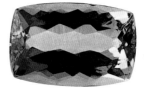

Faceted Topaz

St. Hildegard of Bingen recommended an elixir of Topaz to correct dimness of vision. This crystal encourages trust in the universe that enables you to "be" rather than to "do," cutting through doubt and uncertainty. Directing energy to where it is needed most, it recharges and aligns the meridians of the body and sheds light on your path, tapping into inner resources. Traditionally known as a stone of love and good fortune, it supports affirmations, manifestation and visualization, and helps you discover your own inner riches. Excellent for cleaning the aura and for inducing relaxation, Topaz releases tension at any level and can speed up spiritual development where this has been laborious. Negativity does not survive around joyful Topaz.

Golden (Imperial) Topaz

Crystal system	Orthorhombic
Chemistry	$Al_2(SiO_4)(F, OH)_2$ Aluminum hydroxyl fluoro
Hardness	8
Source	USA, Russia, Mexico, India, Australia, South Africa, Sri Lanka, Pakistan, Myanmar, Germany
Chakra	Solar plexus
Number	9
Zodiac sign	Leo, Sagittarius, Pisces
Planet	Sun, Jupiter
Beneficial for	Cellular structures, solar plexus, nervous exhaustion, insufficient combustion, liver, gallbladder, endocrine glands, astuteness, problem-solving, honesty, forgiveness, self-realization, emotional support, manifesting health, digestion, anorexia, sense of taste, nerves, metabolism, skin, vision.

Natural Golden Topaz

In addition to carrying the generic properties of Yellow Topaz (above), Golden Topaz acts as a battery, recharging you spiritually and physically. An excellent stone for conscious attunement to the highest forces in the universe, it stores information received in this way, reminding you of your divine origins. Golden Topaz assists in recognizing your own abilities and attracts mentors. This stone bestows charisma and confidence while remaining generous and openhearted. It assists in overcoming limitations and in setting great plans afoot.

Rutilated Topaz

Crystal system	Complex
Chemistry	Complex
Hardness	Unknown
Source	Very rare
Chakra	Third eye
Zodiac sign	Gemini, Scorpio, Sagittarius
Beneficial for	Astuteness, problem-solving, honesty, forgiveness, self-realization, emotional support, manifesting health, digestion, anorexia, sense of taste, nerves, metabolism, skin, vision, cell regeneration.

In addition to carrying the generic properties of Yellow Topaz (page 87) and Rutilated Quartz (page 202), this rare stone, in which fine hairs float in transparent crystal, is extremely effective for visualization, protection and manifestation. An excellent stone for scrying, it brings deep insights and can be programmed to attract love and light into one's life. Rutilated Topaz guards against interference from the physical or spirit world.

Note: Rutilated Topaz is a high-vibration stone.

Rutilated Topaz point

Topaz cluster containing rutilated point

Golden Tiger's Eye

Crystal system	Trigonal
Chemistry	$NaFe^{+3}(SiO_3)_2$ Silicon dioxide with impurities
Hardness	4–7
Source	USA, Mexico, India, Australia, South Africa
Chakra	Third eye, solar plexus
Number	4
Zodiac sign	Leo, Capricorn
Planet	Sun
Beneficial for	Brain hemisphere integration, perception, internal conflicts, pride, willfulness, emotional balance, yin–yang, fatigue, hemophilia, hepatitis, mononucleosis, depression, eyes, night vision, throat, reproductive organs, constrictions, broken bones.

In addition to carrying the generic properties of Tiger's Eye (page 206), Golden Tiger's Eye assists in paying attention to detail, warns against overcomplacency and danger, and encourages you to take action from a place of reason rather than emotion. It is excellent for examinations and important meetings. This stone is said to confer invisibility when you are under psychic attack. It draws negative energy from the solar plexus and returns it to its source. Place Golden Tiger's Eye in your car to protect against accidents. It should be worn for short periods of time.

Tumbled Golden Tiger's Eye

Yellow Tourmaline

Crystal system	Trigonal
Chemistry	Complex silicate
Hardness	7–7.5
Source	Sri Lanka, Brazil, Africa, USA, Australia, Afghanistan, Italy, Germany, Madagascar
Chakra	Solar plexus
Number	1, 4, 33
Zodiac sign	Leo
Beneficial for	Intellectual pursuits, business affairs, stomach, liver, spleen, kidneys, gallbladder, protection, detoxification, spinal adjustments, balancing male–female energy, paranoia, dyslexia, hand-eye coordination, assimilation and translation of coded information, bronchitis, diabetes, emphysema, pleurisy, pneumonia, energy flow, enhancement and removal of blockages.

Faceted Yellow Tourmaline

In addition to carrying the generic properties of Tourmaline (page 210), Yellow Tourmaline enhances personal power and opens up the spiritual pathway.

Sulfur

Crystal system	Orthorhombic
Chemistry	S_8 Sulfur
Hardness	2
Source	Italy, Greece, USA, Japan, Indonesia, Russia, South America, volcanic regions
Number	7
Zodiac sign	Leo
Planet	Sun
Beneficial for	Willfulness, exhaustion, serious illness, creativity, infections, fevers, colds, swelling, fibrous and tissue growths, painful swellings and joint problems, skin conditions.

Raw "powder" Sulfur

Sulfur is associated with volcanic regions and has traditionally been used during magical working to drive off demons. An excellent stone for anything that erupts, such as feelings, violence, skin conditions, or fevers, it can bring latent metaphysical abilities to the surface. A powerful stone for karmic cleansing, Sulfur has a negative electrical charge and is extremely useful for absorbing destructive energies, emanations, and emotions. Placed anywhere in the environment, it absorbs negativity and removes barriers to progress. Sulfur identifies negative traits within the personality, reaching rebellious, stubborn, or obstreperous parts, opening the way to conscious change. It blocks repetitive and distracting thought patterns and grounds thought processes into the here and now.

Note: Sulfur is toxic and should not be taken internally.

Crystalline Sulfur

Gold Sheen Obsidian

Crystal system	Amorphous
Chemistry	SiO_2 Silicon dioxide with impurities
Hardness	5–5.5
Source	Mexico, volcanic regions
Chakra	Solar plexus, third eye
Zodiac sign	Sagittarius
Planet	Saturn
Beneficial for	Compassion, strength, detoxification. Works best beyond the physical level.

A scrying stone, Gold Sheen Obsidian takes you into past, present, and future, and deep into the core of a problem. In addition to carrying the generic properties of Obsidian (page 214), it balances energy fields and indicates what requires healing (but other crystals achieve this healing). Gold Sheen eliminates any sense of futility or conflict. By releasing ego involvement, it imparts knowledge of spiritual direction.

Gold Sheen Obsidian ball

Chalcopyrite

Crystal system	Tetragonal
Chemistry	$CuFeS_2$ Copper iron sulfide
Hardness	3.5–4
Source	France, Chile, Namibia, Zambia, Peru, Germany, Spain, USA (Montana and Utah)
Chakra	Crown
Number	9
Zodiac sign	Capricorn
Planet	Venus
Beneficial for	Self-esteem, perception, logical thought, energy blockages, hair growth, thread veins, brain disorders, excretory organs, tumors, infectious diseases, RNA/DNA, arthritis, bronchitis, inflammation, fever.

A copper pyrite named from the Greek *chalkos*, "sparks when struck," Chalcopyrite puts you through "the fires of truth." Excellent for achieving the state of no mind, this stone enhances perception and assimilates spiritual knowledge. Linking to ancient incarnations, it accesses the cause of present-life difficulties or diseases. A powerful energy conduit supporting Tai Chi, acupuncture, or acupressure, it releases energy blockages and enhances the movement of Qi around the body. Used to locate lost objects, it can disappear and reappear in different realities. Chalcopyrite shows you that abundance is a state of mind, creating inner security.

Tumbled Chalcopyrite

Iron Pyrite

Crystal system	Cubic
Chemistry	FeS_2 Iron sulfide
Hardness	6–6.5
Source	USA, Spain, Portugal, Italy, UK, Chile, Peru
Number	3
Zodiac sign	Leo
Planet	Mars
Beneficial for	Energy, diplomacy, despair, fatigue, inferiority complex, servitude, inadequacy, inertia, memory, accessing potential, cooperation, blood, circulation, bones, cell formation, DNA damage, meridians, sleep disturbed owing to gastric upset, digestive tract, ingested toxins, circulatory and respiratory systems, lungs, asthma, bronchitis, oxygenates bloodstream.

Natural Iron Pyrite formation

Known as Fool's Gold, Pyrite comes from the Greek for "firestone" because it was believed that Pyrite, a sparking stone, held fire in its core. An excellent energy shield, Pyrite blocks out negative energy and pollutants at all levels, preventing energy leaks from the physical body and aura, protecting subtle and physical bodies, and deflecting harm. It creates a positive outlook. This stone sees behind a façade to what *is*. Helpful for men who feel inferior, it strengthens confidence in masculinity but may be too powerful for "macho" men, initiating aggression. Pyrite is very fast-acting and is particularly helpful for getting to the root of karmic and psychosomatic disease. Cubic Pyrite expands and structures mental capabilities, balancing instinct with intuition, creativity with analysis.

Iron Pyrite flower

Marcasite

Crystal system	Orthorhombic
Chemistry	FeS_2 Iron sulfide
Hardness	6–6.5
Source	USA, Mexico, Germany, France
Chakra	Base
Number	8
Zodiac sign	Leo
Beneficial for	Yang energy, concentration, memory, hysteria, cleansing the blood, warts, moles, freckles, spleen.

Marcasite crystals on matrix

Derived from the Arabic word *markaschatsa*, "firestone," Marcasite expands metaphysical abilities, especially those of spirit awareness and clairvoyance. Providing a psychic shield that grounds in the everyday world, Marcasite assists those who undertake house-clearing or entity removal. Providing a detached perspective when seeking insight into your Self, it helps to make any adjustments necessary. If you suffer from scattered or confused thinking and impaired memory, Marcasite brings clarity. Increasing willpower, it boldly goes where you have not been before. Excellent for Leos, it encourages you to shine, and helps anyone who suffers from a sense of spiritual lack to find true abundance.

Uranophane

Crystal system	Monoclinic
Chemistry	$Ca(UO_2)_2Si_2O_7\cdot6H_2O$ Hydrated calcium uranyl silicate
Hardness	2–3
Source	Zaire, Germany, USA, Czech Republic, Germany, Australia, France, Italy
Number	5
Beneficial for	Radiation damage. Other properties not yet confirmed.

A radioactive crystal, Uranophane should be stored away from other crystals and is not a mineral to use for prolonged periods. However, under the supervision of a suitably qualified practitioner, it can support nuclear-based medicine and radiation therapy, and act as a homeopathic catalyst for releasing ancient radiation damage.

Raw Uranophane on matrix

Yellow Phantom Quartz

Crystal system	Hexagonal
Chemistry	SiO_2 Silicon dioxide with inclusions
Hardness	7
Source	Worldwide
Chakra	Third eye, crown, past life, solar plexus
Zodiac sign	Gemini
Planet	Sun
Beneficial for	Old patterns, hearing disorders, clairaudience.

In addition to carrying the generic properties of Phantoms (page 239) and Quartz (page 230), Yellow Phantom, an intellectually attuned stone, helps the mind recall and reorganize memories and thought patterns. The inclusion is limonite, a stimulator for intellectual activities of all kinds. This phantom can be used to remove mental attachments from this life or any other.

Yellow Phantom Quartz

Golden Healer Quartz

Crystal system	Hexagonal
Chemistry	SiO_2 Silicon dioxide with impurities
Hardness	7
Source	Africa
Chakra	Third eye, crown, solar plexus, aligns all
Planet	Sun
Beneficial for	Multidimensional healing, a master healer for any condition, cellular memory healer, efficient receptor for programming, cleans and enhances the organs, immune system, brings the body into balance, soothes burns, energy enhancement.

In addition to carrying the generic properties of Quartz (page 230), a naturally coated, transparent Golden Healer facilitates spiritual communication over a long distance, including between the worlds, and empowers multidimensional healing. It is said to access Christ consciousness and to balance yin–yang energies.

Double-terminated Golden Healer Quartz

Sunshine Aura Quartz

Crystal system	Hexagonal
Chemistry	Complex amendment
Hardness	Brittle
Source	Manufactured (may be dyed, not alchemicalized)
Chakra	Solar plexus
Planet	Sun, Moon
Beneficial for	Emotional trauma and hurt, constipation on all levels, toxicity, multidimensional healing, multidimensional cellular memory healer, efficient receptor for programming, cleansing and enhancing the organs, immune system, bringing the body into balance, soothing burns.

In addition to carrying the generic properties of Aura Quartz (page 143) and Quartz (page 230), Sunshine Aura is expansive and protective. Created from gold and platinum, Sunshine Aura Quartz has powerful and extremely active energy.

Opal Aura Quartz

Crystal system	Hexagonal
Chemistry	Complex amendment
Hardness	Brittle
Source	Manufactured
Chakra	Solar plexus
Planet	Sun
Beneficial for	Emotional trauma and hurt, constipation on all levels, toxicity, multidimensional healing, efficient receptor for programming, enhancing muscle-testing, cleansing and enhancing the organs, immune system, bringing the body into balance, soothing burns.

Opal Aura Quartz companion points with diamond window on right-hand point

In addition to carrying the generic properties of Aura Quartz (page 143) and Quartz (page 230), true Opal Aura, produced from platinum, brings about a state of total union with the divine and cosmic consciousness. Like a rainbow signifying hope and optimism, Opal Aura is a crystal of joy. Purifying and balancing all the chakras, it integrates the light body into the physical dimensions and opens a deep state of meditative awareness, grounding the information received in the physical body.

Note: This stone may be dyed Quartz with no additional properties.

Opal Aura long point

Additional yellow stones

Andratite Garnet (page 192), Apophyllite (page 242), Aragonite (page 190), Barite (page 244), Cassiterite (page 139), Cerussite (page 247), Covellite (page 158), Danburite (page 26), Diamond (page 248), Grossular Garnet (page 41), Kyanite (page 152), Lepidocrosite (page 52), Magnesite (page 252), Moonstone (page 251), Moss Agate (page 101), Muscovite (page 31), Onyx (page 219), Opal (page 254), Peridot (page 120), Prehnite (page 122), Smithsonite (page 138), Wavellite (page 123), Wulfenite (page 207), Zoisite (page 56).

Green crystals

Green stones resonate with the heart chakra
and the planet Venus, providing emotional
healing and instilling compassion. Traditionally,
these stones relieved diseases of the eye and
improved vision, as the color mimicked nature
and soothed tired eyes.

alachite

al system	Monoclinic
istry	$Cu_2CO_3(OH)_2$ Hydrous copper carbonate
ness	3.5–4
e	USA (New Mexico), Australia, Zaire, France, Russia, Germany, Chile, Romania, Zambia, Congo, Middle East
ra	Heart, solar plexus, base, sacral
ber	9
ac sign	Scorpio, Capricorn
et	Venus
ficial for	Transformation, psychosexual problems, inhibitions, rebirthing, shyness, detoxifying liver and gallbladder, stress, insomnia, allergies, eyes, circulatory diseases, childbirth, cramps, menstrual problems, labor, female sexual organs, blood pressure, asthma, arthritis, epilepsy, fractures, swollen joints, growths, travel sickness, vertigo, tumors, optic nerve, pancreas, spleen, parathyroid, DNA, cellular structure, immune system, acidification of tissue, diabetes.

Polished Malachite

Malachite is named from the Greek for "mallow," a green herbaceous plant. Reputed to protect against the Evil Eye, witchcraft, and evil spirits, this stone is a powerful cleanser for the emotional body, releasing past-life or childhood trauma, but is best used by a qualified healer. Life is lived more intensely under the influence of Malachite, a powerful energy conduit. It mercilessly shows what is blocking your spiritual growth, drawing out deep feelings and psychosomatic causes, breaking unwanted ties and outworn patterns, and teaching how to take responsibility for your actions, thoughts, and feelings. An important protection stone, Malachite absorbs negative energies and pollutants from the environment and the body, soaking up plutonium and radiation and clearing electromagnetic smog. Malachite has a strong affinity with devic forces and heals the earth.

Malachite can be used for scrying or to access other worlds, inner or outer. Journeying through Malachite's convoluted patterns assists in receiving insights from the subconscious or messages from the future.

Note: Malachite is copper ore, which is toxic to humans if taken in sufficient quantities. However, wearing a polished stone is perfectly safe and will not give a toxic dose.

Malachite has characteristic whorls of color.

Aventurine

Crystal system	Trigonal
Chemistry	SiO_2 Silicon dioxide
Hardness	7
Source	Italy, Brazil, China, India, Russia, Tibet, Nepal
Chakra	Heart, spleen
Number	3
Zodiac sign	Aries
Planet	Mercury
Beneficial for	Balancing male–female energy, prosperity, leadership, decisiveness, compassion, empathy, irritation, creativity, stuttering, severe neurosis, thymus gland, connective tissue, nervous system, blood pressure, metabolism, cholesterol, arteriosclerosis, heart attacks, anti-inflammatory, skin eruptions, allergies, migraine headaches, eyes, adrenals, lungs, sinuses, heart, muscular and urogenital systems.

Raw Green Aventurine

A very positive stone, Aventurine is used to grid gardens or houses against geopathic stress. Wearing Aventurine absorbs electromagnetic smog and protects against environmental pollution. This stone guards against metaphysical vampirism of heart energy and brings together the intellectual and emotional bodies. Aventurine stabilizes one's state of mind, recognizing alternatives and possibilities. It aids emotional recovery and enables living within one's own heart. Aventurine regulates growth from birth to seven years.

Green Aventurine

Crystal system	Trigonal
Chemistry	SiO_2 Silicon dioxide
Hardness	7
Source	Italy, Brazil, China, India, Russia, Tibet, Nepal
Chakra	Heart, spleen
Zodiac sign	Aries
Planet	Mercury
Beneficial for	Negative emotions and thoughts, malignant conditions, nausea, stress, eyes, heart, balancing male–female energy, prosperity, leadership, decisiveness, compassion, empathy, irritation, creativity, stuttering, severe neurosis, thymus gland, connective tissue, nervous system, blood pressure, metabolism, cholesterol, arteriosclerosis, heart attacks, anti-inflammatory, skin eruptions, allergies, migraine headaches, eyes, adrenals, lungs, sinuses, heart, muscular and urogenital systems.

In addition to carrying the generic properties of Aventurine (above), Green Aventurine is a comforter, all-around healer, and general harmonizer, bringing in well-being and emotional calm. This stone assists in establishing exactly what makes you happy or unhappy. Traditionally, it was worn to strengthen eyesight and used as a gambler's talisman. It is an excellent protector for the spleen chakra and should be worn over the base of the sternum or taped beneath the left armpit.

Tumbled Green Aventurine

Rainbow Obsidian

Crystal system	Amorphous
Chemistry	SiO_2 Silicon dioxide with impurities
Hardness	5–5.5
Source	Mexico, volcanic regions around the world
Chakra	Heart
Number	2
Zodiac sign	Libra
Planet	Saturn
Beneficial for	Heartbreak, compassion, strength, digestion of anything that is hard to accept, detoxification, blockages, hardened arteries.

Polished Rainbow Obsidian

In addition to carrying the generic properties of Obsidian (page 214), Rainbow Obsidian, one of the gentler obsidians, nevertheless has strong protective properties and teaches you about the evolution of your spiritual nature. Cutting the cords of old love, it gently releases hooks that others have left in the heart, replenishing the heart energy. Worn as a pendant, Rainbow Obsidian absorbs negative energy from the aura and draws off stress from the body. This stone can be used to facilitate past-life healing and to gain insight into how the past is affecting the present, especially at the level of health and well-being.

Green Obsidian

Crystal system	Amorphous
Chemistry	SiO_2 Silicon dioxide with impurities
Hardness	5–5.5
Source	Mexico, volcanic regions
Chakra	Heart, throat
Number	5
Zodiac sign	Gemini
Planet	Saturn
Beneficial for	Gallbladder, heart, compassion, strength, digestion of anything that is hard to accept, detoxification, blockages, hardened arteries, arthritis, joint pain, cramp, injuries, pain, bleeding, circulation.

In addition to carrying the generic properties of Obsidian (page 214), Green Obsidian removes hooks from other people lodged in the chakras and protects against these being hooked in again. It is especially beneficial for the gallbladder and the heart.

Raw Green Obsidian

Hyalite (Water Opal)

Crystal system	Amorphous
Chemistry	$SiO_2 \cdot nH_2O$ Hydrated silica
Hardness	5.5–6.5
Source	Australia, Brazil, USA, Tanzania, Iceland, Mexico, Peru, UK, Canada, Honduras, Slovakia
Chakra	Links base to crown, past life
Zodiac sign	Cancer
Beneficial for	Mood stabilizer, self-worth, strengthening the will to live, intuition, fear, loyalty, spontaneity, female hormones, menopause, Parkinson's, infections, fevers, memory, purifying blood and kidneys, regulating insulin, childbirth, PMS, eyes, ears.

Raw Hyalite

Hyalite is a wonderful stone for scrying, as its watery depths stimulate intuition, connect with the spiritual realms, and access your life plan. In addition to carrying the generic properties of Opal (page 254), this stone is a mood stabilizer that enhances meditation experience. It aids those who are making the transition out of the body, teaching that the physical overcoat is a temporary vehicle for the soul and facilitating a tranquil passing.

Alexandrite

Crystal system	Hexagonal
Chemistry	$BeAl_2O_4$
Hardness	7.5–8
Source	USA, Brazil, China, Ireland, Switzerland, Australia, Czech Republic, France, Norway
Chakra	Lower, heart
Number	1
Zodiac sign	Scorpio
Planet	Pluto
Beneficial for	Longevity, protection, nervous and glandular systems, inflammation, spleen, pancreas, male reproductive organs, neurological tissue, tension in neck muscles, side effects of leukemia, courage, stress, overanalysis, elimination, pulmonary and circulatory systems, sedation, resistance to toxins and pollutants, liver, stomach, spine, concussion.

Faceted Alexandrite

Alexandrite on matrix

Named for Czar Alexander II of Russia, on whose 21st birthday it was discovered in 1830, pleochroic Alexandrite is dark green shining red in transmitted light, paler when faceted, and may be artificially manufactured. A guardian stone and a useful purifier, harmonizing male and female energies, Alexandrite assists in accurately perceiving emotions. In addition to carrying the generic properties of Beryl (page 81), this regenerative stone rebuilds self-respect, enhancing rebirth of one's Self, which it centers. It intensifies your willpower and your dreams. An emotional comforter, Alexandrite teaches how to expend less effort and find joy in life, inspiring the imagination and attuning to your own inner voice. It brings luck in love.

Raw Alexandrite

Tree Agate

Crystal system	Trigonal
Chemistry	Complex with iron inclusions
Hardness	6
Source	USA, India, Morocco, Czech Republic, Brazil, Africa
Chakra	Earth
Zodiac sign	Virgo
Planet	Mercury
Beneficial for	Immune system, infections, perseverance, fortitude, positive ego, unshakable self-esteem, emotional trauma, self-confidence, concentration, perception, analytical abilities, aura stabilization, negative-energy transformation, emotional disease, digestive process, gastritis, eyes, stomach, uterus, lymphatic system, pancreas, blood vessels, skin disorders.

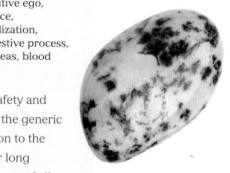

Polished Tree Agate

Tree Agate is an extremely stabilizing stone that instills a feeling of safety and security in the most challenging of situations. In addition to carrying the generic properties of Agate (page 190), this stone makes a powerful connection to the nurturing energy of nature, restoring vitality, and should be worn for long periods. A useful earth-healer, it is an excellent stone for plants and trees of all kinds and can be gridded around a growing area. Offering protection against negativity and imparting strength, it helps you face unpleasant circumstances with equanimity, and overcome them, finding the gift within them.

Green Agate

Crystal system	Trigonal
Chemistry	SiO_2 Silicon dioxide with impurities
Hardness	6
Source	USA, India, Morocco, Czech Republic, Brazil, Africa
Chakra	Sacral, spleen
Zodiac sign	Virgo
Planet	Mercury
Beneficial for	Infertility, emotional trauma, self-confidence, concentration, perception, analytical abilities, aura stabilization, negative-energy transformation, emotional disease, digestive process, gastritis, eyes, stomach, uterus, lymphatic system, pancreas, blood vessels, skin disorders.

Tumbled Green Agate

In ancient times women would drink water in which a Green Agate had been soaked, to guard against sterility. In addition to carrying the generic properties of Agate (page 190), natural Green Agate assists in resolving disputes, enhancing mental and emotional flexibility, and improving decision-making.

Moss Agate

Crystal system	Trigonal
Chemistry	Complex
Hardness	6
Source	USA, India, Morocco, Czech Republic, Brazil, Africa
Chakra	Base, sacral, earth, throat
Number	1
Zodiac sign	Virgo
Planet	Mercury
Beneficial for	Abundance, midwifery, sensitivity to weather and pollutants, self-esteem, fear, depression, recovery, anti-inflammatory, circulatory and elimination systems, flow of lymph, immune system, depression caused by left–right brain imbalance, hypoglycemia, dehydration, infections, colds and flu, fungal and skin infections, energy depletion, stiff neck, emotional trauma, self-confidence, concentration, perception, analytical abilities, aura stabilization, negative-energy transformation, emotional disease, digestive process, gastritis, eyes.

Tumbled Moss Agate

In ancient times Moss Agate was the gardener's talisman and is said to refresh the soul and enable you to see the beauty in all you behold. A birthing crystal, Moss Agate aids midwives in their work, lessening pain and ensuring a good delivery. With the generic properties of Agate (page 190), it is a stone of new beginnings and release from blockages or spiritual fetters. Helping intellectual people access their intuitive feelings, it aids intuitive people in channeling their energy practically. This is a powerfully protective stone during a relationship breakup.

Dendritic Agate

Crystal system	Trigonal
Chemistry	Complex
Hardness	6
Source	USA, India, Morocco, Czech Republic, Brazil, Africa
Chakra	Earth, aligns all
Number	3
Zodiac sign	Gemini
Planet	Mercury
Beneficial for	Peaceful environment, stability, perseverance, disease caused by chakra imbalances, blood vessels, nerves, neuralgia, skeletal disorders, capillary degeneration, circulatory system, pain relief, emotional trauma, self-confidence, concentration, perception, analytical abilities, aura stabilization, negative-energy transformation, emotional disease, digestive process, gastritis, eyes, stomach, uterus, lymphatic system, pancreas, skin disorders. Wear for long periods to gain maximum benefit.

Polished Dendritic Agate

In addition to carrying the generic properties of Agate (page 190), Dendritic Agate, known as the Stone of Plenitude, brings abundance and fullness to all areas of life, including business and agriculture, enhancing the yield of crops and maintaining health of houseplants. Stabilizing the vortexes within the earth's energy field and overcoming geopathic stress or "black ley lines," Dendritic Agate deepens your connection to the earth, urging you to remain connected with your roots as you grow.

Aegirine

Crystal system	Monoclinic
Chemistry	$NaFeS_1$ Sodium iron silicate
Hardness	6
Source	Greenland, USA, Africa
Chakra	Higher heart
Number	5
Zodiac sign	Pisces
Beneficial for	Self-esteem, integrity, sensitivity, focusing goals, immune system, muscles and muscle pain, bones, metabolic system, nerves.

Raw Aegirine in matrix

Named for Aegir, Scandinavian god of the sea, Aegirine is an excellent crystal for generating and focusing energy beams, removing emotional blockages and enhancing positive vibrations. Extremely helpful in cases of psychic attack or negative thinking, it repairs the aura after attachments have been removed. This stone helps you see the bigger picture and assists in healing relationship problems or overcoming the grief of separation. It protects against the energetic incursions of an old love. Empowering the quest for your true Self and the ability to do what is needed from the heart, Aegirine encourages following your own truth without conforming to group pressure. Aegirine can be used to boost the body's own healing systems and the healing energy of other crystals.

Natural Aegirine wand

Annabergite

Crystal system	Monoclinic
Chemistry	$(Ni, Co)_3 (AsO_4)_2$
Hardness	2
Source	Canada, USA, Germany, Sardinia, Italy, Spain, Greece
Chakra	Third eye
Number	6
Zodiac sign	Capricorn
Beneficial for	Radiotherapy, infections, dehydration, tumors, cellular disorders, radionic treatment.

Annabergite shows that everything is perfect exactly as it is and opens all possibilities, especially for healing. This mystical stone enhances visualization and intuition and is said to bring you into contact with wise masters of the universe. It is excellent for past-life regression. Aligning and strengthening the biomagnetic sheath, Annabergite enhances the flow of energy in the physical meridians and harmonizes these with the earth's meridian body.

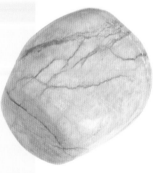

Tumbled Annabergite

Yttrian Fluorite

Crystal system	Cubic
Chemistry	CaF_2 Calcium fluoride with yttrium
Hardness	4
Source	USA, Sweden, England, China, Peru, Brazil
Chakra	Third eye, heart
Zodiac sign	Pisces
Planet	Mercury
Beneficial for	Coordination, self-confidence, shyness, worry, centering, concentration, absorption of nutrients, antiviral, skin and mucous membranes, shingles, nerve-related pain.

Yttrian takes a slightly different form from other fluorites and does not correct disorganization. It does, however, heighten mental activity and is an effective healer, as it is a service-oriented stone. In addition to carrying the generic properties of Fluorite (page 177), it attracts wealth and abundance, teaching the principles of manifestation and enhancing relationships.

Note: Yttrian Fluorite is a high-vibration stone.

Green Fluorite

Shaped Green Fluorite wand

Crystal system	Cubic
Chemistry	CaF_2 Calcium fluoride with impurities
Hardness	4
Source	USA, England, Mexico, Canada, Australia, Germany, Norway, China, Peru, Brazil
Chakra	Earth, spleen, solar plexus, cleanses all
Zodiac sign	Capricorn
Planet	Mercury
Beneficial for	Outworn conditioning, stomach disorders, intestines, balance, coordination, self-confidence, shyness, worry, centering, concentration, psychosomatic disease, absorption of nutrients, bronchitis, emphysema, pleurisy, pneumonia, antiviral, infections, disorders, teeth, cells, bones, DNA damage, skin and mucous membranes, respiratory tract, colds, flu, sinusitis, ulcers, wounds, adhesions, mobilizing joints, arthritis, rheumatism, spinal injuries, pain relief, shingles, nerve-related pain, blemishes, wrinkles, dental work.

Grounding excess energy, Green Fluorite dissipates emotional trauma, clears infections and absorbs negative energies within the environment. In addition to carrying the generic properties of Fluorite (page 177), this stone brings information up from the subconscious mind and accesses intuition. It is an auric, chakra, and mental cleanser and especially protective for the spleen chakra.

Diopside

Crystal system	Monoclinic
Chemistry	$CaMg(Si_2O_6)$ Calcium magnesium silicate
Hardness	5–6.5
Source	USA, Sweden, Canada, Germany, India, Russia
Number	9
Zodiac sign	Virgo
Beneficial for	Mathematics, trust, psychological conditions, physical weakness, acid-alkaline balance, inflammation, muscular aches and spasm, kidneys, heart, hormonal balance, circulation, blood pressure, stress.

The name Diopside comes from the Greek word meaning "two views," reflecting its twofold symmetry. This stone assists you in reconciling with anyone or anything that has hurt you, facilitating your making the first approach if necessary. Diopside increases compassion and humility, opening your heart and mind to the suffering of others, and encourages you to be of service to the planet. An analytical stone that stimulates the intellectual faculties, it is helpful for academic study or creative pursuits. This stone teaches humility and assists in contacting and honoring what you really feel, supporting your own intuition. A useful healing stone for those who cannot show grief, it promotes letting go and forgiveness. If you feel overburdened, it teaches you how to live life lightly.

Diopside formation

Actinolite

Natural Actinolite point

Crystal system	Monoclinic
Chemistry	$Ca_2(MgFe)_5Si_8O_{22}(OH)_2$ Calcium magnesium iron silicate hydroxide
Hardness	5.5–6
Source	USA, Brazil, Russia, China, New Zealand, Canada, Taiwan
Chakra	Heart
Number	4, 9
Zodiac sign	Scorpio
Beneficial for	Self-esteem, stress, asbestos-related cancers, the immune system, liver, kidneys.

An excellent stone for metaphysical shielding, Actinolite expands the aura and crystallizes its edges. Connecting you to higher awareness, it brings body, mind, psyche, and spirit into balance and is an excellent aid to visualization. A useful stone if you have encountered blockages or personal resistance on your spiritual path, it dissolves that which is unwanted or inappropriate. Bringing all the functions of the body into harmony and stimulating growth, Actinolite helps it adjust to changes or traumas.

Raw Actinolite in matrix

Actinolite Quartz

Crystal system	Complex
Chemistry	Complex
Hardness	Combination
Source	USA, Brazil, Russia, China, New Zealand, Canada, Taiwan
Beneficial for	Detoxification, metabolism, self-esteem, stress, asbestos-related cancers, the immune system, liver, kidneys, multidimensional cellular memory healer, efficient receptor for programming, immune system, bringing the body into balance.

Actinolite in Quartz

In addition to carrying the generic properties of Actinolite (left) and Quartz (page 230), Actinolite Quartz is particularly useful if you feel you have lost your way and are looking for a new direction. Instilling a sense of right timing, it shows you the new path you should take and helps you see the value in your mistakes.

Bloodstone (Heliotrope)

Crystal system	Trigonal
Chemistry	Complex
Hardness	7
Source	Australia, Brazil, China, Czech Republic, Russia, India
Chakra	Higher heart, cleanses and realigns lower chakras
Number	4, 6
Zodiac sign	Aries, Libra, Pisces
Planet	Mars
Beneficial for	Revitalizing love, purification, prosperity, insomnia, preventing miscarriage, immune stimulator, acute infections, lymph, metabolic processes, purifies blood, liver, intestines, kidneys, spleen and bladder, blood-rich organs, circulation, overacidification, leukemia, tumors.

Tumbled Bloodstone

This stone assists in living in the present moment, but 3,000 years ago, in ancient Babylon, it was used to overcome enemies and was believed to cause stone walls to fall. It was said to have mystical and magical properties, controlling the weather and conferring the ability to banish evil and negativity and to direct spiritual energies. In ancient times it was regarded as an "audible oracle" that gave warning of danger. Bloodstone is an excellent blood cleanser, immune stimulator, and a powerful healer and revitalizer. With its grounding and protecting properties, Bloodstone keeps out undesirable influences. It teaches how to avoid dangerous situations by strategic withdrawal and flexibility and assists the recognition that chaos often precedes transformation. This stone assists in grounding the heart energy, reducing irritability, aggressiveness, and impatience. It heals the ancestral line.

Raw Bloodstone

Atlantasite

Crystal system	Complex combination
Chemistry	Complex combination
Hardness	Combination
Source	Tasmania
Chakra	Clears all, especially the crown and heart
Beneficial for	Stress, blood disorders, hypoglycemia, diabetes, longevity, detoxification, calcium and magnesium absorption, pain relief (especially dental), PMS, muscular aches, ADHD (Attention Deficit Hyperactivity Disorder), kundalini rise, skin elasticity and stretch marks, hernia, teeth and gums.

In addition to carrying the generic properties of Serpentine (page 205), Infinite Stone (page 124), and Stichtite (page 178), Atlantasite is said to access information and skills from Atlantis and to complete projects set in motion at that time. It accesses other past lives and stimulates spiritual development, lowers stress levels, and enables you to think before you speak. Atlantasite brings enormous peace into the environment and can undertake earth-clearing and energy restructuring in a place of death and destruction. This stone is helpful for assisting children to modify their behavior.

Tumbled Atlantasite

Seraphinite (Seraphina)

Tumbled Seraphinite

Crystal system	Monoclinic
Chemistry	$MgAlFeLiMnNi_{4-6}$ (SiAlBFe) $4O_1O(OHO)_8$ Hydrous magnesium iron aluminum silicate
Hardness	1–4
Source	Russia, Germany, USA
Chakra	Third eye, crown, higher crown, heart
Number	5
Zodiac sign	Sagittarius
Beneficial for	Releasing muscle tension up into the neck; enhancing weight loss; chills; lymph; infections; detoxification; assimilation of Vitamins A and E, iron, magnesium, and calcium; pain; skin growths; liver spots; proliferation of helpful bacteria.

A stone of spiritual enlightenment, Seraphinite's feathery wings whisk you up to a high spiritual vibration, and this stone is excellent for making journeys out of the body, protecting the physical body while you are away. In addition to carrying the generic properties of Chlorite (right), it accesses self-healing and makes angelic connection. Promoting living from the heart, Seraphinite assists in reviewing the progress you have made in life and with identifying the changes needed. In healing, Seraphinite works best at a subtle level, aligning the aura with the light body, and activating the spinal cord and the links to the etheric body situated behind the heart. Its effects are then passed into the physical body.

Note: Seraphinite is a high-vibration stone.

Polished Seraphinite slice

Chlorite

Crystal system	Monoclinic
Chemistry	$MgAlFeLiMnNi_{4-6}(SiAlBFe)_4O_1O(OHO)_8$
Hardness	1–4
Source	Russia, Germany, USA
Number	9
Zodiac sign	Sagittarius
Beneficial for	Detoxification; assimilation of Vitamins A and E, iron, magnesium, and calcium; pain; skin growths; liver spots; proliferation of helpful bacteria.

Raw Chlorite

Found in several crystals, Chlorite is a powerful healing stone that is beneficial for the environmental or personal energy field. Combined with Amethyst, it is particularly useful for removing energy implants and for warding off psychic attack. Used with Carnelian and Ruby, it not only protects against psychic attack but also assists earthbound spirits to make their transition, and is an excellent combination to grid an area against negative energies or entities. Place in the toilet tank to energetically cleanse the whole house.

Green Phantom Quartz

Crystal system	Monoclinic
Chemistry	SiO_2 Silicon dioxide with inclusions
Hardness	7
Source	Worldwide
Chakra	Earth, base, solar plexus, heart, third eye, spleen
Zodiac sign	Sagittarius
Beneficial for	Energy cleansing and enhancement; detoxification; assimilation of Vitamins A and E, iron, magnesium, and calcium; pain; skin growths; liver spots; proliferation of helpful bacteria.

Chlorite-included Green Phantom Quartz absorbs negative energy and toxins and clears a build-up of negative energy anywhere in the body or environment. A large Chlorite Phantom placed point down in the toilet tank energetically cleanses the whole house. In addition to carrying the generic properties of Phantoms (page 239) and Chlorite (above), this stone assists with the removal of energy implants, accessing their source in this or any other lifetime, but should be used under the guidance of an experienced therapist. Green Phantom Quartz ameliorates panic attacks, stabilizes bipolar disorder, and helps in self-realization.

Green Phantom Quartz not formed from Chlorite is a wise and powerful healer that accelerates the recovery process. This stone can be used for angelic contact and for clarifying clairaudient communication. As with all green crystals, it also alleviates despair and helps you feel supported.

Green Phantom Quartz

Green Quartz (Natural)

Crystal system	Hexagonal
Chemistry	SiO_2 Silicon dioxide with impurities
Hardness	7
Source	Seriphos, Greece
Chakra	Heart
Beneficial for	Negative energy, immune system, creativity, endocrine system, new life path, mental clarity, a master healer for any condition, multidimensional cellular memory healer, efficient receptor for programming, enhances muscle testing, cleans and enhances the organs, immune system, brings the body into balance.

Tumbled Green Quartz

One form of natural colored Quartz, a gentle apple green, is found on the small island of Seriphos near Athens and is formed from fibrous hedenbergite and Quartz laid down in pockets in marble. In addition to carrying the generic properties of Quartz (page 230), this stone has traditionally been used for prosperity rituals. Activating an intuitive ability that is imbued with love, Natural Green Quartz opens and stabilizes the heart chakra. Hedenbergite facilitates transitions of all kinds and harmonizes extremes. Green Quartz may also have inclusions of Actinolite.

Siberian Green Quartz

Crystal system	Manufactured
Chemistry	Complex (manufactured)
Hardness	Not established
Source	Manufactured
Chakra	Heart
Beneficial for	Heart, emotions, lung conditions, altitude sickness.

Deep emerald-green Siberian Green Quartz has been regrown in Russia from natural Quartz combined with chemicals to produce the intense color. In addition to carrying the generic properties of Quartz (page 230), this extremely powerful stone brings in a strong love vibration that heals the heart and emotions. It is particularly useful to harmonize disputes or meetings between people who have opposing points of view. Said to create prosperity and abundance, it is a lucky stone for matters of health, love, and money.

Note: Siberian Green Quartz is a high-vibration stone.

Polished Siberian Green Quartz

Green Quartz (Chinese)

Crystal system	Hexagonal
Chemistry	Manufactured
Hardness	Not established
Source	China
Beneficial for	Not established.

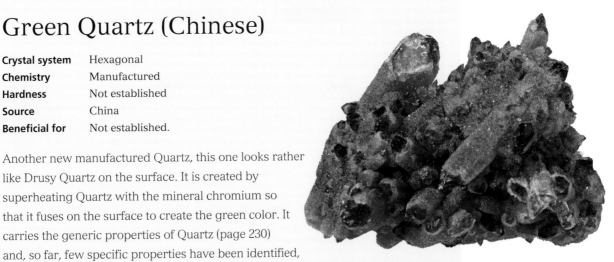

Another new manufactured Quartz, this one looks rather like Drusy Quartz on the surface. It is created by superheating Quartz with the mineral chromium so that it fuses on the surface to create the green color. It carries the generic properties of Quartz (page 230) and, so far, few specific properties have been identified, but chromium is useful for mobilization of heavy metal out of the body, correcting blood sugar imbalances, chronic fatigue, weight regulation, and hormone deficiencies, and Chinese Quartz may well help these conditions.

Artificial formation of Chinese Quartz

Apple Aura Quartz

Crystal system	Hexagonal
Chemistry	Complex amendment
Hardness	Brittle
Source	Manufactured
Chakra	Spleen
Beneficial for	Multidimensional healing, multidimensional cellular memory healing, efficient receptor for programming, cleansing and enhancing the organs, immune system, bringing the body into balance, energy enhancement.

Apple Aura Quartz, formed when nickel is heated onto Quartz, is an excellent protector for the spleen. In addition to carrying the generic properties of Aura Quartz (page 143), this stone, worn over the base of the sternum or taped over the spleen chakra, cuts energy drains and overcomes psychic vampirism.

Note: Apple Aura Quartz is a high-vibration stone.

Apple Aura Quartz

Ouro Verde Quartz

Crystal system	Hexagonal
Chemistry	Complex amendment
Hardness	Not established
Source	Manufactured
Chakra	Harmonizes all, aligns the aura
Beneficial for	Tumors, herpes, allergies, anaphylactic shock, peripheral circulation.

Created by bombarding Quartz with gamma rays, Ouro Verde means "green gold." It is said that this crystal has a very high energy that never requires cleansing or recharging, and that it gives powerful protection to the user, but some people feel nauseous when touching it, and sensitive people may have a strong adverse reaction to it.

For people who are not averse to the stone, which carries the generic properties of Quartz (page 230), it is said to actualize abundance and to "season the character" to experience the deeper meaning of life, and to enable them to shine. It is said to activate intuition and to allow you to view future events in the light of wisdom from the past, leading to more productive choices. Ouro Verde has been used to detect radon gas and the triggers for illness, and to protect against radioactivity.

Note: Ouro Verde Quartz is a high-vibration stone.

Ouro Verde Quartz

Gaia Stone

Crystal system	Artificial
Chemistry	Complex amendment
Hardness	Not established
Source	Mount St. Helens, Washington
Chakra	Earth, heart, harmonizes all
Number	9
Zodiac sign	Aquarius
Beneficial for	Self-healing, emotional wounds, past trauma.

Manufactured from the volcanic ash of Mount St. Helens, Gaia Stone is named for the ancient Greek Earth Mother goddess and is also known as the Goddess Stone. Said to link to the devas and to the *anima terra*, the soul of the earth, this is a stone of prosperity that brings you into close harmony with the earth and the environment. It stimulates healing ability, particularly for earth-healing, and promotes compassion and empathy.

Note: Gaia Stone is a high-vibration stone.

Gaia Stone

Chrysoprase

Crystal system	Trigonal
Chemistry	SiO_2 Silicon dioxide with nickel
Hardness	7
Source	USA, Russia, Brazil, Australia, Poland, Tanzania
Chakra	Heart, sacral
Number	3
Zodiac sign	Taurus
Planet	Venus
Beneficial for	Fluent speech, judgmentalism, forgiveness, compassion, mental dexterity, codependence, detoxifying, stanching blood, pain, arthritis, rheumatism, influenza, eyes, mobilizing heavy metals out of the body, liver function, relaxation, fertility, infertility caused by infection, sexually transmitted diseases, gout, eye problems, mental illness, skin diseases, heart problems, goiter, balancing hormones, digestive system, infirmity, absorption of vitamin C, fungal infections, claustrophobia, nightmares.

Polished Chrysoprase

Said by the ancients to promote love of truth, Chrysoprase promotes optimism and personal insight. Inducing deep meditative states, it imparts a sense of being part of the divine whole. This stone assists in looking at egotistical motives in the past and the effect that has had on your development, and aligns your ideals with your behavior. Chrysoprase heals your inner child, releasing emotions locked in since childhood, and, overcoming compulsive thoughts, turns your attention to positive events. This stone stimulates acceptance of oneself and others.

Andalusite (Green Chiastolite)

Crystal system	Orthorhombic
Chemistry	$Al_2S_1O_5$ Aluminum silicate
Hardness	6.5–7.5
Source	USA, Brazil, China, Spain, Italy, Australia, Chile, Russia
Chakra	All
Number	7
Zodiac sign	Virgo
Beneficial for	Insufficiency of oxygen, chromosome disorders, hands, eyes, guilt, memory, analytic capability, fever, stanching blood flow, overacidification, rheumatism, gout, lactation, immune system, paralysis, nerve fortifier.

The name Andalusite derives from the Spanish province Andalusia. In addition to carrying the generic properties of Chiastolite (page 194), Andalusite is a heart cleanser and balancing stone that releases blockages caused by pent-up anger and old hurts. Helpful in psycho- or crystal therapy and in accessing past-life memories, Andalusite helps sensitive people feel at home on the earth and teaches the non-necessity of self-sacrifice.

Conichalcite

Crystal system	Orthohombic
Chemistry	CaCuAsO$_4$ (OH) Calcium copper arsenate hydroxide
Hardness	4.5
Source	USA, Mexico, Chile, Poland, Zaire
Number	3
Zodiac sign	Pisces
Planet	Venus
Beneficial for	Detoxification, mucus, kidneys, bladder, psoriasis, herpes.

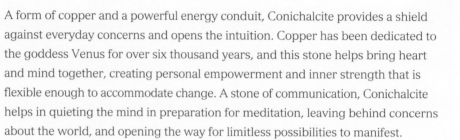

Conichalcite on matrix

A form of copper and a powerful energy conduit, Conichalcite provides a shield against everyday concerns and opens the intuition. Copper has been dedicated to the goddess Venus for over six thousand years, and this stone helps bring heart and mind together, creating personal empowerment and inner strength that is flexible enough to accommodate change. A stone of communication, Conichalcite helps in quieting the mind in preparation for meditation, leaving behind concerns about the world, and opening the way for limitless possibilities to manifest.

Emerald

Crystal system	Hexagonal
Chemistry	Be$_3$Al$_2$Si$_6$O$_{18}$
Hardness	7.5–8
Source	India, Zimbabwe, Tanzania, Brazil, Egypt, Austria, Colombia, Madagascar
Chakra	Heart
Number	4
Zodiac sign	Aries, Taurus, Gemini
Planet	Venus
Beneficial for	Claustrophobia, mental clarity, mutual understanding, group cooperation, memory, discernment, eloquent expression, patience, osteoporosis, recovery after infectious illness, detoxification, sinuses, lungs, heart, spine, muscles, eyes, vision, rheumatism, diabetes, antidote to poisons, epilepsy, malignant conditions.

Raw Emeralds

Faceted Emerald

Emerald derives from the Greek word *smargos*, meaning "green stone," but the oldest known mine is Egyptian, dating back to 3000 BCE. Emeralds were traditionally bound to the left arm to protect travelers or given to people to exorcise their demons. Said to protect from enchantment and the ploys of magicians, it foretold the future. Known as the "Stone of Successful Love," Emerald brings domestic bliss and loyalty; enhances unity, unconditional love and partnership; and promotes friendship. If it changes color, it is said to signal unfaithfulness. A life-affirming stone with great integrity, Emerald enhances mental equilibrium and metaphysical abilities.

Note: Do not wear constantly, as it can overstimulate.

Chrysotile (Chrysotite)

Crystal system	Monoclinic
Chemistry	$Mg_3(S_{12}OS)(OH)_4$ Hydrated silicate (type B asbestos)
Hardness	2.5–4
Source	USA, Canada, India, Russia, Australia
Chakra	Third eye
Number	8, 55
Zodiac sign	Taurus
Beneficial for	Chronic fatigue, irritating coughs, parathyroid, throat, brain stem, central meridian channel, emphysema, inflammation, multiple sclerosis.

Polished Chrysotile

Named from the Greek *chrysos* (gold) and *tilos* (fiber), Chrysotile is mentioned in Revelations as a foundation of the New Jerusalem and as one of the stones of the breastplate of the High Priest in Exodus. Banded Chrysotile is a visual stone with ancient writing inscribed upon it that links you to the knowledge of the ages and, below that, your power animal waiting to make itself known so that you can embody it. This stone helps you clear away the debris of the past to reveal your core Self. It also shows you where you seek to control others and works on the etheric blueprint to correct imbalances and blockages that could manifest as physical disease.

Note: Toxic; use as tumbled stone.

Datolite

Crystal system	Monoclinic
Chemistry	$CaB(SiO_4)(OH)$ Hydrous calcium borosilicate
Hardness	5–5.5
Source	Mexico, USA, South Africa, Tanzania, Scotland, Russia, Germany, Norway, Canada
Chakra	Third eye, soma
Number	5
Zodiac sign	Aries
Beneficial for	Concentration, problem-solving, diabetes, hypoglycemia.

Datolite on matrix

Named from the Greek *dateisthai*, "divide," when meditated with, Datolite facilitates retrieval of information encoded in subtle DNA, connecting to ancestral patterns and events and soul memory. The stone assists in accepting the transience of all things, knowing that "this too will pass," and is useful during violent upheaval or tumultuous change. Its attributes include clarity of thought and enhanced concentration, leading to an ability to remember important detail. This stone is said to bring you closer to loved ones.

Epidote

Crystal system	Monoclinic
Chemistry	$Ca_2 (Al,Fe)Al_2O(SiO_4)(Si_2O_7)(OH)$ Hydrous calcium iron aluminum silicate
Hardness	6–7
Source	Bulgaria, Austria, France, Russia, Norway, USA, South Africa
Chakra	Heart
Number	2
Zodiac sign	Gemini
Beneficial for	Convalescence, emotional body, self-pity, anxiety, realistic goals, emotional trauma, grief, stamina, nervous and immune systems, dehydration, brain, thyroid, liver, gallbladder, adrenal glands. As an elixir, it softens the skin.

Tumbled Epidote

Epidote arises from the Greek words *epi* and *donal*, because one side is often larger than the other. In those who are attuned, this stone enhances perception and personal power, and dispels criticalness, enabling you to look objectively at your strengths and weaknesses. Removing ingrained resistance to spiritual awakening, a powerful catharsis or abreaction of negative energy may be experienced, and this is best undertaken with a crystal therapist. Epidote assists you in staying centered in any situation and is ideal for those who fall into victimhood or martyrdom. It supports the body's healing processes and helps you look after yourself.

Epidote in Quartz

Crystal system	Complex combination
Chemistry	Complex
Hardness	Not established
Source	Bulgaria, Austria, France, Russia, Norway, USA, South Africa
Beneficial for	Bruises, sprains, pain, convalescence, emotional body, self-pity, anxiety, realistic goals, emotional trauma, grief, stamina, nervous and immune systems, dehydration, brain, thyroid, liver, gallbladder, adrenal glands.

Epidote crystals in Quartz on matrix

Bringing together the regenerative properties of Quartz (page 230) and Epidote, this hopeful stone provides rejuvenation and the courage to bounce back after enormous setbacks, adding a new impetus to soul growth.

Green Zircon

Crystal system	Tetragonal
Chemistry	$ZrSiO_3$ Zirconium silicate
Hardness	6.5–7.5
Source	Australia, USA, Sri Lanka, Ukraine, Canada (may be heat-treated)
Chakra	Heart
Zodiac sign	Virgo
Beneficial for	Synergy, constancy, jealousy, possessiveness, victimization.

Green Zircon (see also page 261) is an attractor of abundance.

Green Opalite

Crystal system	Amorphous
Chemistry	SiO_2 nH_2O Hydrated silica
Hardness	5.5–6.5
Source	Australia, Brazil, USA, Tanzania, Iceland, Mexico, Peru, UK, Canada, Honduras, Slovakia
Chakra	Higher heart
Number	3
Zodiac sign	Aries, Sagittarius
Beneficial for	Immune system, colds and flu, self-worth, strengthening the will to live, intuition, fear, loyalty, spontaneity, female hormones, menopause, Parkinson's, infections, fevers, memory, purifying blood and kidneys, regulating insulin, childbirth, PMS, eyes, ears.

Tumbled Green Opalite

In addition to carrying the generic properties of Opal (page 254), Green Opalite, a cleansing and rejuvenating stone, promotes emotional recovery and assists relationships. With the ability to filter information and reorient the mind, it gives meaning to everyday life and brings about a spiritual perspective.

Howlite

Crystal system	Monoclinic
Chemistry	$Ca_2B_5SiO_9(OH)_5$
Hardness	3.5
Source	USA
Chakra	Third eye
Number	2
Zodiac sign	Gemini
Beneficial for	Turbulent emotions, rage, patience, selfishness, positive character traits, memory, insomnia, calcium levels, teeth, bone, soft tissue.

Howlite encourages you to set aside the personality mask you don to face the world, allowing you to be true to yourself and your inner *knowing*. This stone opens attunement and prepares the mind to receive wisdom. Aiding journeys out of the body and accessing past lives, focusing your eyes into Howlite transports you to another time or dimension. On the third eye, it opens memories of other lives, including those in the between-life state. A piece placed in the pocket absorbs your own anger and any that is directed toward you. Howlite formulates ambitions, both spiritual and material, and assists in achieving them, and facilitates calm and reasoned communication.

Tumbled

Tumbled Howlite

Jade

Crystal system	Monoclinic
Chemistry	$Na(AlFe)Si_2O_6$ with impurities
Hardness	6
Source	USA, China, Italy, Myanmar, Russia, Middle East
Chakra	Third eye, soma (varies according to color)
Number	1 (Jadeite 9, Nephrite 5)
Zodiac sign	Aries, Taurus, Gemini, Libra (Jadeite Aries, Nephrite Libra)
Planet	Venus
Beneficial for	Longevity, self-sufficiency, detoxification, filtration, elimination, kidneys, suprarenal glands, cellular and skeletal systems, stitches, fertility, childbirth, hips, spleen, water–salt–acid–alkaline ratio.

Polished Green Jade

Polished Green Jade

Jade has long been a sacred stone in the Orient, and it was included with Chinese grave goods to give vitality to the deceased. It was used for weather magic, being forcefully thrown into water to call up snow, mist, or rain. A protector against danger for children, Jade can undo physical harm. This stone is a symbol of purity, serenity, and nurturing and is a "dream stone." Placed on the soma chakra, it brings insightful dreams. Jade stabilizes the personality and integrates mind and body. This stone encourages you to become who you really are, recognizing yourself as a spiritual being on a human journey.

Peridot (Olivine)

Crystal system	Orthorhombic
Chemistry	$(Mg,Fe)_2 SiO_4 Mg_2 SiO_4$
Hardness	6.5–7
Source	Canada, Russia, USA, Italy, Pakistan, Brazil, Egypt, Ireland, Sri Lanka, Canary Islands
Chakra	Heart, solar plexus
Number	5, 6
Zodiac sign	Virgo, Leo, Scorpio, Sagittarius
Planet	Venus
Beneficial for	Jealousy, resentment, spitefulness, anger, stress, lethargy, confidence, assertion, tissue regeneration, metabolism, skin, heart, thymus, lungs, gallbladder, spleen, intestinal tract, ulcers, eyes, birth contractions, bipolar disorder, hypochondria, melancholia, digestive problems.

Faceted Peridot

Believed in ancient times to keep away evil spirits, Peridot is still a protective stone for the aura and a powerful cleanser. Releasing and neutralizing toxins, it purifies the subtle and physical bodies, and the mind. Showing how to detach oneself from outside influences and to look to your own higher energies for guidance, Peridot teaches that holding on to people, or the past, is counterproductive. This visionary crystal helps you understand your destiny and spiritual purpose. It is particularly helpful to healers.

Polished Peridot

Moldavite

Crystal system	Noncrystalline meteorite
Chemistry	Extraterrestrial
Hardness	5
Source	Czechoslovakia, Bavaria, Moldavia
Chakra	All
Number	2, 6
Zodiac sign	All, especially Scorpio
Beneficial for	Compassion, security, empathy, finding the gift in an illness, diagnosis, emotional trauma.

Natural Moldavite

Formed when a giant meteorite struck the earth and the heat of impact metamorphosed surrounding rocks, Moldavite fuses extraterrestrial energies with Mother Earth and takes you way beyond your limits and boundaries. Used since Stone Age times as a talisman and amulet for good fortune and fertility, this is a stone of the New Age. Bringing you into communication with your higher self and with extraterrestrials, Moldavite has its own cosmic connection, which puts you in touch with Ascended Masters and cosmic messengers, facilitating the ascension process. It integrates the divine blueprint and accelerates spiritual growth by downloading information from the Akashic Record and the light body, which has to be processed and made conscious. Under the influence of Moldavite you can go forward to a future life to see the results of actions taken in the present, or to learn what is needed now to prevent destruction in the future. Moldavite is a useful stone for sensitive people who find it difficult being in incarnation on earth, and it assists in developing detachment from security issues such as money and worries for the future. Providing an overview of reasons for incarnating and spiritual purposes, and integrating this into earthly life, Moldavite releases fixed ideas and outworn belief systems and can neutralize hypnotic commands instilled in the past.

Note: Moldavite is a high-vibration stone.

Green Sapphire

Crystal system	Hexagonal
Chemistry	Al_2O_3 Aluminum oxide with impurities
Hardness	9
Source	Myanmar, Czech Republic, Brazil, Kenya, India, Australia, Sri Lanka, Canada, Thailand, Australia, Madagascar
Chakra	Heart
Zodiac sign	Gemini, Leo
Planet	Moon, Saturn
Beneficial for	Vision, serenity, peace of mind, concentration, multidimensional cellular healing, overactive body systems, glands, eyes, stress.

Faceted Green Sapphire

In addition to carrying the generic properties of Sapphire (page 160), Green Sapphire, known as "the stone of fidelity," enhances compassion and an understanding of the vulnerability and unique qualities of others, helping you trust and honor other people's belief systems. This stone improves inner and outer vision and aids dream recall.

Prehnite

Crystal system	Orthorhombic
Chemistry	$Ca_2Al_2S_{13}O_1O(OH)_2$ Hydrous calcium aluminum
Hardness	6–6.5
Source	USA, New Zealand, India, Scotland, Switzerland, South Africa
Chakra	Third eye
Number	5
Zodiac sign	Libra
Beneficial for	Hyperactive children, precognition, nightmares, phobias, fears, diagnosis, root causes, kidneys, bladder, thymus gland, shoulders, chest, lungs, gout, blood disorders, connective tissue, malignancy.

Natural Prehnite

Named after Hendrik von Prehn, a Dutch mineralogist, Prehnite is a stone of unconditional love and the crystal that heals the healer. When meditating with this crystal, you are put in touch with the universe's energy grid. It is said to connect to the Archangel Raphael and to spiritual and extraterrestrial beings, enabling you always to be prepared, no matter what. This crystal seals the auric field in a protective shield and is useful for gridding the environment. It teaches how to be in harmony with nature and the elemental forces, revitalizing and renewing your surroundings. A good Feng Shui stone, Prehnite is helpful for "decluttering," aiding those who hoard possessions or love because of an inner lack, and restoring belief in divine manifestation.

Variscite

Crystal system	Orthorhombic
Chemistry	$Al(PO_{42}H_2)$
Hardness	3.5–4.5
Source	USA, Germany, Austria, Czech Republic, Bolivia
Chakra	Past life, third eye, heart
Number	7
Zodiac sign	Taurus, Gemini, Scorpio
Beneficial for	Chronic fatigue, nervousness, clear thinking, perception, peaceful sleep, postoperative conditions, clearing anesthetics, depleted energy reserves, nervous system, abdominal distension, constricted blood flow, elasticity of veins and skin, overacidification, gout, gastritis, ulcers, rheumatism, male impotence, cramp.

Tumbled Variscite

Variscite encourages an invalid and helps carers deal with the disease an illness can create, bringing unconditional love into the situation. Helpful for past-life exploration, it facilitates visual images while going deeply into the feelings of appropriate lives, stimulating insights into the cause of disease and reframing situations. This stone facilitates moving out of deep despair and into a position of trust in the universe. It does away with pretense, enabling you to show yourself to the world exactly as you are. Variscite supports sobriety and yet has a lively energy that prevents one from becoming too serious.

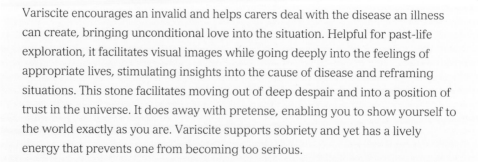

Wavellite

Crystal system	Orthorhombic
Chemistry	$Al_3\text{-}(PO_4)_2(OH)_3\text{-}(H_2O)_5$
Hardness	3.5–4
Source	USA, Bolivia, UK
Chakra	Past life, soma
Number	1
Zodiac sign	Aquarius
Planet	Moon
Beneficial for	Energy flow from auric to physical bodies, blood flow, white cell count, dermatitis.

Natural Wavellite rosettes

Said to be at its most effective at the new moon, Wavellite facilitates deep soul healing and an overview of core attitudes that lead to disease. A useful stone for emotional healing, clearing the effects of trauma or abuse from the emotional body, it assists in maintaining well-being. If you need an overview of a situation before making a move, hold Wavellite, which will also assist you to manage challenging situations with ease.

Fuchsite (Green Muscovite)

Crystal system	Monoclinic
Chemistry	$KA_{l2}(AlSi_3O_{10})(F,OH)_2$
Hardness	2–3.5
Source	Switzerland, Russia, Austria, Czech Republic, Brazil, New Mexico, Canada, India, Italy, Scotland, Germany, Austria, Finland, Madagascar, Afghanistan, Dominican Republic
Chakra	Past life
Number	9
Zodiac sign	Aquarius
Planet	Mercury
Beneficial for	Codependency, emotional blackmail, resilience, trauma, self-worth, emotional shock, red–white blood cell ratio, carpal tunnel syndrome, repetitive strain injury, spine realignment, tendonitis, flexibility in musculoskeletal system, dyspraxia and left–right confusion, problem-solving, quick-wittedness, insomnia, allergies, anger, insecurity, self-doubt, nervous stress, hair, eyes, weight, blood sugar, pancreatic secretions, dehydration, fasting, kidneys.

Raw Fuchsite

Carrying the generic properties of Muscovite (page 31), Fuchsite amplifies the energy of crystals and facilitates its transfer to speed up the healing process, channeling practical information regarding herbal treatment and holistic remedies. Demonstrating how to be of service without becoming embroiled in power struggles or false humility, it helps you deal with issues of servitude from past or present lives, reversing a tendency to martyr/savior/rescuer roles. Combining unconditional and tough love, Fuchsite shows how to stand by placidly while someone else learns his or her own lessons. It is helpful for "the identified patient" within a family or group situation on whom disease and tension are projected. Fuchsite gives the identified patient the strength to find wellness and helps restore emotional equilibrium after confrontation.

Infinite Stone (Light Green Serpentine)

Crystal system	Monoclinic
Chemistry	(MgFe) $3Si_2O_5$ (OH) 4 Magnesium iron silicate hydroxide
Hardness	3–4.5
Source	UK, Norway, Russia, Zimbabwe, Italy, USA, Switzerland, Canada
Chakra	Past life, soma
Number	8
Zodiac sign	Gemini
Planet	Saturn
Beneficial for	Pain relief, especially dental; PMS; muscular aches; longevity; detoxification; parasite elimination; calcium and magnesium absorption; hypoglycemia; diabetes.

Tumbled Infinite Stone

In addition to carrying the generic properties of Serpentine (page 205), Infinite Stone brings you into contact with angelic guidance, accessing and integrating past, present, and future. Holding this stone takes you into the between-life state so that healing of a former life which was not undertaken at the time can be completed. This stone is excellent for all past-life exploration, as it promotes forgiveness for oneself and what you went through. It heals imbalances from past lives and clears emotional baggage from previous relationships. Use Infinite Stone if you need to confront anyone from your past, as it brings a gentle touch to the meeting.

Leopardskin Serpentine

Crystal system	Monoclinic
Chemistry	(MgFe) $3Si_2O_5$ (OH) 4 Magnesium iron silicate hydroxide
Hardness	3–4.5
Source	UK, Norway, Russia, Zimbabwe, Italy, USA, Switzerland, Canada
Chakra	Crown, clears all
Number	8
Zodiac sign	Gemini
Planet	Saturn
Beneficial for	Longevity, detoxification, parasite elimination, calcium and magnesium absorption, hypoglycemia, diabetes.

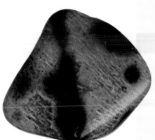

Tumbled Leopardskin Serpentine

In addition to carrying the generic properties of Serpentine (page 205), Leopardskin Serpentine is a shamanic stone that helps you access Leopard energy and travel with the Leopard as a power or healing animal. As such, it is of enormous assistance in reclaiming power, especially where this has been misplaced or misused in previous lives or in other dimensions. Leopardskin Serpentine facilitates trancework and meditation, opening a direct channel to spiritual guidance, and is an excellent tool for multidimensional journeys.

Verdelite (Green Tourmaline)

Crystal system	Trigonal
Chemistry	Complex silicate
Hardness	7–7.5
Source	Sri Lanka, Brazil, Africa, USA, Australia, Afghanistan, Italy, Germany, Madagascar
Chakra	Heart
Zodiac sign	Virgo, Capricorn
Beneficial for	Compassion, tenderness, patience, sense of belonging, fears, openness, rejuvenation, restful sleep, claustrophobia, panic attacks, hyperactivity, detoxification, constipation, diarrhea, nervous system, eyes, heart, thymus, brain, immune system, weight loss, relieves chronic fatigue and exhaustion, spinal realignment, strained muscles, gallbladder, liver, protection, detoxification, spinal adjustments, balancing male–female energy, paranoia, dyslexia, hand-eye coordination, assimilation and translation of coded information, bronchitis, diabetes, emphysema, pleurisy, pneumonia, energy flow, removal of blockages.

Raw Verdelite

Helpful for visualization and creativity, Green Tourmaline is a powerful healer and protector during detoxification on all levels. In addition to carrying the generic properties of Tourmaline (page 210), it facilitates the study of herbalism, enhances the application of remedies, has the power to heal plants, and prepares for a vibrational shift. This stone can be used to heal past-life trauma in the emotional body and to reprogram negative emotional patterns. With Green Tourmaline you are able to see all possible solutions and to select the most constructive. It magnetizes the wearer to prosperity and abundance. This nurturing stone brings balance and *joie de vivre*, transforming negative energy to positive. Green Tourmaline overcomes problems with authority and father figures.

Uvarovite Garnet

Crystal system	Cubic
Chemistry	Complex silicate
Hardness	6–7.5
Source	Europe, USA (Arizona and New Mexico), South Africa, Australia
Chakra	Heart
Number	7
Zodiac sign	Aquarius
Planet	Mars
Beneficial for	Detoxification, anti-inflammatory, fever, acidosis, leukemia, frigidity, heart, lungs, kidney and bladder infections, attracting love, dreaming, blood diseases, regenerating the body, metabolism, spinal and cellular disorders, blood, regeneration of DNA, assimilation of minerals and vitamins.

In addition to carrying the generic properties of Garnet (page 47), emerald-green Uvarovite Garnet, named after Russian mineral collector Count S. S. Uvarov, promotes individuality without egocentricity, and at the same time links the soul into its universal nature. It enhances spiritual relationships. This peaceful stone assists in experiencing solitude without loneliness.

Uvarovite Garnet

Green Amber

Green Amber

Crystal system	Noncrystalline
Chemistry	Heat-amended CHO with impurities
Hardness	2–2.5
Source	Manufactured
Number	3
Zodiac sign	Aquarius
Beneficial for	No specific benefits (see below).

Green Amber is heat-treated Amber that has no specific properties and which has a weaker effect than in its natural state (see page 79 for generic properties).

Green Spinel

Crystal system	Cubic
Chemistry	$MgAl_2O_4$ Magnesium aluminum oxide
Hardness	7.5–8
Source	Sri Lanka, Myanmar, Canada, USA, Brazil, Pakistan, Sweden (may be synthetic)
Chakra	Heart
Number	7
Zodiac sign	Libra
Planet	Pluto
Beneficial for	Muscular and nerve conditions, blood vessels.

In addition to carrying the generic properties of Spinel (page 260), Green Spinel stimulates love, compassion, and kindness.

Green Selenite

Crystal system	Monoclinic
Chemistry	$CaSo_{4-2}$ (H_2O) Hydrated calcium sulfate
Hardness	2
Source	England, USA, Mexico, Russia, Austria, Greece, Poland, Germany, France, Sicily (may be dyed)
Chakra	Higher crown
Zodiac sign	Taurus
Planet	Moon
Beneficial for	Effects of aging on the skin and skeleton, judgment, insight, aligning the spinal column, flexibility, epilepsy, mercury poisoning from dental amalgam, free radicals, breastfeeding. Its finest healing occurs at the energetic levels.

In addition to carrying the generic properties of Selenite (page 257), Green Selenite is oriented to working for the highest good. It makes one feel good about oneself.

Note: Green Selenite is a high-vibration stone.

Green Selenite Cluster

Hiddenite (Green Kunzite)

Crystal system	Monoclinic
Chemistry	$LiAl(SiO_2)_2$ with impurities (contains lithium)
Hardness	6.5–7
Source	USA, Madagascar, Brazil, Myanmar, Afghanistan
Chakra	Third eye, heart
Number	7
Zodiac sign	Taurus, Leo, Scorpio
Planet	Venus, Pluto
Beneficial for	Thymus; chest; combining intellect, intuition, and inspiration; humility; service; tolerance; self-expression; creativity; stress-related anxiety; bipolar disorder; psychiatric disorders and depression; geopathic stress; introspection; immune system; witness for radionic practitioners; joint pain; anesthetic; circulatory system; heart muscle; neuralgia; epilepsy.

Natural Hiddenite

In addition to carrying the generic properties of Kunzite (page 30), Hiddenite supports new beginnings and grounds spiritual love. Assisting the transfer of knowledge from the higher realms and beneficial for intellectual and emotional experiences, it gently releases feelings of failure, helping people who "put a brave face" on things to accept comfort and support from people and the universe. With the power to link the intellect with love, it births the unknown. Hiddenite aids diagnosis when gently "combed" over the body, showing areas of weakness.

Note: Hiddenite is a high-vibration stone.

Tibetan Turquoise

Crystal system	Triclinic
Chemistry	$CuAl_6(PO_4)_4(OH)_8 5(H_2O)$ Hydrous copper aluminum phosphate
Hardness	5–6
Source	Tibet
Chakra	Throat
Zodiac sign	Scorpio, Sagittarius, Pisces
Planet	Jupiter, Venus, Neptune
Beneficial for	Friendship, loyalty, purification, subtle energy fields, physical and metaphysical immune systems, tissue regeneration.

Natural Tibetan Turquoise

Greener than most Turquoises (see page 134 for generic properties), Tibetan Turquoise carries a slightly different vibration from vivid blue. It is especially useful for healing throat chakra blockages and suppressed self-expression, going back down the ancestral line until the original source of the problem is cleared.

Additional green stones

Amazonite (page 130), Apatite (page 133), Apophyllite (page 242), Aquamarine (page 133), Aragonite (page 190), Beryl (page 81), Chrysocolla (page 137), Diopside (page 104), Dioptase (page 136), Grossular Garnet (page 41), Hemimorphite (page 197), Kyanite (page 152), Moonstone (page 251), Unakite (page 36), Zoisite (page 56).

Green-blue and turquoise crystals

Green-blue and turquoise crystals resonate with higher levels of being. They stimulate spiritual awareness and metaphysical abilities. Many turquoise stones connect to cosmic consciousness, drawing it down to earth, and all instill profound peace and relaxation. These stones work at the third eye, uniting the heart and intuition.

Amazonite

Crystal system	Triclinic
Chemistry	$KA(AlSi_3O_8)$ + copper
Hardness	6–6.5
Source	USA, Russia, Canada, Brazil, India, Mozambique, Namibia, Austria
Chakra	Spleen, solar plexus, heart, connects higher heart to throat
Number	5
Zodiac sign	Virgo
Planet	Uranus
Beneficial for	Electromagnetic smog, emotional trauma, worry, fear, negative energy, aggravation, universal love, alcoholism, thyroid and parathyroid, liver, nervous system, osteoporosis, tooth decay, calcium balance, calcium deposits, metabolic deficiencies, calcium deficiencies, muscle spasm.

Raw Amazonite

With its powerful filtering action, Amazonite blocks geopathic stress and, placed between you and the source, absorbs microwaves and cellphone emanations, protecting against electromagnetic pollution. It is particularly useful for illnesses caused by oversensitivity to environmental influences and electromagnetic smog. Filtering information passing through the brain, and combining intellect with intuition, Amazonite allows you to see both sides of an argument and reach your own conclusions, supporting self-determination. Releasing grief from the emotional body, from whatever time span it occurred, this stone creates emotional balance and facilitates constructive expression of what has formerly been left unsaid. Aligning the physical body with the etheric, Amazonite assists in maintaining optimum health. It is of particular benefit to musicians and writers.

Raw Amazonite

Brilliant Turquoise Amazonite

Crystal system	Triclinic
Chemistry	$KA(AlSi_3O_8)$ + copper
Hardness	6–6.5
Source	USA, Russia, Canada, Brazil, India, Mozambique, Namibia, Austria
Chakra	Spleen, solar plexus, heart, connects higher heart to throat
Number	5
Zodiac sign	Aquarius
Planet	Uranus
Beneficial for	Electromagnetic smog, emotional trauma, negative energy, aggravation, universal love, alcoholism, thyroid and parathyroid, liver, nervous system, deficiencies.

In addition to carrying the generic properties of Amazonite (above), this rare and refined form of Amazonite provides spiritual protection at a very high level. Enfolding you safely as you traverse the higher realms of consciousness and the other planes of existence, it brings you into perfect alignment with cosmic consciousness. It is an excellent stone for divesting yourself of karmic entanglements, and for protecting against reconnection.

Brilliant Turquoise Amazonite

Ajoite

Crystal system	Triclinic
Chemistry	$(K,Na)Cu_7 Al(Si_3O_8)_3 (OH)_{63}H_2O$
Hardness	7
Source	South Africa, USA
Chakra	Third eye, crown, links heart and throat
Number	6
Zodiac sign	Virgo
Beneficial for	Releasing toxic emotions, serenity, stress, cellular structures.

Raw Ajoite in Quartz

A rare crystal, especially as the African mine has now flooded, and one that ushers in the age of Aquarius, translucent Ajoite has an extremely high vibration that wraps the soul in universal love and brings about a profound spiritual revelation. A stone of infinite peace, creating deep emotional and environmental calm, Ajoite can draw negative energy, karmic wounds, or implants out of the body, no matter at what level or from which time frame they originate. Excellent for dissipating stress from the physical and emotional bodies, it harmonizes the etheric blueprint with the physical body. Ajoite assists in resolving conflict, highlighting the need for self-forgiveness and compassion that can then encompass others.

Note: Ajoite is a high-vibration stone.

Ajoite with Shattuckite

Crystal system	Complex
Chemistry	Complex
Hardness	Not established
Source	USA
Chakra	Higher heart
Beneficial for	Stress-related illness, bowel blockages, constipation, releasing toxic emotions, serenity, stress, cellular structures, syphilitic miasm, minor health complaints, balance, spring tonic, tonsillitis, blood clotting, intercellular structures.

In addition to carrying the generic properties of Ajoite (above) and Shattuckite (page 132), Ajoite with Shattuckite is one of the most powerful protections against electromagnetic smog and psychic attack, especially when worn over the thymus. It creates a protective bubble around the aura that keeps you safe, no matter where you may be, and yet allows you to remain open spiritually. Putting on this stone allows you to sink into profound peace. The combination teaches the difference between atonement and at-onement.

Note: Ajoite with Shattuckite is a high-vibration stone.

Raw Ajoite with Shattuckite

Shattuckite

Crystal system	Orthorhombic
Chemistry	$Cu_5(SiO_3)_4(OH)_2$ Copper silicate hydroxide
Hardness	3.5
Source	USA
Chakra	Aligns third eye and throat; crown, higher crown, higher heart
Number	11
Zodiac sign	Taurus, Libra
Planet	Venus
Beneficial for	Syphilitic miasm, minor health complaints, balance, spring tonic, tonsillitis, blood clotting, intercellular structures.

Tumbled Shattuckite

Shattuckite is named for the Shattuck mine, where it was first discovered. Channeled sources say that this stone is excellent for stimulating cell division, repairing genetic information and healing genetically transmitted diseases, including those brought about by radiation damage. This highly spiritual stone heightens vibration and amplifies thought, bringing clear metaphysical vision and assisting in communicating what is seen. Shattuckite can clear past-life curses and commands to secrecy and is particularly useful in cases where past-life experience has closed down metaphysical abilities, as it removes hypnotic commands and edicts. During channeling, Shattuckite's powerful energy ensures that the entity does not take over the physical body. An excellent energy conduit, it reaches a high vibration, insisting that the purest source is contacted. This stone develops automatic writing and telepathy and is said to facilitate clear communication with extraterrestrials.

Chrysopal (Blue-green Opal)

Crystal system	Amorphous
Chemistry	$SiO_2\,nH_2O$ Hydrated silica with impurities
Hardness	5.5–6.5
Source	Australia, Brazil, USA, Tanzania, Iceland, Mexico, Peru, UK, Canada, Honduras, Slovakia
Chakra	Third eye
Zodiac sign	Cancer, Pisces
Beneficial for	Emotional burdens, detoxification, liver, constriction in heart and chest, self-worth, strengthening the will to live, intuition, fear, loyalty, spontaneity, female hormones, menopause, Parkinson's, infections, fevers, memory, purifying blood and kidneys, regulating insulin, childbirth, PMS, eyes, ears.

In addition to carrying the generic properties of Opal (page 254), Chrysopal helps you observe the world with new eyes, opening to new impressions and encouraging openness to other people.

Raw Chrysopal

Apatite

Crystal system	Hexagonal
Chemistry	$Ca_5 (PO_4)_3 (F,CL,OH)$
Hardness	5
Source	Canada, USA, Mexico, Norway, Russia, Brazil
Chakra	Third eye, base
Number	9
Zodiac sign	Gemini
Beneficial for	Motivation, nervous exhaustion, irritability, humanitarian attitude, apathy, service, communication, energy depletion, pain, bones, cells, calcium absorption, cartilage, bone, teeth, motor skills, arthritis, joint problems, rickets, appetite suppression, metabolic rate, glands, meridians, organs, hypertension.

Raw Apatite

The name Apatite is derived from the Greek *apate,* meaning "deceit," because it can be confused with gems such as Peridot and Beryl. The interface between consciousness and matter, Apatite is a stone of manifestation attuned to the future, yet connects to past lives. Developing metaphysical abilities and spiritual attunement, it deepens meditation and raises kundalini. Releasing energy in the base chakra, Apatite clears frustration and supports passion without guilt. It balances the physical, emotional, mental, and spiritual bodies. Promoting a humanitarian attitude, this stone aids communication and induces openness and social ease, dissolving aloofness and alienation. It draws off negativity about oneself and others and is helpful for hyperactive and autistic children.

Aquamarine

Faceted Aquamarine

Crystal system	Hexagonal
Chemistry	$Be_3Al_2Si_6O_{18}$ + iron
Hardness	7.5–8
Source	USA, Mexico, Russia, Brazil, India, Ireland, Zimbabwe, Afghanistan, Pakistan
Chakra	Aligns all, clears throat chakra, opens third eye
Number	1
Zodiac sign	Aries, Gemini, Pisces
Planet	Moon
Beneficial for	Pollutants, stress, intuition, fear, sore throats, swollen glands, thyroid, pituitary, hormones, growth, elimination, eyes, jaw and teeth, near- or farsightedness, stomach, immune system, autoimmune diseases.

Aquamarine's color comes from minute traces of iron. Said to protect sailors at sea and to guard against drowning, it was the stone of the sea goddess and counteracted the forces of darkness, gaining favor from the spirits of light. A wonderful stone for meditation, Aquamarine shields the aura, invokes high states of consciousness, and encourages service to humanity. With an affinity to sensitive people, it invokes tolerance and supports anyone overwhelmed by responsibility. Breaking self-defeating programs, it leads to dynamic change. Useful for closure on all levels, this stone is helpful in understanding underlying emotional states and interpreting how you feel. Removing extraneous thought, Aquamarine filters information reaching the brain and clarifies perception.

Raw Aquamarine

Atacamite

Crystal system	Orthorhombic
Chemistry	$Cu_2(OH)_3Cl$ Copper chloro-hydroxide
Hardness	3–3.5
Source	USA, Australia, Mexico, Chile, Italy, England, Russia, Namibia, Peru
Chakra	Third eye, higher heart
Number	6
Beneficial for	Thymus, immune system, kidneys, fear, elimination, genitals, herpes, venereal disease, hypothyroidism, nervous system, stress.

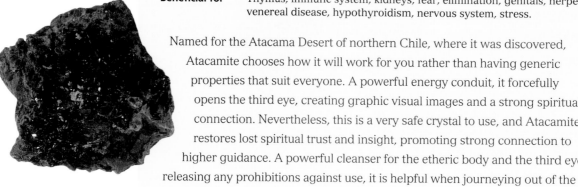

Named for the Atacama Desert of northern Chile, where it was discovered, Atacamite chooses how it will work for you rather than having generic properties that suit everyone. A powerful energy conduit, it forcefully opens the third eye, creating graphic visual images and a strong spiritual connection. Nevertheless, this is a very safe crystal to use, and Atacamite restores lost spiritual trust and insight, promoting strong connection to higher guidance. A powerful cleanser for the etheric body and the third eye, releasing any prohibitions against use, it is helpful when journeying out of the body. Atacamite brings unconditional love into your life.

Atacamite crystals on matrix

Turquoise

Crystal system	Triclinic
Chemistry	$CuAl_6(PO_4)_4(OH)_8 5(H_2O)$ Hydrous copper aluminum phosphate
Hardness	5–6
Source	USA, Egypt, Mexico, China, Iran, Peru, Poland, Russia, France, Tibet, Afghanistan, Arabian Peninsula, Iran
Chakra	Throat, third eye
Number	1
Zodiac sign	Scorpio, Sagittarius, Pisces
Planet	Jupiter, Venus, Neptune
Beneficial for	Friendship, loyalty, self-realization, mood swings, romantic love, purification, electromagnetic smog, exhaustion, depression, panic attacks, shame, guilt, anti-inflammatory, detoxification, meridians of body, subtle energy fields, physical and metaphysical immune systems, tissue regeneration, assimilation of nutrients, pollution, viral infections, eyes, neutralizes overacidity, gout, rheumatism, stomach, cramp, pain, sore throat.

Raw Turquoise

Turquoise comes from the French *turquoise*, meaning "Turkey," which in ancient times encompassed Persia (Iran). This stone bridges earth and heaven and is sacred to Native Americans. To be given a Turquoise brings good fortune and peace. It is protective and has been used for amulets since time began, defending against injury, outside influences, or atmospheric pollutants. Promoting spiritual attunement and enhancing communication with the physical and spiritual worlds, Turquoise is an efficient healer, providing solace for the spirit and well-being for the body. A powerful energy conduit, it releases old vows, inhibitions, and prohibitions, dissolves a martyred attitude or self-sabotage, and allows the soul to express itself once more. Turquoise shows how the creation of our "fate" depends on what we do at each moment.

Tumbled Turquoise

Eilat Stone

Crystal system	Complex combination
Chemistry	Complex combination
Hardness	Variable
Source	Israel, Jordan
Chakra	Higher heart, heart, thymus, throat
Number	3
Zodiac sign	Sagittarius
Beneficial for	Creativity; stress; coping with incest, rape, physical violence, misogyny, sexual repression and depression; bone and tissue regeneration; sinus; reorders cellular growth rate; fever; pain; tumors; transformation; psychosexual problems; inhibitions; rebirthing; detoxifying liver and gallbladder; stress; insomnia; allergies; eyes; circulatory diseases; childbirth; labor; female sexual organs; blood pressure; asthma; arthritis; epilepsy; fractures; swollen joints; growths; travel sickness; vertigo; optic nerve; pancreas; spleen; parathyroid; DNA; cellular structure; acidification of tissue; diabetes; friendship; loyalty; self-realization; mood swings; purification; electromagnetic smog; exhaustion; depression; panic attacks; shame; guilt; anti-inflammatory; meridians of body; subtle energy fields; physical and metaphysical immune systems; tissue regeneration; assimilation of nutrients; pollution,; viral infections; eyes; neutralizes overacidity; gout, rheumatism; stomach; cramp; pain; sore throat; personal power; creativity; self-awareness; confidence; motivation; letting go; phobias; guilt; mental tension; miasms; grief; lungs; breathing capacity; pain; regulating insulin; reoxygenating blood; blood pressure; cellular structure; Alzheimer's; bone disease; muscle spasm; digestive tract; ulcers; blood disorders; liver; kidneys; intestines; pancreas; muscles; infections; throat and tonsils; burns; thyroid; metabolism.

Raw Eilat Stone

Polished Eilat Stone

Eilat Stone instills a sense of wonderment at the beauty all around. In addition to carrying the generic properties of Malachite (page 96), Turquoise (left) and Chrysocolla (page 137), it flushes out hurt, fear, and loss; removes detritus created from soul-shattering events in the current or previous lives; and calls soul fragments home. These traumas can then be wiped from the Akashic Record. Known as the "sage stone," it offers wisdom and creative solutions for problem-solving. Eilat Stone balances yin and yang and brings about a lightness of being. It harmonizes and stimulates your emotional life, ensuring that it is never dull.

Blue-green Obsidian

Crystal system	Amorphous
Chemistry	SiO_2 Silicon dioxide with impurities
Hardness	5–5.5
Source	Mexico, volcanic regions (may be artificially created)
Chakra	Heart, crown, third eye, throat
Beneficial for	Reiki healing.

In addition to carrying the generic properties of Obsidian (page 214), natural and rare Blue-green Obsidian promotes understanding from the heart and speaking one's truth. However, Blue-green Obsidian may be artificially made glass with no therapeutic properties.

Cavansite

Crystal system	Orthorhombic
Chemistry	$Ca(VO)Si_4O_{10}(H_2O)_4$ Hydrated calcium vanadium silicate
Hardness	3–4
Source	Poona (India), USA (Oregon), Brazil, New Zealand
Chakra	Third eye, throat, past life
Number	5
Zodiac sign	Aquarius
Beneficial for	Endorphin release, self-respect, purification, regeneration, recurrent disease, stabilizing the pulse, cellular healing, tinnitus, sore throat, kidneys, bladder, fragmented DNA, eyes, blood, calcium deficiency, teeth, joint flexibility.

Cavansite on matrix

Tumbled Cavansite

With its wonderful turquoise color, Cavansite brings optimism and inspiration to your life. Named for its component minerals, calcium and Vanadinite, it was discovered in the 1970s. Stimulating intuition and encouraging astral journeying, it facilitates pragmatic learning and logical thought. A self-reflective stone, it redresses destructive behavior or thought patterns, whether from previous or current lives, enabling you to be more comfortable in your physical body. This life-affirming crystal facilitates past-life exploration and helps you reframe trauma at its source. Cavansite protects a healer or past-life therapist during a healing session and also protects your home or car. Sensitizing you to the need to look after the environment, it helps you think before you act and instills an appreciation of beauty.

Note: Toxic stone; use with care.

Dioptase

Crystal system	Hexagonal
Chemistry	$CuSiO_2(OH)_2$ Hydrous copper silicate
Hardness	5
Source	Iran, Russia, Namibia, Congo, North Africa, Chile, Peru, Zaire
Chakra	Third eye, higher heart
Number	8
Zodiac sign	Scorpio, Sagittarius
Beneficial for	Grief, betrayal, abandonment, spiritual attunement, metaphysical vision, positive attitude, shock, addiction, stress, detoxification, cell disorders, T-cells, thymus, Ménière's disease, high blood pressure, pain, migraine, heart attacks, fatigue, nausea, liver.

Dioptase crystals on matrix

The name Dioptase comes from the Greek *diopteia*, "to see through." An excellent energy conduit, this stone is a powerful healer for the heart, especially for the child within, and it has a dramatic effect on the human energy field. Dioptase encourages you to live in the present moment and, paradoxically, activates past-life memories. A strong mental cleanser and detoxifier, it releases the need to control others. Its green ray reaches deep within the heart to absorb festering wounds and forgotten hurts. Teaching that pain and difficulty in relationships mirror separation from one's Self, Dioptase heals an emotional black hole that is desperate for love and clears away perceptions as to how love ought to be, ushering in a new vibration of love.

Chrysocolla

Crystal system	Orthorhombic
Chemistry	$CuSiO_3H_2O$ + Al, Fe, P Hydrated copper
Hardness	2–4
Source	USA, UK, Mexico, Chile, Peru, Zaire, Russia
Chakra	Cleanses and activates all, aligning with divine
Number	5
Zodiac sign	Gemini, Virgo, Taurus
Planet	Venus
Beneficial for	Personal power, creativity, self-awareness, confidence, motivation, letting go, phobias, guilt, mental tension, miasms, grief, lungs, breathing capacity, pain, regulating insulin, reoxygenating blood, blood pressure, cellular structure, Alzheimer's, arthritis, bone disease, muscle spasm, digestive tract, ulcers, blood disorders, liver, kidneys, intestines, pancreas, blood, muscles, infections, throat and tonsils, burns, thyroid, metabolism, PMS, menstrual cramps.

Raw Chrysocolla

Chrysocolla is named from the Greek words *chrynos*, "gold," and *kola*, "glue," as it resembled material used for soldering gold. An excellent auric cleanser and powerful energy conduit, this is a useful stone for meditation and communication. Accepting with serenity situations that are constantly changing, it helps you remain impartial and speak your truth. Beneficial to relationships, it draws off negative energies, stabilizing the home. Drawing out negative emotions, it reverses destructive programming, heals heartache, and increases the capacity to love. Assisting communication yet aiding in keeping silent when appropriate, it attunes you to the song lines of the earth.

Drusy Chrysocolla

Crystal system	Orthorhombic
Chemistry	Complex hydrated crystalline copper
Hardness	2
Source	USA, UK, Mexico, Chile, Peru, Zaire, Russia
Chakra	Soma, higher crown
Beneficial for	Personal power, creativity, self-awareness, confidence, motivation, letting go, phobias, guilt, mental tension, miasms, grief, lungs, breathing capacity, pain, regulating insulin, reoxygenating blood, blood pressure, cellular structure, Alzheimer's, arthritis, bone disease, muscle spasm, digestive tract, ulcers, blood disorders, liver, kidneys, intestines, pancreas, blood, muscles, infections, throat and tonsils, burns, thyroid, metabolism, PMS, menstrual cramps, self-imposed limitations, periodontal disease, lethargy.

Raw Drusy Chrysocolla on matrix

Combining the properties of Drusy Quartz (see page 63 for generic properties) and Chrysocolla (above), this fast-working stone speeds things up and intensifies the purpose behind applications, making it a useful healer for trauma.

Crystalline Chrysocolla (Gem Silica)

Crystal system	Orthorhombic
Chemistry	$CuSiO_3H_2O$ + Al, Fe, P Hydrated copper
Hardness	2–4
Source	USA, UK, Mexico, Chile, Peru, Zaire, Russia
Chakra	Crown, higher crown
Zodiac sign	Gemini, Virgo, Taurus
Planet	Venus
Beneficial for	Personal power, creativity, self-awareness, confidence, motivation, letting go, phobias, guilt, mental tension, miasms.

Crystalline Chrysocolla

In addition to carrying the generic properties of Chrysocolla (page 137), Crystalline Chrysocolla, the most evolved form of Chrysocolla, increases the rate at which energies are stabilized, balancing the physical with the etheric. A powerful healing stone for women, it is excellent for sexual and emotional trauma stemming from a present or past life, especially where this was intertwined with magical ritual. Gem Silica prevents trauma from settling onto the etheric blueprint to become an ingrained karmic pattern in the future. It connects with the Goddess and enhances the deep joy of being a woman.

Note: Crystalline Chrysocolla is a high-vibration stone.

Smithsonite

Crystal system	Trigonal
Chemistry	$ZnCO_3$ Zinc carbonate
Hardness	4–5
Source	USA, Australia, Greece, Italy, Mexico, Namibia, Germany, South Africa
Chakra	Higher heart, crown, third eye
Number	7
Zodiac sign	Virgo, Pisces
Beneficial for	Rebirthing, birth, leadership qualities, tact, harmony, diplomacy, alcoholism, stress, mental breakdown, immune system, sinus, digestive disorders, osteoporosis, elasticity to veins, muscles.

Smithsonite on matrix

Smithsonite is named after the American mineralogist James Smithson, founder of the Smithsonian Institution. This stone has an extremely gentle presence and forms a buffer against life's problems. It heals the inner child and alleviates emotional abuse and misuse. Strengthening metaphysical abilities, it can act as a witness for the truth of a metaphysical communication and connect to the angelic realm. This stone aids difficult relationships and remedies unpleasant situations. It is an excellent immune stimulator and can be gridded around the bed to bring healing and protection.

Cassiterite

Crystal system	Tetragonal
Chemistry	SnO_2 Tin oxide
Hardness	6–7
Source	Brazil
Chakra	Heart, solar plexus
Number	2
Zodiac sign	Sagittarius
Beneficial for	Eating disorders, compulsive behavior, obesity, malnutrition, nervous and hormonal systems, secretions.

Cassiterite on matrix

Cassiterite assists in manifesting your dreams. Traditionally linked to astrology and astronomy, it imparts the mathematical precision needed to see into the heart of a problem, objectively perceiving how, and why, things were as they were, opening the way for compassion and forgiveness for yourself and others. An excellent stone for anyone suffering from rejection, abandonment, prejudice, or alienation, or who was disapproved of, Cassiterite dissolves the resulting pain. Facilitating tough love, it encourages you to do exactly what is necessary and no more for yourself and others.

Blue-green Jade

Crystal system	Monoclinic
Chemistry	$Na(AlFe)Si_2O_6$
Hardness	6
Source	USA, China, Italy, Myanmar, Russia, Middle East
Chakra	Third eye
Zodiac sign	Taurus, Libra
Planet	Venus
Beneficial for	Longevity, self-sufficiency, detoxification, filtration, elimination, kidneys, suprarenal glands, cellular and skeletal systems, stitches, fertility, childbirth, hips, spleen, water–salt–acid–alkaline ratio.

Polished Blue-green Jade

Blue-green Jade symbolizes peace and reflection. In addition to carrying the generic properties of Jade (page 120), this stone brings inner serenity and patience, ensuring slow but steady progress and assisting if you feel overwhelmed by situations beyond your control.

Blue and indigo crystals

Blue stones resonate with the throat chakra and are excellent for self-expression. Traditionally these stones were a tonic—and a symbol of chastity. Reflecting the blue of heaven, they procured the assistance of spirits of light to counteract darkness. Indigo stones link to the highest states of consciousness and to the depths of space. Stimulating intuition and metaphysical abilities, they bring about a mystical perception of the world when placed at the third eye and cohere spiritual identity at the soma chakra.

Azurite

Tumbled Azurite

Crystal system	Monoclinic
Chemistry	$Cu_3(CO_3)_2(OH)_2$ Copper hydroxyl-carbonate
Hardness	3.5–4
Source	USA, Australia, Chile, Peru, France, Namibia, Russia, Egypt, Italy, Germany
Chakra	Third eye, crown, higher crown, soma
Number	1
Zodiac sign	Sagittarius
Planet	Venus
Beneficial for	Healing crisis, the mind and mental processes, mental healing, stress relief, fears, phobias, memory, self-expression, grief, detoxification, throat problems, arthritis, joint problems, spinal alignment, brain structure, kidney, gallbladder, spleen, liver, thyroid, bones, teeth, skin, embryonic development. If palpitations occur, remove immediately.

Raw Azurite

Named from *azure*, meaning "blue," Azurite has long been used to guide psychic development and increase metaphysical powers, especially when placed on the third eye. A favorite stone in ancient Egypt, it raises consciousness to the highest level, facilitates a meditative channeling state, urges the soul toward enlightenment, and controls spiritual unfoldment. The stone can bring about profound multidimensional cellular reprogramming. A powerful healing stone and energy conduit, Azurite facilitates understanding of the effect of the mind on the body and, with its high copper content, amplifies energy flow through the nervous system. This crystal enables journeys out of the body to take place safely.

Excellent for the mind and mental processes, Azurite challenges your view of reality, releasing programmed belief systems so that you move into the unknown without fear. It assists someone who talks too much out of nervousness and provides mental healing at many levels. Drawing out emotional debris and ancient fears, it cleanses the emotional body and brings about inner peace. If a healing crisis occurs, Azurite will gently bring things back into balance.

Raw Azurite looks like the night sky.

Aura Quartz

Crystal system	Hexagonal
Chemistry	Complex amendment
Hardness	Brittle
Source	Manufactured
Chakra	Depends on type
Beneficial for	Multidimensional healing, a master healer for any condition, multidimensional cellular memory healer, efficient receptor for programming, brings the body into balance, energy enhancement.

Carrying the generic properties of Quartz (page 230), Aura Quartz is artificially enhanced but is nevertheless powerful, with an intense energy resulting from the alchemical process that bonds gold or other metals onto pure Quartz. Each Aura Quartz has its own specific properties related to color and gold, platinum, or other alchemicalized metal.

Aura Quartz

Note: Aura Quartz is a high-vibration stone.

Aqua Aura Quartz

Crystal system	Hexagonal
Chemistry	Complex amendment
Hardness	Brittle
Source	Manufactured
Chakra	Throat, third eye, soma, higher crown
Beneficial for	Balancing polarities, fulfilling potential, thymus, immune system, carpal tunnel syndrome, strokes, multidimensional healing, a master healer for any condition, multidimensional cellular memory healing, efficient receptor for programming, bringing the body into balance.

A stone of spiritual abundance and communication created from gold bonded to Quartz (see page 230 for generic properties), Aqua Aura activates soul energy, frees you from limitation, and generates space for something new. Stimulating channeling and self-expression, it deepens spiritual attunement and communication. Aqua Aura safeguards against metaphysical or psychological attack and bestows profound peace during meditation. Releasing negativity from the subtle energetic bodies, and healing auric "holes," Aqua Aura activates the chakras, especially at the throat, to encourage communication from the heart. Used in conjunction with other crystals, Aqua Aura enhances their healing properties.

Note: Aqua Aura Quartz is a high-vibration stone.

Aqua Aura Quartz

Rainbow Aura Quartz

Crystal system	Hexagonal
Chemistry	Complex amendment
Hardness	Brittle
Source	Manufactured
Chakra	Higher crown, heart, soma
Beneficial for	Multidimensional healing, a master healer for any condition, multidimensional cellular memory healing, efficient receptor for programing, bringing the body into balance.

Created by bonding gold and titanium onto Quartz (see page 230 for generic properties), Rainbow Aura Quartz activates all the energy centers in the body, clearing a path for the life force to manifest multidimensionally, bringing in vibrant energy and zest for life. Rainbow Aura is beneficial for dysfunctional relationships, as it highlights projections and releases negative emotions such as resentment or grief, bringing deep insights into relationships at all levels and releasing karmic ties that are hindering relationships in the present life. The transformed relationship is vital and harmonious.

Note: Rainbow Quartz is a high-vibration stone.

Rainbow Aura Quartz

Flame Aura Quartz

Crystal system	Hexagonal
Chemistry	Complex amendment
Hardness	Brittle
Source	Manufactured
Chakra	Higher crown, third eye, soma
Beneficial for	Diabetes, multidimensional healing, a master healer for any condition, multidimensional cellular memory healing, efficient receptor for programming, bringing the body into balance.

Sharing many properties with Rainbow Aura Quartz (see above and page 230 for generic properties), very deep blue Flame Aura Quartz, created from titanium and niobium, is an excellent crystal for use in spiritual initiations and rituals and for deepening meditation and spiritual attunement.

Note: Flame Aura Quartz is a high-vibration stone.

Flame Aura Quartz double-terminated twinflame formation

Siberian Blue Quartz

Crystal system	Hexagonal
Chemistry	Complex
Hardness	Not ascertained
Source	Manufactured
Chakra	Throat, third eye, crown
Beneficial for	Throat infections (as an elixir), stomach ulcers, stress. Applied externally: depression, inflammation, sunburn, stiff neck or muscles.

A brilliant blue laboratory-regrown crystal created from Quartz (see page 230 for generic properties) and cobalt, Siberian Blue Quartz brings about intense visionary experiences and accesses cosmic consciousness, stimulating metaphysical vision and telepathy. Lifting the spirit and instilling deep peace, this stone facilitates speaking your truth and being heard.

Note: Siberian Blue Quartz is a high-vibration stone.

Polished Siberian Blue Quartz

Blue Quartz (natural)

Tumbled Blue Quartz

Crystal system	Hexagonal
Chemistry	SiO_2 Silicon dioxide with impurities
Hardness	7
Source	Africa, England, USA, Russia
Chakra	Throat
Number	44
Beneficial for	Organs in upper body, detoxification, depression, bloodstream, throat, immune system, overstimulation, spleen, endocrine system. A master healer for any condition, multidimensional cellular memory healer, and efficient receptor for programming. If Blue Quartz is rutilated, it is said to restrain premature ejaculation.

In addition to carrying the generic properties of Quartz (page 230), Blue Quartz reaches out to others and inspires hope, calms the mind, assuages fear, and assists in understanding your spiritual nature during metamorphosis. Excellent for overcoming disorganization, it instills mental clarity and self-discipline and fires creativity. Natural Blue Quartz may have Dumortierite, Aerinite, Rutile, or Indicolite included within it. See also Dumortierite (page 150).

Note: Blue Quartz is a high-vibration stone.

Blue Quartz on matrix

Blue Phantom Quartz

Crystal system	Hexagonal
Chemistry	SiO_2 Silicon dioxide with inclusions
Hardness	7
Source	Worldwide
Chakra	Throat
Number	77
Zodiac sign	Sagittarius, Aquarius
Beneficial for	Ameliorating anger, anxiety, throat, endocrine and metabolic systems, spleen, blood vessels, multidimensional cellular memory healing, efficient receptor for programming, immune system, bringing the body into balance, old patterns, hearing disorders, clairaudience.

Blue Phantom Quartz point

In addition to carrying the generic properties of Phantoms (page 239) and Quartz (page 230), Blue Phantom is useful for enhancing telepathic communication between people, or earth and the spiritual realms, assisting you in multidimensional travel and facilitating retrieval of knowledge. Supporting any form of divination, in making you feel a part of the perfect whole this stone helps you reach out to others with compassion and tolerance.

Indicolite Quartz

Crystal system	Complex
Chemistry	Complex
Hardness	Not determined
Source	Sri Lanka, Brazil, Africa, USA, Australia, Afghanistan, Italy, Germany, Madagascar
Chakra	Third eye, throat
Beneficial for	Multidimensional cellular memory healing, efficient receptor for programming, energy enhancement, immune system, bringing the body into balance, speech impediments, sadness, blocked feelings, pulmonary and immune systems, brain, fluid imbalances, kidney, chronic sore throat, insomnia, night sweats, sinusitis, bacterial infections. Place where there is disease or congestion. A master healer for any condition.

The inclusions of Blue Tourmaline within Indicolite Quartz stimulate out-of-body experiences and journeys through different realms of consciousness. In addition to carrying the generic properties of Tourmaline (page 210) and Quartz (page 230), it transports you to a very high vibration, offering an overview of your lives and indicating why you have chosen to incarnate again. Meditating with Indicolite Quartz puts you in touch with your life purpose and spiritual guides.

Note: Indicolite Quartz is a high-vibration stone.

Indicolite Quartz

Indicolite (Blue Tourmaline)

Crystal system	Hexagonal
Chemistry	Complex silicate
Hardness	7–7.5
Source	Sri Lanka, Brazil, Africa, USA, Australia, Afghanistan, Italy, Germany, Madagascar
Chakra	Throat, third eye, higher heart
Number	6, 55
Zodiac sign	Taurus, Libra
Beneficial for	Speech impediments, sadness, blocked feelings, pulmonary and immune systems, brain, fluid imbalances, kidney, bladder, thymus, thyroid, chronic sore throat, insomnia, night sweats, sinusitis, bacterial infections, throat, larynx, lungs, esophagus, eyes, burns, protection, detoxification, spinal adjustments, balancing male–female energy, paranoia, dyslexia, hand-eye coordination, assimilation and translation of coded information, bronchitis, diabetes, emphysema, pleurisy, pneumonia, energy flow, removal of blockages. Place where there is disease or congestion.

Polished Indicolite

In addition to carrying the generic properties of Tourmaline (page 210), this stone promotes metaphysical awareness, encourages visions, and opens the way for service to others while encouraging those who constantly give also to receive. Assisting in developing an inner sense of responsibility and living in harmony with the environment, Indicolite supports fidelity, ethical behavior, tolerance, and a love of truth. Stimulating the urge for spiritual freedom and clarity of self-expression, it is an excellent stone for healers, as it prevents negativity from sticking. Bright Blue Tourmaline is a useful diagnostic tool, as it identifies underlying causes of disease, especially grief and emotional blockages, and facilitates emotional and cellular memory healing.

Blue Halite

Crystal system	Cubic
Chemistry	NaCl Sodium chloride
Hardness	2
Source	USA, France, Germany
Chakra	Third eye
Zodiac sign	Pisces
Beneficial for	Iodine absorption, thyroid, thymus, hypothalamus, anxiety, detoxification, metabolism, water retention, intestinal problems, bipolar disorders, respiratory disorders, skin.

Blue Halite

In addition to carrying the generic properties of Halite (page 250), Blue Halite opens the metaphysical gates, heightens intuition, and encourages mystical awareness. Extremely useful for reprogramming a distorted vision of reality, Blue Halite cleanses mental attachments or undue influence from the third eye.

Note: Blue Halite is a high-vibration stone.

Blue Calcite

Crystal system	Hexagonal
Chemistry	$CaCO_3$ Calcium carbonate
Hardness	3
Source	USA, UK, Belgium, Czech Republic, Slovakia, Peru, Iceland, Romania, Brazil
Chakra	Third eye, throat
Zodiac sign	Cancer
Planet	Venus
Beneficial for	Recuperation, blood pressure, pain on all levels, study, motivation, laziness, emotional stress, organs of elimination, calcium uptake in bones, dissolving calcification, skeleton, joints, intestinal conditions, skin, tissue healing, immune system, growth in small children.

Tumbled Blue Calcite

A powerful healing and purification stone, Blue Calcite absorbs energy, filters it, and returns it to benefit the sender. In addition to carrying the generic properties of Calcite (page 245), this stone quiets mental chatter and brings about clarity. Excellent for initiating spiritual growth and for relaxation, Blue Calcite soothes nerves and lifts anxieties. Releasing negative emotions, it assists clear communication of thoughts and feelings, especially where there is dissent, and facilitates adapting to necessary change.

Angelite

Crystal system	Orthorhombic
Chemistry	$CaSO_4$
Hardness	3.5
Source	Peru
Chakra	Throat, third eye
Number	1
Zodiac sign	Aquarius
Beneficial for	Compassion, rebirthing, meridians and energetic pathways, throat, inflammation, thyroid and the parathyroids, tissue and blood vessels, fluid balance, diuretic, weight control, lungs, arms, sunburn.

Tumbled Angelite

Formed from Celestite that has been compressed over millions of years into one of the stones of awareness for the New Age, Angelite represents peace and brotherhood. Facilitating conscious contact with the angelic realm, it enhances telepathic communication and enables out-of-body journeys to take place while still in contact with everyday reality. Angelite has been used to enhance astrological understanding and to bring deeper understanding of mathematics. This is a powerful stone for healers, as it deepens attunement, heightens perception, and provides protection for the environment or the body. It encourages you to speak your truth and to be more accepting. Alleviating psychological pain and counteracting cruelty, Angelite transmutes disorder into wholeness.

Polished Angelite slice

Celestite

Crystal system	Orthorhombic
Chemistry	$SrSO_4$
Hardness	3–3.5
Source	UK, Egypt, Mexico, Peru, Poland, Libya, Madagascar
Chakra	Third eye, crown, higher crown, throat
Number	2, 8
Zodiac sign	Gemini
Planet	Venus, Neptune
Beneficial for	The arts, worry, conflict resolution, peaceful coexistence, balance, alignment, mental clarity, pain, detoxification, mental torment, eyes, ears, cellular order, muscle tension, throat.

Celestite geode

A high-vibration stone and a teacher for the New Age, Celestite brings divine energy into the environment and stimulates spiritual development and metaphysical abilities. It stresses trust in the infinite wisdom of the divine. Healing the aura, it promotes purity of heart and maintains a harmonious atmosphere in times of stress. Celestite assists dysfunctional relationships, opening a space for negotiation and urging greater openness to new experiences. With its calming effect, Celestite cools fiery emotions and synthesizes the intellect with the instincts, promoting mental balance. It provides excellent support when speaking in front of large crowds.

Note: Celestite is a high-vibration stone.

Andean Blue Opal

Crystal system	Amorphous
Chemistry	SiO_2 nH_2O Hydrated silica with impurities
Hardness	5.5–6.5
Source	Peru
Chakra	Throat, heart, higher heart, third eye
Number	2
Beneficial for	"Right action," water retention, muscular swelling, heart, lungs, thymus, self-worth, strengthening the will to live, intuition, spontaneity, female hormones, menopause, purifying blood and kidneys, regulating insulin, eyes, ears.

Polished Andean Blue Opal slice

Mined deep in the mountains of Peru and an excellent journeying stone, Andean Opal induces a relaxed, receptive state and enhances divination. In addition to carrying the generic properties of Opal (page 254), this stone promotes acting for the highest good and is excellent for stimulating communication from the heart. Particularly useful for healing old emotional wounds, from this life or another, it creates inner serenity to carry you through troubled times or stress. This stone is said to smooth the auric field, enhancing connection and communication with others. Increasing awareness of the need for healing the earth, it is a useful tool for facilitating that healing and for those who manifest and transmute the changing vibration through their own body.

Dumortierite

Crystal system	Orthorhombic
Chemistry	(Al_7O_3) $(BO_3)(SiO_4)$ 3 Aluminum borosilicate hydroxide
Hardness	7
Source	USA, Brazil
Chakra	Past life, throat, third eye
Number	4
Zodiac sign	Leo
Beneficial for	Clairaudience, self-confidence, cellular memory healing, filing, organizational abilities, stage fright, shyness, stress, phobias, insomnia, panic, fear, depression, overexcitability, detachment, *joie de vivre*, patience, self-discipline, mental clarity, sunburn, stubbornness, hypersensitivity, wasting disorders, epilepsy, headaches, nausea, vomiting, cramping, colic, diarrhea, palpitations.

Tumbled Dumortierite

Named after the French paleontologist Eugene Dumortier, Dumortierite communicates with angelic or spirit guides, helping you see the worth in each human being. This stone takes you back to the beginning of your soul journey and breaks ties that are no longer useful. It is particularly helpful for releasing past-life causes of disease, difficult circumstances, and addiction. Stabilizing a rocky relationship, it is said to attract a soulmate. Dumortierite assists in standing up for yourself and adapting to your present reality, and helps you remain young at heart. Excellent for promoting a positive attitude to life, it is useful for people who deal with crisis and trauma, calming and focusing effort. Dumortierite develops your linguistic capabilities so that you can communicate with other cultures.

Raw Dumortierite

Iolite

Crystal system	Orthorhombic
Chemistry	$Mg_2Al_4Si_5O_{18}$
Hardness	7
Source	USA
Chakra	Third eye, aligns all
Number	7
Zodiac sign	Taurus, Libra, Sagittarius
Beneficial for	Strong constitution, visualization, discord in relationships, fatty deposits, detoxification, alcohol excesses, liver regeneration, malaria, fevers, pituitary, sinus, respiratory system, migraine headaches, bacterial infection.

Tumbled Iolite

A vision stone, Iolite stimulates inner knowing. Useful in shamanic ceremonies, it assists journeying and clears thought forms. Iolite gives off an electrical charge that reenergizes the auric field and aligns the aura. This stone releases causes of addiction and codependency, expressing your true Self freed from the expectations of those around you.

Raw Iolite

Blue Aventurine

Crystal system	Trigonal
Chemistry	SiO_2 Silicon dioxide with impurities
Hardness	7
Source	Italy, Brazil, China, India, Russia, Tibet, Nepal
Chakra	Third eye, crown, past life
Zodiac sign	Aries
Planet	Mercury
Beneficial for	Mental healing, balancing male–female energy, prosperity, leadership, decisiveness, compassion, empathy, creativity, stuttering, severe neurosis, thymus gland, connective tissue, nervous system, blood pressure, metabolism, cholesterol, arteriosclerosis, heart attacks, anti-inflammatory, skin eruptions, allergies, migraine headaches, eyes, adrenals, lungs, sinuses, heart, muscular and urogenital systems.

Raw Blue Aventurine

In addition to carrying the generic properties of Aventurine (page 97), Blue Aventurine is a powerful mental healer that supports male shamanic energy and enhances the masculine side of men or women, increasing vitality and positivism.

Blue Fluorite

Crystal system	Cubic
Chemistry	CaF_2 Calcium fluoride
Hardness	4
Source	USA, England, Mexico, Canada, Australia, Germany, Norway, China, Peru, Brazil
Chakra	Third eye
Zodiac sign	Pisces
Planet	Mercury
Beneficial for	Eye problems, nose, ears, throat, balance, coordination, self-confidence, shyness, worry, centering, concentration, psychosomatic disease, absorption of nutrients, bronchitis, emphysema, pleurisy, pneumonia, antiviral, infections, disorders, teeth, cells, bones, DNA damage, skin and mucous membranes, respiratory tract, colds, flu, sinusitis, ulcers, wounds, adhesions, mobilizing joints, arthritis, rheumatism, spinal injuries, pain relief, shingles, nerve-related pain, blemishes, wrinkles, dental work, sexual libido, electromagnetic stress.

Tumbled Blue Fluorite

Enhancing creative, orderly thought and clear communication, Blue Fluorite amplifies your healing potential by tightly focusing brain activity, and can invoke spiritual awakening. This dual-action stone calms or revitalizes energy as needed for the physical body or the aura. Extremely useful for reprogramming karmic patterns, Blue Fluorite heals soul fragmentation from the present or past lives and promotes cellular memory healing. See also Fluorite, page 177.

Blue Fluorite on matrix

Kyanite (Disthene)

Crystal system	Triclinic
Chemistry	Al_2SiO_5 Aluminum silicate
Hardness	5.5–7
Source	USA, Brazil, Switzerland, Austria, Italy, India
Chakra	Opens throat, aligns all with aura
Number	4
Zodiac sign	Aries, Taurus, Libra
Beneficial for	Metaphysical abilities, logical and linear thought, victimhood, frustration, anger, stress, resignation, pain, dexterity, muscular disorders, fevers, urogenital system, thyroid and parathyroid, adrenal glands, throat, brain, blood pressure, infections, excess weight, cerebellum, motor responses, yin–yang balance, larynx, hoarseness, motor nerves.

Natural Kyanite wand

Excellent for attunement and meditation, and a powerful transmitter and amplifier of high-frequency energies, Kyanite never needs cleaning. Tuning into causal connections, this stone detaches from the idea of blind fate or implacable karma, showing how you created your present experience by past behavior. Facilitating the ascension process, it draws the light body into the physical realm and connects the higher mind to multidimensional frequencies. Kyanite points to your true identity and a fulfilling vocation. This crystal connects to guides, instills compassion, and facilitates spiritual maturation. Assisting dream recall and promoting healing dreams, it is helpful for those making the transition through death. Kyanite clears meridians, restores Qi to the physical body and its organs, and stabilizes the biomagnetic field. Kyanite encourages speaking one's truth; cutting through fears, blockages, and ignorance; and opens to spiritual and psychological truth. Slicing through confusion and dispelling blockages, illusion, and anger, Kyanite releases frustration and stress.

Crystalline Kyanite

Crystal system	Triclinic
Chemistry	Al_2SiO_5 Aluminum silicate
Hardness	5.5–7
Source	USA, Brazil, Switzerland, Austria, Italy, India
Chakra	Higher
Number	2
Zodiac sign	Aries, Taurus, Libra
Beneficial for	Ovarian or ovulation pain, metaphysical abilities.

In addition to carrying the generic properties of Kyanite (above), Crystalline Kyanite is excellent for making connections of all kinds and is a useful stone to assist in smoothing the way for lasting relationships. It has a very light and fast vibration that links you to your life path and true vocation.

Note: Crystalline Kyanite is a high-vibration stone.

Tumbled Crystalline Kyanite

Larimar (Pectolite)

Crystal system	Triclinic
Chemistry	$NaCa_2Si_3O_8 (OH)$
Hardness	5
Source	Dominican Republic, Bahamas
Chakra	Throat, heart, third eye, solar plexus, crown
Number	6, 55
Zodiac sign	Leo
Beneficial for	Energy blockages in the chest, head and neck pain, free flow of energy, coldness, serenity, martyrdom, guilt, fear, self-healing, bipolar disorders, cartilage, throat conditions, constricted joints, blocked arteries.

Tumbled Larimar

Inspiring Larimar is deeply nurturing, radiating love as it restores your strength especially after extended spiritual work, harmonizing body and soul to new vibrations. Effortlessly inducing a deeply meditative state, it guides the soul on its true pathway. Larimar releases self-sabotaging behavior, self-imposed bonds, and inappropriate burdens, and removes attached entities. Awakening inner wisdom and the ability to manifest, when moving through periods of stress and change, it enables challenges to be met with equanimity. Larimar draws a soulmate to you, healing relationship karma or heart trauma. An antidote to emotional extremes, it reconnects joyful childlike energy. Stimulating creativity and encouraging "going with the flow," Larimar brings calmness and equilibrium. This stone connects to the energy of the earth goddess, helping women reattune to innate femininity and restoring connection with nature. Dissipating geopathic stress and blockages, it is excellent for earth evolution and healing. As a reflexology tool, Larimar pinpoints the site of disease and clears meridians.

Note: Larimar is a high-vibration stone.

Lazulite

Crystal system	Monoclinic
Chemistry	$(MgFe)Al_2 (PO_4) 2 (OH) 2$ Hydroxy magnesium aluminum phosphate
Hardness	5–6
Source	Brazil, Austria, Switzerland, USA, Canada
Number	7
Zodiac sign	Gemini, Sagittarius
Beneficial for	Sun-sensitivity, cellular memory healing, immune system, fractures, thyroid, pituitary, lymphatic system, liver.

Derived from the Persian *lazhward*, meaning "blue," Lazulite is often called the Stone of Heaven and, as with many blue stones, draws in pure cosmic energy. Opening the intuition and bringing about profound states of meditative bliss, this stone creates a serene inner being, firmly anchored in the divine, and promotes balance and cosmic alignment. It boosts confidence and self-esteem and offers intuitive solutions to underlying problems, assisting in finding the reasons behind addiction, particularly if these lie in previous lives, and in detaching from the desire for more.

Raw Lazulite

Scapolite

Crystal system	Tetragonal
Chemistry	$(NaCa)_4 (SiAl)_{12}O_{24} (Cl,X_{03}SO_4)$
Hardness	5–5.5
Source	Madagascar, USA, Norway, Italy
Chakra	Third eye
Number	1
Zodiac sign	Taurus
Beneficial for	Dyslexia, meditation, postoperative recovery, calcium assimilation, varicose veins, eyes, cataracts, glaucoma, bone disorders, shoulders, dyslexia, incontinence.

Polished Scapolite slice

Stimulating the ability to be independent and set achievable goals, cool and calm Blue Scapolite provides the clarity to see what is needed in any situation. An excellent stone if you wish to make conscious change or to remove blockages from the left-hand side of the brain, it increases analytic ability and facilitates transformation. This stone is particularly helpful in convalescence and postoperative healing. Clearing the effects of old emotional trauma, and eliminating it from the subtle body, Scapolite reprograms the emotional blueprint. It facilitates release of energy blockages or build-up from the physical body, especially in legs and veins. Scapolite overcomes self-sabotage and scapegoating.

Girasol (Blue Opal)

Crystal system	Amorphous
Chemistry	$SiO_2 nH_2O$ Hydrated silica with impurities
Hardness	5.5–6.5
Source	Australia, Brazil, USA, Tanzania, Iceland, Mexico, Peru, UK, Canada, Honduras, Slovakia
Chakra	Third eye
Number	3, 9
Zodiac sign	Taurus
Beneficial for	Panic, phobias, confidence, creativity, assimilation of iron, vision, hair loss, metabolism, fatigue, lymph nodes, strengthening the will to live, intuition, female hormones, menopause, Parkinson's, infections, self-worth, fever, memory, purifying blood and kidneys, regulating insulin.

The blue tinge to Girasol comes from aluminum. In addition to carrying the generic properties of Opal (page 254), this visioning stone reveals solutions to present difficulties, especially where these arise from previously unvoiced causes. Revealing hidden feelings and psychic impressions inadvertently received, it assists in recognizing the deeper causes of discontent and strengthens psychic boundaries. This stone identifies connections between souls, and shows how the potential of these can be maximized. An emotional pacifier, it facilitates satisfying emotional needs and realigns your spiritual purpose. Helpful when past-life experiences or injuries are affecting the present life, Girasol reprograms cellular memory and the etheric blueprint, allowing the physical body to release a condition. An excellent stone for stimulating creativity, Girasol creates a quiet space in which to work and meditate.

Blue Aragonite

Crystal system	Orthorhombic
Chemistry	CaCo$_3$ Calcium carbonate with impurities
Hardness	3.5–4
Source	USA (Arizona and New Mexico), Namibia, UK, Spain, Morocco
Chakra	Third eye, throat, heart
Number	9
Zodiac sign	Capricorn
Beneficial for	Patience, emotional stress, anger, reliability, acceptance, flexibility, tolerance, pain (especially lower back), grounding, wound-healing, Reynaud's disease, chills, bones, calcium absorption, disc elasticity, night twitches, muscle spasm, immune system, regulates processes.

Raw Blue Aragonite

A powerful energy conduit that heightens and grounds spiritual communication, beautiful Blue Aragonite is colored by copper, the Venus metal, and can be programmed to attract your spiritual twinflame. In addition to carrying the generic properties of Aragonite (page 190), this stone uplifts your emotions and assists you in finding the source of any problems you may be encountering, instilling optimism and turning them into opportunities to grow. This stone purifies and aligns all the subtle bodes with the physical, and balances yin–yang energies, leading to optimum well-being.

Note: Blue Aragonite may be dyed.

Blue Chalcedony

Crystal system	Trigonal
Chemistry	SiO$_2$ Silicon dioxide
Hardness	7
Source	USA, Austria, Czech Republic, Slovakia, Iceland, England, Mexico, New Zealand, Turkey, Russia, Brazil, Morocco
Zodiac sign	Cancer, Capricorn
Planet	Moon
Beneficial for	Lactation, depression, nightmares, regeneration of mucous membrane, disease caused by pressure, glaucoma, immune system, lymph and edema, anti-inflammatory, high temperature, blood pressure, lungs, the effects of smoking, diabetes, generosity, hostility, lawsuits, nightmares, fear of the dark, hysteria, negative thoughts, turbulent emotions, maternal instinct, mineral assimilation, mineral build-up in veins, dementia, senility, holistic healing, eyes, bones.

Polished Blue Chalcedony

Traditionally used in weather magic, Blue Chalcedony is excellent for clearing illnesses associated with weather and pressure changes. Warding off psychic attack, including spells and incantations, it is protective during times of political unrest. In addition to carrying the generic properties of Chalcedony (page 247), creative Blue Chalcedony facilitates acceptance of new situations and improves self-perception. Opening the mind, it stimulates the ability to learn new languages and improves memory and assimilation of new ideas. Imparting mental flexibility and verbal dexterity and enhancing listening skills, Blue Chalcedony imparts lightheartedness and the ability to look forward optimistically.

Raw Blue Chalcedony

Avalonite (Drusy Blue Chalcedony)

Crystal system	Trigonal
Chemistry	SiO₂ Silicon dioxide
Hardness	7
Source	USA, Austria, Czech Republic, Slovakia, Iceland, England, Mexico, New Zealand, Turkey, Russia, Brazil, Morocco
Chakra	Links sacral and heart, soma, past life
Number	9
Zodiac sign	Cancer, Sagittarius, Capricorn
Planet	Moon
Beneficial for	Sensitivity to weather or pressure changes, love, wisdom, joy, lactation, depression, nightmares, regeneration of mucous membrane, immune system, lymph, edema.

Avalonite is at the center of this geode.

In addition to carrying the generic properties of Chalcedony (page 247) and Blue Chalcedony (page 155), Avalonite accesses the mythical realms where fairy tales and legends live, and this stone acts as facilitator for creatively reworking the myths. Contacting fairies, elves, and devas, it links into ancient magic. Metaphysical awareness is opened by the contours of Avalonite, enhancing visualization. To contact your inner wise woman or explore priestess incarnations, gaze into Drusy Blue Chalcedony. This stone enhances practical wisdom and presence of mind, especially when faced with new situations. Perfect for those who fear to love or dread failure, it opens the heart and discovers your true, perfect Self, and assists you in recognizing that you are never alone. Use Avalonite to harmonize emotional, mental, and spiritual wisdom at the center of your being.

Note: Avalonite is a high-vibration stone.

Blue Howlite

Crystal system	Monoclinic
Chemistry	Amended stone
Hardness	3.5
Source	USA
Chakra	Third eye
Number	2
Zodiac sign	Gemini
Beneficial for	Turbulent emotions, rage, patience, selfishness, positive character traits, memory, insomnia, calcium levels, teeth, bone, soft tissue.

Tumbled Blue Howlite

In addition to carrying the generic properties of Howlite (page 115), Blue Howlite, an artificially colored stone, encourages dream recall and accessing the insights that dreams offer.

Blue Lace Agate

Crystal system	Trigonal
Chemistry	SiO_2 Silicon dioxide with inclusions
Hardness	6
Source	USA, India, Morocco, Czech Republic, Brazil, Africa
Chakra	Throat, third eye, heart and crown
Zodiac sign	Gemini, Pisces
Planet	Mercury
Beneficial for	Nurturing, shoulder and neck problems caused by blocked self-expression, thyroid deficiencies, throat and lymph infections, anger-based infection, inflammation, fever, blockages of nervous system, arthritic and bone deformity, skeletal system, fractures, capillaries, pancreas, emotional trauma, self-confidence, concentration, perception, analytical abilities, aura stabilization, negative-energy transformation, emotional disease, digestive process, gastritis, eyes, stomach, uterus, pancreas, blood vessels, skin disorders. As an elixir: brain fluid imbalances and hydrocephalus.

Tumbled Blue Lace Agate

An excellent stone for starting over, the gentle energy of Blue Lace Agate instills peace of mind. In addition to carrying the generic properties of Agate (page 190), this stone opens the way to higher energies and facilitates expression of spiritual and personal truth. Fear of being judged often leads to nonexpression of feelings, and Blue Lace Agate counteracts fear of rejection. Blocked self-expression settles in the throat chakra and may induce a feeling of suffocation. Blue Lace Agate gently dissolves the old pattern and counteracts mental stress. It helps men accept their sensitive, feeling nature. The peaceful energies exuded from this stone neutralize feelings of anger. Focusing and directing sound to the appropriate place, Blue Lace Agate enhances sound healing.

Raw Blue Lace Agate

Blue Agate

Crystal system	Trigonal
Chemistry	SiO_2 Silicon dioxide with inclusions (may be dyed)
Hardness	6
Source	USA, India, Morocco, Czech Republic, Brazil, Africa
Chakra	Third eye
Zodiac sign	Gemini
Planet	Mercury
Beneficial for	Emotional trauma, self-confidence, concentration, perception, analytical abilities, aura stabilization, negative-energy transformation, emotional disease, digestive process, gastritis, eyes, stomach, uterus, lymphatic system, pancreas, blood vessels, skin disorders.

Tumbled Blue Agate

In addition to carrying the generic properties of Agate (page 190), Blue Agate is helpful in a family that quarrels frequently, as it invokes harmony and peacefulness in each member.

Covellite

Crystal system	Hexagonal
Chemistry	CuS Cupric sulfide
Hardness	1–1.5
Source	Italy, USA, Germany, Sardinia, Wales
Chakra	Third eye, sacral, solar plexus
Number	4, 7
Zodiac sign	Sagittarius
Beneficial for	Communication, creativity, rebirthing, sexuality, detoxification, radiation-induced disease, despondency, anxiety, birth, rebirth, digestion, cancer, ears, eyes, nose, mouth, sinuses, throat.

Tumbled Covellite

Named after its discoverer, Italian mineralogist N. Covelli, this stone facilitates energy flow through cells, detoxifying and removing stagnant energy. Connecting to the higher self, Covellite transforms dreams into realities and stimulates metaphysical abilities. This reflective stone opens a doorway to the past and to the wisdom you acquired then, releasing anything holding you back, particularly ingrained beliefs from other lives. Covellite harmonizes body, mind, and soul and facilitates loving yourself unconditionally while eliminating vanity and arrogance. This is a helpful stone if you feel vulnerable and too easily stimulated by others. Covellite overcomes discontent, instilling satisfaction with your life. Mentally, Covellite facilitates rational analytic thought and the decision-making process. It protects the body against radiation.

Blue Jade

Crystal system	Monoclinic
Chemistry	$Na(AlFe)Si_2O_6$
Hardness	6
Source	USA, China, Italy, Myanmar, Russia, Middle East
Chakra	Third eye
Zodiac sign	Taurus
Planet	Venus
Beneficial for	Longevity, self-sufficiency, detoxification, filtration, elimination, kidneys, suprarenal glands, cellular and skeletal systems, stitches, fertility, childbirth, hips, spleen, water–salt–acid–alkaline ratio.

Tumbled Blue Jade

In addition to carrying the generic properties of Jade (page 120), Blue Jade symbolizes peace and reflection and brings inner serenity and patience. The stone for slow but steady progress, it assists people who feel overwhelmed by situations beyond their control.

Lapis Lazuli

Crystal system	Cubic
Chemistry	$(Na,Ca)_8 (Al,Si)_{12}O_{24}S_2$ FeS $CaCO_3Al_2O_3$ Sodium calcium aluminosilicate
Hardness	5–6
Source	Russia, Afghanistan, Chile, Italy, USA, Middle East, Chile
Chakra	Throat, third eye, crown
Number	3
Zodiac sign	Sagittarius
Planet	Venus
Beneficial for	Objectivity, clarity, stress, self-awareness, self-expression, anxiety, female hormones, menopause, PMS, immune system, insomnia, pain, migraine, depression, respiratory and nervous systems, throat, larynx, thyroid, organs, bone marrow, thymus, hearing loss, blood, vertigo, blood pressure.

Polished Lapis Lazuli

The name Lapis Lazuli comes from the Persian *lazuward*, "blue." Prized for thousands of years, it was a favored stone in ancient Egypt, where it was believed to lead the soul into immortality and open the heart to love. The royal stone, it was said to contain the soul of the gods. A metaphysical stone *par excellence*, Lapis Lazuli is a key to spiritual attainment. Enhancing dreamwork and metaphysical abilities, it facilitates spiritual journeying and stimulates personal and spiritual power. Possessing enormous serenity, Lapis Lazuli is protective. Alerting to psychic attack, it returns the energy to its source. This stone highlights the power of the spoken word, and can reverse curses or disease caused by not speaking out. Harmonizing body, emotions, mind, and spirit, it brings deep inner self-knowledge and multidimensional cellular healing. A powerful thought amplifier, Lapis Lazuli stimulates higher mental faculties and encourages creativity. This stone teaches the value of active listening and helps you confront truth, wherever you find it, and accept its teaching. Facilitating expressing your own opinions and harmonizing conflict, Lapis Lazuli aids in taking charge of life. If repressed anger is causing difficulties in the throat, it releases these. This stone brings honesty, compassion, and uprightness to the personality. A bonding stone in love and friendship, it dissolves martyrdom, cruelty, suffering, self-mortification, and emotional bondage.

Note: Lapis Lazuli is a high-vibration stone.

Raw Lapis Lazuli

Faceted Sapphire

Sapphire

Crystal system	Hexagonal
Chemistry	Al_2O_3 Aluminum oxide
Hardness	9
Source	Myanmar, Czech Republic, Brazil, Kenya, India, Australia, Sri Lanka, Canada, Thailand, Madagascar
Chakra	Throat (see colors)
Number	2 (varies according to color)
Zodiac sign	Virgo, Libra, Sagittarius (varies according to color)
Planet	Moon, Saturn
Beneficial for	Serenity, peace of mind, concentration, multidimensional cellular healing, overactive body systems, glands, eyes, stress, blood disorders, excessive bleeding, veins, elasticity.

Sapphire is named from the Sanskrit *sanipriya*, meaning "dear to the planet Saturn," and is an important Vedic healing gem. In the West it was used to frighten away demons and evil. Traditionally worn on the right side of the body, it was said to protect its owner from imprisonment and to assist with legal matters. Known as the wisdom stone, Sapphire focuses and calms the mind, releasing unwanted thoughts and mental tension. This stone alleviates depression and spiritual confusion, attracting prosperity and gifts of all kinds. Placed on the throat, it releases frustration and aids self-expression.

Indigo Sapphire

Crystal system	Hexagonal
Chemistry	Al_2O_3 Aluminum oxide
Hardness	9
Source	Myanmar, Czech Republic, Brazil, Kenya, India, Australia, Sri Lanka, Canada, Thailand, Madagascar
Chakra	Third eye, cleanses all
Zodiac sign	Sagittarius
Planet	Moon, Saturn
Beneficial for	Dyslexia, the brain, serenity, peace of mind, concentration, multidimensional cellular healing, overactive body systems, glands, eyes, stress.

In addition to carrying the generic properties of Sapphire (above), Indigo Sapphire accesses truth and promotes intuition, helping you take responsibility for your thoughts and feelings.

Faceted Sapphire

Blue Sapphire

Crystal system	Hexagonal
Chemistry	Al_2O_3 Aluminum oxide
Hardness	9
Source	Myanmar, Czech Republic, Brazil, Kenya, India, Australia, Sri Lanka, Canada, Thailand, Madagascar
Chakra	All, especially throat; earth
Zodiac sign	Gemini
Planet	Moon, Saturn
Beneficial for	Thyroid, serenity, peace of mind, concentration, multidimensional cellular healing, overactive body systems, glands, eyes, stress, blood disorders, excessive bleeding, veins, elasticity.

Raw Blue Sapphire

Shaped Sapphires

In addition to carrying the generic properties of Sapphire (left), Blue Sapphire is a stone for the seeker after spiritual truth and is traditionally associated with love and purity. This tranquil stone assists in staying on the spiritual path and is used in shamanic ceremonies to transmute negative energies. Extremely effective for earth and chakra healing, it stimulates the thyroid, and facilitates self-expression and speaking one's own truth.

Royal Blue Sapphire

Crystal system	Hexagonal
Chemistry	Al_2O_3 Aluminum oxide
Hardness	9
Source	Myanmar, Czech Republic, Brazil, Kenya, India, Australia, Sri Lanka, Canada, Thailand, Madagascar
Chakra	All, especially third eye and soma
Zodiac sign	Libra
Planet	Moon, Saturn
Beneficial for	Brain disorders, dyslexia, serenity, peace of mind, concentration, multidimensional cellular healing, overactive body systems, glands, eyes, stress.

In addition to carrying the generic properties of Sapphire (left), Royal Sapphire eliminates negative energies from chakras, and stimulates the third eye to access information for growth. This stone teaches self-responsibility for one's thoughts and feelings.

Raw Royal Blue Sapphire

Sodalite

Polished Sodalite

Crystal system	Cubic
Chemistry	$Na_4Al_3 (SiO_4)_3Cl$ Sodium aluminum silicate chloride
Hardness	5.5–6
Source	USA, Canada, France, Brazil, Greenland, Russia, Myanmar, Romania, Italy
Chakra	Throat
Number	4
Zodiac sign	Sagittarius
Planet	Venus
Beneficial for	Sick-building syndrome, electromagnetic stress, self-esteem, panic attack, phobias, guilt, self-acceptance, self-trust, mental confusion, cellular memory healing, rational thought, objectivity, intuitive perception, balancing male–female polarities, absorption of fluid, glandular system, nerve endings, central nervous system, metabolism, calcium deficiencies, hoarseness, digestive disorders, fevers, lymphatic system, organs, immune system, radiation damage, insomnia, throat, vocal cords, larynx, lowers blood pressure.

Uniting logic with intuition, Sodalite opens spiritual perception, bringing the higher mind down to the physical. This stone stimulates the pineal and pituitary glands, harmonizes with the third eye, and deepens meditation to understand the circumstances in which you find yourself. Instilling a drive for truth and an urge toward idealism, Sodalite encourages being true to yourself and standing up for your beliefs. Eliminating confusion and intellectual bondage, it releases mental conditioning and rigid beliefs, creating space to put new insights into practice. Bringing about emotional balance, Sodalite transforms a defensive or oversensitive personality, releasing core fears and control mechanisms and integrating shadow qualities. Useful for groups, it brings harmony and solidarity of purpose, stimulating trust and companionship and encouraging interdependence. Sodalite clears electromagnetic pollution and can be placed on computers.

Raw Sodalite

Blue Spinel

Crystal system	Cubic
Chemistry	$MgAl_2O_4$ Magnesium aluminum oxide
Hardness	7.5–8
Source	Sri Lanka, Myanmar, Canada, USA, Brazil, Pakistan, Sweden (may be synthetic)
Chakra	Throat
Zodiac sign	Gemini
Planet	Pluto
Beneficial for	Muscular and nerve conditions, blood vessels.

In addition to carrying the generic properties of Spinel (page 260), Blue Spinel stimulates communication and channeling. It calms sexual desire.

Blue Spinel on matrix

Dark-blue Spinel

Crystal system	Cubic
Chemistry	$MgAl_2O_4$ Magnesium aluminum oxide
Hardness	7.5–8
Source	Sri Lanka, Myanmar, Canada, USA, Brazil, Pakistan, Sweden (may be synthetic)
Chakra	Third eye
Number	5
Zodiac sign	Sagittarius
Planet	Pluto
Beneficial for	Muscular and nerve conditions, blood vessels.

Natural Dark-blue Spinel

In addition to carrying the generic properties of Spinel (page 260), Dark-blue Spinel enhances metaphysical powers and induces astral journeying.

Blue Topaz

Crystal system	Orthorhombic
Chemistry	$Al_2 (SiO_4)(F, OH)_2$ Aluminum hydroxyl fluoro with impurities
Hardness	8
Source	USA, Russia, Mexico, India, Australia, South Africa, Sri Lanka, Pakistan, Myanmar, Germany
Chakra	Throat, third eye
Zodiac sign	Sagittarius
Planet	Sun, Jupiter
Beneficial for	Throat, astuteness, problem-solving, honesty, forgiveness, self-realization, emotional support, manifesting health, digestion, anorexia, sense of taste, nerves, metabolism, skin, vision.

In addition to carrying the generic properties of Topaz (page 87), Blue Topaz connects to the angels of truth and wisdom, strengthens the third eye and throat chakras, and assists verbalization of thoughts and feelings. An excellent stone for meditation and attuning to the higher self, it assists in living according to your own aspirations, identifying the scripts you have been living by, and helps you recognize where you have strayed from your own truth. Where this is the case, Blue Topaz gently assists you in forgiving and letting go.

Polished Blue Topaz

Blue Selenite

Crystal system	Monoclinic
Chemistry	$CaSO_{4\text{-}2}$ (H_2O) Hydrated calcium sulfate
Hardness	2
Source	England, USA, Mexico, Russia, Austria, Greece, Poland, Germany, France, Sicily
Chakra	Third eye, higher crown
Zodiac sign	Taurus
Planet	Moon
Beneficial for	Insight, aligning the spinal column, flexibility, epilepsy, mercury poisoning from dental amalgam, free radicals, breastfeeding. Its finest healing occurs at the energetic levels.

Blue Selenite (see also page 257) quiets the intellect, facilitates shutting off mind chatter during meditation, and quickly reveals the core of a problem.

Note: Blue Selenite is a high-vibration stone.

Natural Blue Selenite

Blue Jasper

Crystal system	Trigonal
Chemistry	SiO_2 Silicon dioxide with impurities
Hardness	7
Source	Worldwide
Chakra	Throat, third eye, sacral
Beneficial for	Degenerative diseases, mineral deficiency, electromagnetic and environmental pollution, radiation, stress, prolonged illness or hospitalization, circulation, digestive and sexual organs, balancing mineral content of the body.

Blue Jasper (see also page 45) connects you to the spiritual world. Positioning this stone on the sacral and heart chakras facilitates astral journeying. Balancing yin–yang energy, it stabilizes the aura and sustains energy during a fast.

Tumbled Blue Jasper

Blue Tiger's Eye

Crystal system	Trigonal
Chemistry	$NaFe+_3$ (SiO_3) $_2$ Silicon dioxide with impurities
Hardness	4–7
Source	USA, Mexico, India, Australia, South Africa
Chakra	Third eye
Zodiac sign	Leo, Capricorn
Planet	Sun
Beneficial for	Metabolic healing, brain hemisphere integration, perception, internal conflicts, pride, willfulness, emotional balance, yin–yang, fatigue, hemophilia, hepatitis, mononucleosis, depression, eyes, night vision, throat, reproductive organs, constrictions, broken bones.

Tumbled Blue Tiger's Eye

Calming and stress-releasing, Blue Tiger's Eye (page 206) assists the overanxious, the quick-tempered, and those suffering from phobias. This stone slows the metabolism, cools an overactive sex drive, and dissolves sexual frustrations.

Blue Obsidian

Crystal system	Amorphous
Chemistry	SiO_2 Silicon dioxide with impurities
Hardness	5–5.5
Source	Mexico, volcanic regions (may be artificial)
Chakra	Third eye, throat
Zodiac sign	Aquarius
Planet	Saturn
Beneficial for	Pain, speech defects, eye disorders, Alzheimer's, schizophrenia, multiple personality disorder, compassion, strength, detoxification, blockages, enlarged prostate.

In addition to carrying the generic properties of Obsidian (page 214), Blue Obsidian assists in astral journeying, facilitates divination, enhances telepathy, and opens the aura to receive healing energy. This stone supports communication skills.

Electric-blue Obsidian

Crystal system	Amorphous
Chemistry	SiO_2 Silicon dioxide with impurities
Hardness	5–5.5
Source	Mexico, volcanic regions (may be artificial)
Chakra	Third eye, crown
Number	1
Zodiac sign	Aquarius
Planet	Saturn
Beneficial for	Radionic treatment, spinal misalignment, impacted vertebrae, circulatory disorders, growths, spasmodic conditions, detoxification, blockages. As an elixir, it heals eyes.

An intuitive stone, Electric-blue Obsidian opens the third eye, assisting divination, trance states, shamanic journeying, metaphysical communication, and past-life regression. In addition to carrying the generic properties of Obsidian (page 214), this stone accesses the roots of difficulties and balances energy fields. Making a patient more receptive, it is an effective pendulum for dowsing.

Additional blue and indigo stones

Apatite (page 133), Barite (page 244), Beryl (page 81), Boji Stones (page 191), Chrysocolla (page 137), Diamond (page 248), Fire Agate (page 63), Idocrase (page 116), Moss Agate (page 101), Onyx (page 219), Pyrolusite (page 224), Shattuckite (page 132), Smithsonite (page 138), Vivianite (page 116), Wavellite (page 123), Zeolite (page 261), Zoisite (page 56).

Purple, lavender, and violet crystals

Purple stones resonate with the crown and higher crown chakras, the planet Jupiter, and multidimensional realities, drawing spiritual energy into the physical plane, and encouraging service to others. Lavender and violet stones have a lighter and finer vibration that links to the highest states of awareness.

Amethyst

Crystal system	Trigonal
Chemistry	SiO_2 Silicon dioxide with iron
Hardness	7
Source	Worldwide
Chakra	Third eye, soma, crown and higher crown
Number	3
Zodiac sign	Aquarius, Pisces
Planet	Jupiter, Neptune
Beneficial for	Physical, emotional, and psychological pain; decision-making; recurrent nightmares; geopathic stress; protection against thieves; anger; rage; fear; anxiety; grief; neural transmission; dreams; alcoholism; hormone production; endocrine system; metabolism; cleansing and eliminating organs; immune system; blood; headache; bruises; injuries; swellings; burns; hearing disorders; lungs; respiratory tract; skin complaints; cellular disorders; digestive tract; regulating flora; removing parasites; reabsorption of water; insomnia; psychiatric conditions other than paranoia or schizophrenia.

Amethyst point

Amethyst derives from the Greek for "to be intoxicated" and was worn to prevent drunkenness. Promoting love of the divine, Amethyst encourages selflessness and spiritual wisdom. Opening multidimensional awareness, it enhances metaphysical abilities and is an excellent stone for meditation and scrying. Sleeping with Amethyst facilitates out-of-body experiences, helps dream recall, and assists visualization. It guards against psychic attack, transmuting it into love. A natural tranquilizer, Amethyst blocks geopathic stress and negative environmental energies. Harmonizing the physical, mental, and emotional bodies and linking them to the spiritual, it purifies the aura. Amethyst is helpful for people about to make the transition through death and supports coming to terms with loss.

This stone has a sobering effect on overindulgence and overcomes addictions. Beneficial to the mind, it calms or stimulates as appropriate, helping to feel more focused, assisting assimilation of new ideas, and connecting cause with effect. Amethyst enhances memory and improves motivation. This stone balances emotional highs and lows.

Amethyst cluster

Vera Cruz Amethyst

Crystal system	Trigonal
Chemistry	SiO_2 Silicon dioxide with impurities
Hardness	7
Source	Mexico
Chakra	Third eye, soma, crown, higher crown
Number	3
Zodiac sign	Pisces
Planet	Jupiter, Neptune
Beneficial for	Metaphysical gifts, brain function, multidimensional healing. Vera Cruz Amethyst works at a high energetic level beyond the physical.

In addition to carrying the generic properties of Amethyst (left), Vera Cruz Amethyst, an extremely high-vibration stone, is said to take you instantly into a state of beta brain waves, facilitating meditation and journeying.

Note: Vera Cruz Amethyst is a high-vibration stone.

Vera Cruz Amethyst points

Amethyst Phantom Quartz

Crystal system	Trigonal
Chemistry	SiO_2 Silicon dioxide with inclusions
Hardness	7
Source	Worldwide
Chakra	Past life, crown, third eye
Zodiac sign	Virgo, Capricorn, Aquarius, Pisces
Planet	Jupiter, Neptune
Beneficial for	Getting out of old patterns; hearing disorders; clairaudience; physical, emotional, and psychological pain; decision-making; recurrent nightmares; geopathic stress; anger; rage; fear; anxiety; grief; neural transmission; dreams; alcoholism; hormone production; endocrine system; metabolism; cleansing and eliminating organs; immune system; headache; bruises; injuries; swellings; burns; hearing disorders; lungs; respiratory tract; skin complaints; cellular disorders; regulating flora; removing parasites; reabsorption of water; insomnia; psychiatric conditions other than paranoia or schizophrenia.

Meditating with Amethyst Phantom Quartz accesses the prebirth state and the plan for the present lifetime, assisting evaluation of the progress you are making with the spiritual lessons for the current incarnation. In addition to carrying the generic properties of Amethyst (left) and Phantoms (page 239), this stone brings about multidimensional cellular healing.

Note: Amethyst Phantom Quartz is a high-vibration stone.

Amethyst Phantom in Brandenburg Quartz point

Amethyst Spirit Quartz

Crystal system	Trigonal
Chemistry	SiO_2 Silicon dioxide with impurities
Hardness	7
Source	South Africa
Chakra	Higher crown, soma
Number	3
Zodiac sign	Aquarius, Pisces
Planet	Jupiter, Neptune
Beneficial for	Ascension, rebirthing, self-forgiveness, patience, purifying and stimulating the auric bodies, insightful dreams, reframing the past, blending male and female, yin and yang.

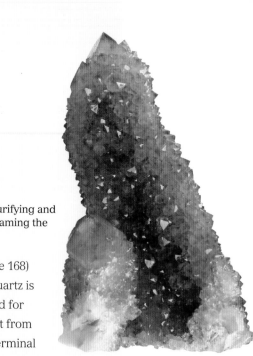

In addition to carrying the generic properties of Amethyst (page 168) and Spirit Quartz (page 237), compassionate Amethyst Spirit Quartz is particularly helpful for the transition to other states of being and for accessing higher consciousness. It can be programmed to assist from afar anyone who is facing death, and is particularly useful for terminal illness, as it offers immense support and comfort throughout the process. Used as a carrier for flower essences, it gently dissolves karma, attitudes, and emotions that would be detrimental if carried into the next world.

Note: Amethyst Spirit Quartz is a high-vibration stone.

Amethyst Spirit Quartz

Brandenberg Amethyst

Brandenberg Amethyst

Crystal system	Trigonal
Chemistry	SiO_2 Silicon dioxide with inclusions
Hardness	7
Source	Namibia, South Africa
Chakra	Third eye, crown, higher crown
Zodiac sign	Aquarius, Pisces
Planet	Jupiter, Neptune
Beneficial for	Convalescence, autoimmune disease, ME, severe depletion, multidimensional cellular memory healing, limbic brain. Brandenberg Amethyst works best beyond the physical level.

Geologically speaking, Brandenberg Amethyst is a young stone but has a very old soul and extremely high vibration. A useful aid to multidimensional spiritual work, "inner windows" or phantoms assist in looking within or traversing the spiritual planes. Emanating infinite compassion to all of creation, Brandenberg brings about deep soul healing and forgiveness. In addition to carrying the generic properties of Amethyst (page 168), this stone speeds recovery from illness or accident and is excellent for house clearing. A Smoky Brandenberg is the finest tool available for removing implants, attachments, spirit possession, or mental influence, and this is the stone *par excellence* for transformation or transition.

Note: Brandenberg Amethyst is a high-vibration stone.

Amethyst Elestial

Crystal system	Trigonal
Chemistry	SiO_2 Silicon dioxide with iron
Hardness	7
Source	Worldwide
Chakra	Higher crown and upward
Zodiac sign	Aquarius, Pisces
Planet	Jupiter, Neptune
Beneficial for	Physical, emotional, and psychological pain; decision-making; recurrent nightmares; geopathic stress; protection against thieves; anger; rage; fear; anxiety; grief; neural transmission; dreams; alcoholism; hormone production; endocrine system; metabolism; cleansing and eliminating organs; immune system; blood; headache; bruises; injuries; swellings; burns; hearing disorders; lungs; respiratory tract; skin complaints; cellular disorders; digestive tract; regulating flora; removing parasites; reabsorption of water; insomnia; psychiatric conditions other than paranoia or schizophrenia.

Shaped Amethyst Elestial point

An extremely powerful healing combination, Amethyst Elestial stimulates the pineal gland, activates the highest chakras, and opens a connection to interplanetary beings, guides, and helpers. In addition to carrying the generic properties of Amethyst (page 168) and Elestial (page 233), this stone disperses negative energy, providing reassurance and calm. The perfect Elestial to assist multidimensional cellular healing and brain integration, it ameliorates the effects of drugs or alcohol.

Note: Amethyst Elestial is a high-vibration stone.

Smoky Amethyst

Crystal system	Trigonal
Chemistry	SiO_2 Silicon dioxide with iron, aluminum, and lithium
Hardness	7
Source	Worldwide
Chakra	Third eye
Zodiac sign	Virgo, Scorpio, Sagittarius, Capricorn, Aquarius, Pisces
Planet	Jupiter, Neptune, Pluto
Beneficial for	Nightmares, stress, geopathic stress, X-ray exposure, psychological pain, protection, grief, neural transmission, alcoholism, hormone production, endocrine system, metabolism, cleansing organs, immune system.

Smoky Amethyst

In addition to carrying the generic properties of Amethyst (page 168), Smoky Quartz (page 186), and Brandenberg Amethyst (left), Smoky Amethyst grounds spiritual energy into the body and assists in contacting the highest spiritual energies. An efficient stone for entity clearing, especially at the third eye, it calls in beneficial influences. Protecting against psychic attack and alien invasion, it repels negative energy, calling in positive vibrations. Contacting guides and angelic helpers, this stone assists disconnection between those who have previously made a mystic marriage and are intertwined at the higher spiritual chakras. Smoky Amethyst amplifies and directs sound healing, creating a two-way flow of energy.

Note: Smoky Amethyst is a high-vibration stone.

Lavender Amethyst

Crystal system	Trigonal
Chemistry	SiO_2 Silicon dioxide with impurities
Hardness	7
Source	South Africa
Chakra	Higher crown, throat
Zodiac sign	Aquarius, Pisces
Planet	Jupiter, Neptune
Beneficial for	Physical, emotional, and psychological pain; decision-making; recurrent nightmares; geopathic stress; anger; rage; fear; anxiety; grief; metabolism; cleansing and eliminating organs; cellular disorders.

In addition to carrying the generic properties of Amethyst (page 168), Lavender Amethyst has a particularly high vibration, and double-terminated lavender crystals take you instantly into beta brain-wave states. These flowers bring light and love into the environment.

Note: Lavender Amethyst is a high-vibration stone.

Lavender Amethyst "flower"

Amethyst Herkimer

Crystal system	Trigonal
Chemistry	SiO_2 Silicon dioxide with impurities
Hardness	7
Source	Himalayas
Chakra	Third eye, higher heart, higher crown
Number	3
Zodiac sign	Pisces
Planet	Jupiter, Neptune
Beneficial for	Inner vision; telepathy; stress; detoxification; multidimensional cellular healing; protection against radioactivity and disease caused by contact; insomnia from geopathic stress or electromagnetic pollution; corrects DNA; cellular disorders; metabolic imbalances; recall of past-life injuries and disease that affect the present; physical, emotional, and psychological pain.

In addition to carrying the generic properties of Amethyst (page 168) and Herkimer Diamond (page 241), Herkimers fine-tune the third eye. A powerful metaphysical tool that facilitates soul retrieval from any lifetime, it induces deep-core soul healing, integrating all the disparate parts of the Self. Freeing the incarnated soul of earthly burdens and aligning with other soul dimensions to cohere the soul as a vehicle for spirit, Amethyst Herkimers can bring about profound spiritual evolution. As with all Herkimers, this stones creates a powerful soul shield when journeying or meditating, and restores and purifies energy after undertaking any form of spiritual or healing work. It is perfect for programming to attract your twinflame and soul companions.

Note: Amethyst Herkimer is a high-vibration stone.

Amethyst Herkimer on matrix

Ametrine

Crystal system	Trigonal
Chemistry	SiO_2 + (Al, Fe, Ca, Ma, Li, Na) Silicon dioxide with impurities
Hardness	7
Source	Worldwide
Chakra	Third eye, solar plexus
Number	4
Zodiac sign	Libra
Planet	Jupiter, Neptune, Pluto, Sun
Beneficial for	Vitality; chronic illness; insight into causes of disease; blockages in the physical, emotional, and mental aura including negative emotional programming; blood cleanser and energizer; physical body regeneration; metabolism; immune system; autonomic nervous system; physical maturation; stabilizing DNA/RNA; oxygenation; ME; burning sensations; gastric disturbances; ulcers; fatigue; lethargy; tension headaches; stress-related disease; sensitivity to environmental influences; optimism; letting go of the past; self-esteem; self-confidence; concentration; fears; phobias; individuality; motivation; creativity; self-expression; nightmares; Alzheimer's; itching; male hormones; detoxification; elimination; energizing; recharging; degenerative disease; spleen; pancreas; kidney and bladder infections; eye problems; blood circulation; thymus; thyroid; nerves; constipation; cellulite; alleviating fatigue; physical, emotional, and psychological pain; decision-making; recurrent nightmares; geopathic stress; protection against thieves; anger; rage; anxiety; grief; neural transmission; dreams; alcoholism; endocrine system; metabolism; cleansing and eliminating organs; bruises; injuries; swellings; burns; hearing disorders; lungs; respiratory tract; skin complaints; cellular disorders; digestive tract; regulating flora; removing parasites; reabsorption of water; insomnia; psychiatric conditions other than paranoia or schizophrenia. As an elixir: menstrual problems, menopause, hot flashes, balancing hormones.

Tumbled Ametrine

In addition to carrying the generic properties of Amethyst (page 168) and Citrine (page 72), Ametrine promotes healing and divination, connecting the physical realm with higher consciousness. Strongly protective, it assists during journeying, is extremely effective against psychic attack, and brings greater focus to meditation. Taking the mind beyond everyday reality to link into higher awareness, Ametrine facilitates transformation, and brings insight into underlying causes of emotional distress. This stone gets to the bottom of things, and holding Ametrine brings deep-seated issues to the surface. Its powerful cleansing properties disperse negativity from the aura and toxins from the body.

An extremely energetic stone, Ametrine stimulates creativity and supports taking control of your life. It imbues mental clarity, harmonizing perception and action and overcoming apparent contradictions. Promoting optimism and a well-being that is not disturbed by stressful external influences, Ametrine strengthens concentration. This stone aids thinking things through, encouraging exploration of all possibilities. Ametrine enhances acceptance of others and overcomes prejudice. It unites masculine and feminine energies.

Lavender Quartz

Crystal system	Trigonal
Chemistry	SiO$_2$ Silicon dioxide with impurities
Hardness	7
Source	South Africa
Chakra	Heart, throat, third eye, higher crown
Zodiac sign	Taurus, Libra
Planet	Venus
Beneficial for	Heartache, emotional-body healing, brain-wave and brain frequency disharmonies, inducing love, reducing tension, overcoming trauma, sexual imbalances, grief, addiction, overcoming rape.

Lavender Quartz refines the vibrations of Rose Quartz (see page 22 for generic properties) and takes you to an even higher spiritual connection, bringing about profound emotional healing and assisting in loving yourself. A stone of self-remembering and heightened self-awareness, it enables you to recall what you do in the different dimensions of consciousness. An excellent stimulator for all metaphysical gifts, Lavender Quartz takes meditation into multidimensional realities.

Note: Lavender Quartz is a high-vibration stone.

Natural Lavender Quar[tz]

Lithium Quartz

Crystal system	Hexagonal
Chemistry	SiO$_2$ Silicon dioxide with lithium inclusions or coating
Hardness	7
Source	Worldwide
Chakra	All
Beneficial for	Ancient anger and grief; cleansing chakras; purifying water, plants, and animals; a master healer; multidimensional cellular memory healer; efficient receptor for programming; cleans and enhances the organs; brings the body into balance; energy enhancement.

Lithium in Quartz point

In addition to carrying the generic properties of Quartz (page 230), spotted Lithium Quartz is an excellent balancing crystal that returns you to perfect equilibrium and is a natural antidepressant. Reaching back into past lives to dissolve the roots of emotional disease pervading the present life, its powerful healing energies gently lift to the surface the conditions underlying depression. An extremely efficient stone to program to facilitate a smooth transition, particularly where this is from a terminal illness, it can act as a carrier for a transitional flower essence. Giving comfort both to the dying and to those who are being bereaved, Lithium Quartz brings an awareness that death is part of a cycle. This stone is said to resonate with every note on the musical scale and to give off a spiral ray of golden energy.

Titanium Quartz

Crystal system	Hexagonal
Chemistry	SiO_2 Silicon dioxide with titanium inclusions or coating
Hardness	7
Source	Worldwide
Chakra	Harmonizes all, aligns the aura
Planet	Sun, Moon
Beneficial for	Mercury poisoning in nerves, muscles, blood, and intestinal tract; immune system; chronic conditions; impotence; infertility; exhaustion; energy depletion; respiratory tract; bronchitis; thyroid; parasites; cell regeneration; torn tissues; encourages upright posture.

Naturally or artificially "spotted" onto or into Quartz (see page 230 for generic properties), Titanium Quartz has the same powers as Rainbow Aura Quartz. (Titanium, also known as Rutile, is part of Rutilated Quartz; see page 202.)

Quartz spotted with Titanium

Charoite

Crystal system	Monoclinic
Chemistry	$(KNa)_5 (CaBaSr)_8 Si_{18}O_{46} (OHF) nH_2O$
Hardness	5
Source	Russia
Chakra	Synthesizes heart and crown, higher crown
Number	7
Zodiac sign	Virgo, Scorpio, Sagittarius
Planet	Chiron
Beneficial for	Autism, auric cleansing, unconditional love, drive, vigor, spontaneity, stress, worry, manic depression, emotional turmoil, transforming negative energy, exhaustion, integrating dualities, blood pressure, eyes, heart, liver, pancreas, liver damage caused by alcohol, cramps, aches, pain, insomnia, autonomous nervous system dysfunction affecting the heart.

Teaching you to accept the present moment as perfect, Charoite assists in walking your destiny, and links you to your karma, revealing the life plan your soul is working to. Grounding the spiritual Self into everyday reality, it urges service to humanity. This stone brings insightful visions of past lives and suggests ways to redress karma on a personal and collective level. Facilitating vibrational change and links to higher realities, it simultaneously provides deep physical, emotional, and cellular memory healing. This stone of transformation overcomes fear, integrates negative qualities, and takes back projections, assisting in coping with fundamental change. It masters compulsions and obsessions and ameliorates alienation or frustration, and is particularly helpful in cases of scapegoating or abasement. Assisting anyone who is driven by other people's thoughts rather than their own, it removes mental attachments. Charoite facilitates fast decisions, perceptive observations, and analysis.

Polished Charoite slice

Lavender-pink Smithsonite

Lavender-pink
Smithsonite

Crystal system	Trigonal
Chemistry	$ZnCO_3$ Zinc carbonate
Hardness	4–5
Source	USA, Australia, Greece, Italy, Mexico, Namibia, Germany, South Africa
Chakra	Heart, higher heart
Number	7
Zodiac sign	Virgo, Pisces
Beneficial for	Heart, addictions, rebirthing, birth, tact, harmony, diplomacy, alcoholism, stress, mental breakdown, immune system, sinus, digestive disorders, osteoporosis, elasticity to veins, muscles.

In addition to the generic properties of Smithsonite (page 138), Lavender-pink Smithsonite holds a vibration of unconditional love that facilitates feeling loved and supported by the universe, heals the heart, and overcomes experiences of abandonment and abuse, rebuilding trust and security. The stone is helpful in convalescence and soothes pain. Lavender-pink Smithsonite ameliorates drug and alcohol problems and the emotions that lie behind them. It is an excellent stone for gridding a sickroom.

Lavender-pink
Smithsonite on matrix

Lavender-violet Smithsonite

Crystal system	Trigonal
Chemistry	$ZnCO_3$ Zinc carbonate
Hardness	4–5
Source	USA, Australia, Greece, Italy, Mexico, Namibia, Germany, South Africa
Chakra	Past life, heart, crown
Number	7
Zodiac sign	Virgo, Pisces
Beneficial for	Neuralgia, inflammation, rebirthing, birth, leadership qualities, tact, harmony, diplomacy, alcoholism, stress, mental breakdown, immune system, sinus, digestive disorders, osteoporosis, elasticity to veins, muscles.

With a gentle vibration, Lavender-violet Smithsonite cleanses negative energy, facilitates joyful spiritual service and higher states of consciousness, and offers guidance and protection. In addition to carrying the generic properties of Smithsonite (page 138), this stone assists soul healing and return to past lives to regain soul energy that did not make the transition away from a past-life death, and is excellent for multidimensional cellular healing.

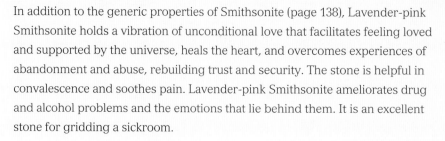

Lavender-violet
Smithsonite

Fluorite

Crystal system	Cubic
Chemistry	CaF_2 Calcium fluoride
Hardness	4
Source	USA, England, Mexico, Canada, Australia, Germany, Norway, China, Peru, Brazil
Chakra	Heart, cleanses all (varies according to color)
Number	9
Zodiac sign	Capricorn, Pisces
Planet	Mercury
Beneficial for	Balance, coordination, self-confidence, shyness, worry, centering, concentration, psychosomatic disease, absorption of nutrients, bronchitis, emphysema, pleurisy, pneumonia, antiviral, infections, teeth, cells, bones, DNA damage, skin and mucous membranes, respiratory tract, colds, flu, sinusitis, ulcers, wounds, adhesions, mobilizing joints, arthritis, rheumatism, spinal injuries, pain relief, shingles, nerve-related pain, blemishes, wrinkles, dental work, libido.

Tumbled Fluorite

Polished Fluorite

An effective crystal to overcome any form of disorganization, Fluorite draws off negative energies and stress, incorporating structure into daily life. It purifies and reorganizes anything within the physical or subtle bodies that is not in perfect order, and cleanses and stabilizes the aura. It brings stability to groups, linking them into a common purpose. Fluorite discerns when outside influences are at work and shuts off psychic manipulation and undue mental influence. Grounding and integrating spiritual energies, it promotes unbiased impartiality and heightens intuitive powers, making you aware of higher spiritual realities. It dissolves fixed patterns of behavior and brings suppressed feelings to the surface for resolution. An excellent learning aid, it increases concentration and promotes quick thinking and absorbtion of new information. This stone is extremely effective against computer and electromagnetic stress and, appropriately positioned, blocks geopathic stress.

Fluorite Wand

Crystal system	Cubic
Chemistry	CaF_2 Calcium fluoride
Hardness	4
Source	USA, England, Mexico, Canada, Australia, Germany, Norway, China, Peru, Brazil (artificially shaped)
Chakra	Heart, cleanses all (varies according to color)
Number	9
Zodiac sign	Capricorn, Pisces
Planet	Mercury
Beneficial for	Pain, inflammation, balance, coordination, psychosomatic disease, antiviral, infections, DNA damage, shingles, nerve-related pain.

Shaped Fluorite wand

Fluorite wands are artificially shaped and have a soothing energy. They carry the varying energy of Fluorite according to color. They can be stroked over the skin to relieve pain and inflammation from joints and muscles or used for reflexology or acupressure. A wand absorbs an enormous amount of negativity and, if not cleansed frequently, may crack under the strain. See also Wands (page 279).

Stichtite

Crystal system	Trigonal
Chemistry	$Mg_6Cr_2Co_3(OH)_{16-4}H_2$
Hardness	1.5–2
Source	USA, Tasmania, Canada, South Africa
Chakra	Earth, base, heart, raises kundalini through all
Number	5
Zodiac sign	Virgo
Beneficial for	ADHD (Attention Deficit Hyperactivity Disorder), kundalini rise, skin elasticity and stretch marks, hernia, teeth and gums.

Raw Stichtite

A useful stone to keep in your pocket if you live alone, Stichtite provides companionship and has a calming influence on the environment. This stone supports manifesting your true Self, living in accordance with your soul-contract for the present life. Assisting in keeping your mind and opinions open and your emotional awareness acute, it shows how emotions and ingrained attitudes affect your well-being. If a child, or you, needs guiding onto a different path, Stichtite is the perfect tool, and it is excellent for Indigo children who suffer from hyperactivity or similar spiritual diseases.

Purpurite

Crystal system	Orthorhombic
Chemistry	$(Mn,Fe)PO_4$ Manganese iron phosphate
Hardness	4–4.5
Source	Namibia, Western Australia, USA, France
Chakra	Crown
Number	9
Zodiac sign	Virgo
Beneficial for	Exhaustion, despair, bruises, bleeding, pustules, cardio-thoracic system and blood flow, blood purification, stabilizing the pulse.

Purpurite helps you speak in public with clarity and confidence, safe in the knowledge that no outside influence can interfere with the dissemination of your views. This stone facilitates a house sale when adverse environmental and neighborhood forces block the sale, especially where past-life conflict is being re-created. Purpurite can also break old habits or attitudes that keep you imprisoned or mired in old ways. Opening the way to spiritual evolution and enlightenment, it helps you reach a high spiritual vibration and progress without hindrance. With excellent energizing properties for the physical and mental bodies, Purpurite overcomes tiredness and despondency at any level. It increases alertness and receptivity to guidance and new ideas.

Raw Purpurite

Faceted Tanzanite

Tanzanite (Lavender-blue Zoisite)

Crystal system	Orthorhombic
Chemistry	$Ca_2Al_3Si_3O_{12}$ (OH) Hydrous calcium aluminum silica
Hardness	6–6.5
Source	Tanzania (may be artificially created)
Chakra	All, especially soma; links crown and higher crown to base
Number	2
Zodiac sign	Gemini, Libra, Sagittarius, Pisces
Beneficial for	Hearing, trust, workaholics, depression, anxiety, reducing inflammation, immune system, cell regeneration, spleen, pancreas. Tanzanite works best at a nonphysical level.

Polished Tanzanite

Discovered in 1967 and now apparently mined out, pleochroic Tanzanite may be artificially produced. It is said that ancient legends link the shamans of Tanzania, dolphins, and Lemuria with this stone. In addition to carrying the generic properties of Zoisite (page 56), this very high-vibration stone facilitates altered states of consciousness, metaphysical abilities, profoundly deep meditation, and interdimensional travel. Accessing Christ-consciousness and the Ascended Masters, it facilitates living with more awareness. Downloading information from the Akashic Record, this stone opens the subtle chakras so the next level of spiritual awareness can be accessed. Ascertaining your true vocation, Tanzanite assists in coming to terms with life as you are living it now, rather than what might be. Particularly helpful to overworked people, it evens out fluctuations of energy and assists in taking time for oneself. Added to Iolite and Danburite and applied during past-life healing, Tanzanite dissolves old patterns of karmic disease and creates the space for new patterns to be integrated. It is best worn on the right side of the body, but confirm by dowsing.

Raw Tanzanite

Note: Tanzanite is a high-vibration stone.

Tumbled Tanzanite

Purple Sapphire

Crystal system	Hexagonal
Chemistry	Al_2O_3 Aluminum oxide
Hardness	9
Source	Myanmar, Czech Republic, Brazil, Kenya, India, Australia, Sri Lanka, Canada, Thailand, Madagascar
Chakra	Crown, higher crown, soma
Number	9
Zodiac sign	Virgo
Planet	Moon, Saturn
Beneficial for	Bipolar disorder, serenity, peace of mind, concentration, multidimensional cellular healing, overactive body systems, glands, stress.

Raw Purple Sapphire

In addition to carrying the generic properties of Sapphire (page 160), Purple Sapphire, a stone of awakening, deepens meditation, stimulates kundalini rise, and opens spirituality. Activating the pineal gland with its link to metaphysical abilities, it encourages visionary qualities. Purple Sapphire calms the emotionally labile.

Tanzine Aura Quartz

Crystal system	Hexagonal
Chemistry	Complex combination
Hardness	Brittle
Source	Manufactured
Chakra	Higher crown, soma, opens and aligns all
Zodiac sign	Virgo, Pisces
Beneficial for	Stress, balance, metabolism, thyroid deficiency, immune system, ADHD (Attention Deficit Hyperactivity Disorder), immune system, convalescence, diabetes, vision, pancreas, multidimensional cellular memory healing, efficient receptor for programming, cleansing and enhancing the organs, bringing the body into balance.

Tanzine Aura Quartz

A mystical new Aura Quartz alchemicalized from indium, a rare metal that falls at the center of the periodic table, Tanzanite brings about multidimensional balance. In addition to carrying the generic properties of Aura Quartz (page 143), this stone opens and aligns the very highest of the subtle crown chakras, drawing cosmic energy into the physical body and to earth. With a powerful regulatory effect on the pituitary, hypothalamus, and pineal glands, Tanzine brings about profound spiritual interconnection and physical equilibrium. Placed on the soma chakra, it redraws the etheric blueprint. Indium, used as a homeopathic remedy for many years, assists in the assimilation of minerals, bringing about optimal metabolic and hormonal balance and resulting in physical and mental well-being, and is believed to be anticarcinogenic. This stone would appear to be excellent for overcoming the effects of thyroid, spleen, pancreas, and mineral deficiency.

Note: Tanzine Aura Quartz is a high-vibration stone.

Lilac Kunzite

Crystal system	Monoclinic
Chemistry	LiAl(SiO$_2$)$_2$ (contains lithium)
Hardness	6.5–7
Source	USA, Madagascar, Brazil, Myanmar, Afghanistan
Chakra	Crown, higher crown, third eye, soma
Number	7
Zodiac sign	Taurus, Leo, Scorpio
Planet	Venus, Pluto
Beneficial for	Intellect, intuition and inspiration, humility, service, tolerance, self-expression, creativity, stress-related anxiety, bipolar disorder, psychiatric disorders and depression, geopathic stress, introspection, immune system, witness for radionic practitioners, anesthetic, circulatory system, heart muscle, neuralgia, epilepsy, joint pain.

Natural Lilac Kunzite

As well as carrying the generic properties of Kunzite (page 30), Lilac Kunzite breaks through barriers of time into the infinite. Forming a celestial doorway, it aids transition for the dying, imparting the knowledge the soul needs and helping them move over into enlightenment. It is excellent for all multidimensional work.

Note: Lilac Kunzite is a high-vibration stone.

Lepidolite

Crystal system	Monoclinic
Chemistry	$AlSi_3O_{10}(OH,F)_2$ Hydrated potassium aluminum silicate
Hardness	5
Source	USA, Czech Republic, Brazil, Madagascar, Dominican Republic
Chakra	All
Number	8
Zodiac sign	Libra
Planet	Jupiter, Neptune
Beneficial for	Addictions, anorexia, emotional or mental dependency, bipolar disorders, nightmares, stress, obsessive thoughts, despondency, emotional lability, digestion, muscle relaxation, allergies, anger, depression, immune system, restructuring DNA, generation of negative ions, exhaustion, epilepsy, Alzheimer's, nerve pain, sciatica, neuralgia, joint problems, detoxification of skin and connective tissue, menopause, illnesses caused by sick-building syndrome, computer stress, repetitive strain injury, and tendonitis.

Tumbled Lepidolite

Lepidolite derives from the Greek *lepidos*, meaning scale. Dissipating negativity and inducing calm, it is excellent for clearing electromagnetic pollution and should be placed on computers or gridded around the house. A stone of transition, Lepidolite insists on being used for the highest good and brings about reconciliation. Activating and opening all chakras, it brings in cosmic awareness. Lepidolite assists in shamanic or spiritual journeying, and accesses the Akashic Record. Showing you thoughts and feelings from other lives that are creating a blockage in your life now, it can take you forward into the future. Containing lithium, it is helpful in stabilizing bipolar disorders. Lepidolite gently removes and restructures outworn behavioral patterns, encouraging independence and the achievement of goals without outside help. Placed over the site of disease, it gently vibrates. With its power of objectivity and concentration, it aids analytic processes and decision-making, focusing on what is important and filtering out distractions.

Raw Lepidolite

Lavender Jade

Crystal system	Monoclinic
Chemistry	$Na(AlFe)Si_2O_6$
Hardness	6
Source	USA, China, Italy, Myanmar, Russia, Middle East
Chakra	Third eye, crown
Zodiac sign	Libra
Planet	Venus
Beneficial for	Emotional healing, longevity, self-sufficiency, detoxification, filtration, elimination, kidneys, suprarenal glands, cellular and skeletal systems, stitches, water–salt–acid–alkaline ratio.

Polished Lavender Jade

In addition to carrying the generic properties of Jade (page 120), Lavender Jade alleviates emotional pain and trauma and bestows inner peace. It teaches subtlety and restraint in emotional matters and helps you set clear boundaries.

Purple-violet Tourmaline

Natural Purple-violet Tourmaline

Crystal system	Trigonal
Chemistry	Complex silicate
Hardness	7–7.5
Source	Sri Lanka, Brazil, Africa, USA, Australia, Afghanistan, Italy, Germany, Madagascar
Chakra	Past life, third eye, connects base and heart
Zodiac sign	Libra
Beneficial for	Multidimensional cellular healing, depression, obsessional thoughts, Alzheimer's, epilepsy, chronic fatigue, protection, detoxification, spinal adjustments, balancing male–female energy, paranoia, dyslexia, hand-eye coordination, assimilation and translation of coded information, energy flow, removal of blockages.

Stimulating healing of the heart, Purple Tourmaline induces loving consciousness and increases devotion and spiritual aspiration. In past-life healing, it takes you to the heart of the problem and then disperses it. In addition to carrying the generic properties of Tourmaline (page 210), this stone is extremely effective in removing, and can protect against, spirit attachments, alien implants, and entity possession. This stone stimulates creativity and the intuition. It activates the pineal gland, and strips away illusions.

Purple Jasper

Crystal system	Trigonal
Chemistry	SiO_2 Silicon dioxide with impurities
Hardness	7
Source	Worldwide
Chakra	Crown
Zodiac sign	Sagittarius
Beneficial for	Electromagnetic and environmental pollution, radiation, stress, prolonged illness or hospitalization, circulation.

In addition to carrying the generic properties of Jasper (page 45), Purple Jasper is a useful stone for eliminating contradictions of all kinds.

Purple Jasper

Royal Plume Jasper

Crystal system	Trigonal
Chemistry	SiO_2 Silicon dioxide
Hardness	7
Source	Worldwide
Chakra	Crown
Beneficial for	Electromagnetic and environmental pollution, radiation, stress.

Royal Plume Jasper aligns your spiritual energies to your soul purpose. In addition to carrying the generic properties of Jasper (page 45), this stone eliminates contradictions and aids in preserving one's dignity. It brings emotional and mental stability, and facilitates achieving status and power.

Sugilite (Luvulite)

Crystal system	Hexagonal
Chemistry	$KNa_2Li_3 (FeMnAl)_2S_{12}O_{30}$ Potassium sodium lithium
Hardness	6–6.5
Source	Japan, South Africa
Chakra	Heart, third eye, crown, aligns all
Number	2, 3, 7
Zodiac sign	Virgo, Sagittarius
Planet	Jupiter
Beneficial for	Self-forgiveness, learning difficulties, Asperger's autism, accelerating body's natural healing ability, spirituality, addiction, eating disorders, dyslexia, mental fatigue, despair, hostility, paranoia, schizophrenia, pain relief, headaches, epilepsy, motor disturbances, nerves, brain alignment. Light-colored Sugilite purifies lymph and blood.

Polished slice of Sugilite

Tumbled Sugilite

Excellent for autism and dyslexia, or anyone who feels they do not fit in, Sugilite has a purple ray vibration of unconditional love. It helps sensitive people and light workers adapt to the earth vibration without becoming despondent, bringing light into the darkest situations, and is helpful for learning difficulties or overcoming brain dysfunction. It helps with living in the present instead of the past, and transcends the limits of time. Sugilite heals the body via the mind, facilitating karmic healing through the mental blueprint. It helps you remember why you came into this life and teaches how to live from your truth. A useful companion in spiritual quests, it protects the soul from disappointments and shocks. It also resolves group difficulties and encourages forgiveness and loving communication. Imparting the ability to face up to unpleasant matters, it encourages positive thoughts and reorganizes brain patterns. It benefits cancer sufferers, as it gently releases emotional turmoil and can alleviate despair, channeling multidimensional healing energy.

Violet Spinel

Crystal system	Cubic
Chemistry	$MgAl_2O_4$ Magnesium aluminum oxide
Hardness	7.5–8
Source	Sri Lanka, Myanmar, Canada, USA, Brazil, Pakistan, Sweden (may be synthetic)
Chakra	Crown, higher crown, soma
Zodiac sign	Virgo, Pisces
Planet	Pluto
Beneficial for	Muscular and nerve conditions, blood vessels.

In addition to carrying the generic properties of Spinel (page 260), Violet Spinel stimulates spiritual development and facilitates astral journeying.

Additional violet stones

Apatite (page 133), Chiastolite (page 194), Dumortierite (page 150), Iolite (page 150), Lilac Danburite (page 26), Opal (page 254).

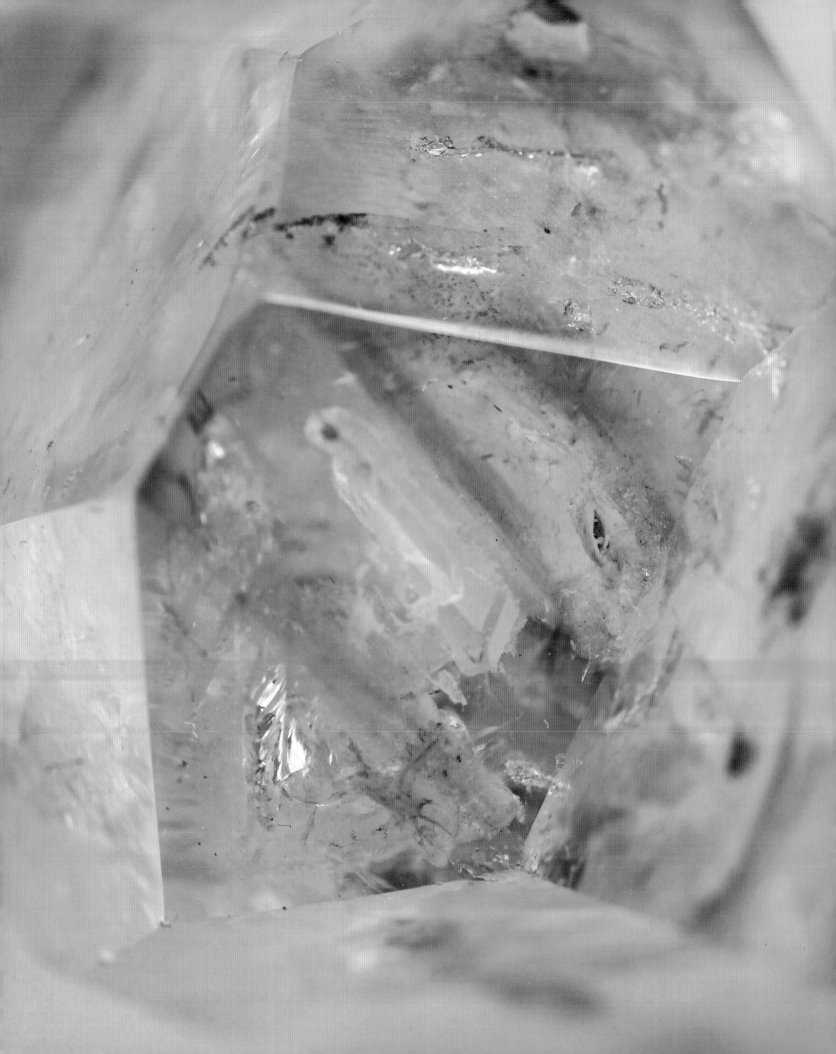

Brown crystals

Brown stones are connected with the earth chakra and with cleansing and purifying energies. Grounding and protecting, they absorb noxious substances and induce stability and centeredness. They are traditionally associated with the pragmatic planet Saturn and also resonate with transformative Pluto.

Smoky Quartz

Crystal system	Trigonal
Chemistry	SiO_2 Silicon dioxide with lithium and aluminum
Hardness	7
Source	Worldwide
Chakra	Earth, base
Number	2, 8
Zodiac sign	Scorpio, Sagittarius, Capricorn
Planet	Pluto
Beneficial for	Concentration, nightmares, geopathic stress, X-ray exposure, hips, chemotherapy, libido, pain relief, fear, depression, abdomen, legs, headaches, stress, reproductive system, muscle, nerve tissue, heart, cramp, the back, nerves, assimilation of minerals, fluid regulation.

Tumbled Smoky Quartz

Natural Smoky Quartz point

A psychopomp for conducting souls to the otherworld, Smoky Quartz is one of the most efficient grounding and cleansing stones. This protective stone has a strong link with the earth, promoting concern for the environment and suggesting ecological solutions. It blocks geopathic stress, absorbs electromagnetic smog, and assists elimination and detoxification at all levels, bringing in a positive vibration to fill the space. Smoky Quartz can be used to protect the earth chakra below the feet or gridded around an area of disturbed earth energy. It teaches how to leave behind anything that no longer serves you. A superb antidote to stress, alleviating suicidal tendencies and ambivalence about being in incarnation, Smoky Quartz helps tolerate difficult times with equanimity, fortifying resolve. It assists acceptance of the physical body and the sexual nature, enhancing virility and cleaning the base chakra so that passion can flow naturally. Facilitating pragmatic thought, it facilitates moving between alpha and beta states of mind. As Smoky Quartz is often naturally irradiated, it is excellent for treating radiation-related illness or supporting chemotherapy and radiotherapy. A layout of slow-release Smoky Quartz pointing out from the body can prevent a healing crisis from occurring.

Smoky Quartz Wand

Crystal system	Trigonal
Chemistry	SiO_2 Silicon dioxide
Hardness	7
Source	Worldwide (artificially shaped)
Chakra	Earth, base
Number	2, 8
Zodiac sign	Scorpio, Sagittarius, Capricorn
Planet	Pluto
Beneficial for	Stress, geopathic stress, X-ray exposure, chemotherapy, radiotherapy, pain relief, fear, depression.

An excellent tool for grounding negative energy and removing entities, a Smoky Quartz wand (see Wands, page 279, and Smoky Quartz, above) connects the energy of the base chakra to the earth chakra beneath your feet. Purifying this chakra, it neutralizes the effect of geopathic stress or earth energy disturbance. It can be used anywhere on the body where negative energy needs to be removed.

Smoky Quartz wand

Smoky Elestial

Crystal system	Trigonal
Chemistry	SiO_2 Silicon dioxide
Hardness	7
Source	Worldwide
Chakra	Earth, base, crown, bridges the flow of energy between all
Number	2, 8
Zodiac sign	Scorpio, Sagittarius, Capricorn
Planet	Pluto
Beneficial for	Concentration, nightmares, stress, geopathic stress, X-ray, energy cleansing, exposure, chemotherapy, radiotherapy, pain relief, fear, depression.

Shaped Smoky Elestial point

Carrying the generic properties of Smoky Quartz (left) and Elestial Quartz (page 233), Smoky Elestial releases karmic enmeshment and magic rituals that are no longer helpful. Particularly useful during past-life healing, it works equally well in present-life adjustments. An extremely efficient tool for mopping up negative energy and healing its effects wherever they may manifest, Smoky Elestial draws past-life trauma out of the present-life physical body and heals the etheric blueprint and the aura, with the beneficial effect traveling back to the source of the problem to reframe it. Working in a similar way, it cleanses and heals the ancestral line of trauma and emotional pain and is the perfect stone for multidimensional cellular memory healing. This intense stone can take you back into past lives to reclaim your power, to purify negativity, and to release you from anyone who has enslaved you in their power, no matter when that may be. It links you to beneficial guides and helpers in the spiritual worlds.

Smoky Herkimer

Crystal system	Trigonal
Chemistry	SiO_2 Silicon dioxide with impurities
Hardness	7
Source	Worldwide
Chakra	Earth, base
Number	2, 3, 8
Zodiac sign	Scorpio
Planet	Pluto
Beneficial for	Stress, geopathic stress, X-ray exposure, chemotherapy, radiotherapy, libido, pain relief, inner vision, detoxification, multidimensional cellular healing, protection against radioactivity and disease caused by contact, insomnia from geopathic stress or electromagnetic pollution, corrects DNA, cellular disorders, metabolic imbalances, recall of past-life injuries and disease that affect the present.

Carrying the generic properties of Smoky Quartz (left) and Herkimer Diamond (page 241), Smoky Herkimer is an excellent psychic clearing tool and an earth-healer. It protects against electromagnetic or geopathic pollution and draws its effects out of the subtle bodies.

Smoky Herkimer

Smoky Phantom (Black) Quartz

Crystal system	Trigonal
Chemistry	SiO_2 Silicon dioxide with inclusions
Hardness	7
Source	Worldwide
Chakra	Past life, earth
Zodiac sign	Scorpio, Sagittarius, Capricorn
Planet	Pluto
Beneficial for	Old patterns, hearing disorders, clairaudience, stress, geopathic stress, X-ray exposure, chemotherapy, radiotherapy, libido, pain relief, depression, reproductive system.

Carrying the generic properties of Phantoms (page 239) and Smoky Quartz (page 186), Smoky Phantom Quartz is a useful entity remover. This stone takes you back to your original soul group, linking into the purpose of the group incarnations. Helping you identify and attract members of your soul group in the present life so that you can fulfill your karmic or spiritual task, it removes any negative energies that have intervened in the group purpose, going back to its original purity of intention. The phantom can also take an individual back to a time before a problem or pattern originated to reconnect to a state of wholeness and harmony.

Smoky Phantom (Black) Quartz

Smoky Spirit Quartz

Crystal system	Trigonal
Chemistry	SiO_2 Silicon dioxide with impurities
Hardness	7
Source	South Africa
Chakra	Base, soma, third eye
Number	2, 4, 8
Zodiac sign	Scorpio
Planet	Pluto
Beneficial for	Multidimensional healing, ascension, rebirthing, self-forgiveness, pain relief, patience, purifying and stimulating the auric bodies, insightful dreams, reframing the past, blending male and female, yin and yang, healing discord, astral projection, detoxification, obsessive behavior, X-ray exposure, geopathic stress, chemotherapy, radiotherapy, libido.

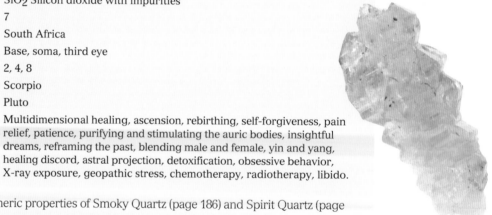

Carrying the generic properties of Smoky Quartz (page 186) and Spirit Quartz (page 237), this stone is protective, grounding, and cleansing, promoting integration and multidimensional cellular healing. A most effective psychopomp, it accompanies transitions and conveys the soul safely to the next world, cleansing the subtle bodies as it does so, removing layers of karmic and emotional debris to reprogram cellular memory and ensuring a good rebirth. Beneficial for any work that entails visiting the underworld or exploring the subconscious mind, it cleanses and releases deeply held emotions and states of disease or traumatic memories, including those that have passed down the ancestral line. Such work may need the guidance of a practitioner, as it may create catharsis. Smoky Spirit Quartz can be used to stabilize and purify areas of environmental imbalance or pollution, no matter what the cause.

Note: Smoky Spirit Quartz is a high-vibration stone.

Smoky Spirit Quartz

Ammolite

Crystal system	Fossil
Chemistry	CaCO$_3$ with impurities (complex)
Hardness	3.5–4 (7–8.5 if Quartz- or Spinel-capped)
Source	Canada, Morocco (synthetic Ammolite is available)
Chakra	Third eye, soma
Number	9
Zodiac sign	Aquarius
Beneficial for	Abundance, craniosacral work, longevity, centering, awakening kundalini energy, prosperity, creativity, well-being, stamina, vitality, health, stabilizing the pulse, degenerative disorders, depression, labor pain, rebirthing, osteomyelitis, ostitis, tinnitus, cranium and inner ear, cell metabolism, lungs, limbs.

Polished Ammolite

A powerful earth-healing stone, Ammolite is created by compression and mineralization of an ammonite fossil. Reputedly named after the spiral horn of the Egyptian god Amon, Ammolite also derives from the Greek for "horn." In ancient Greece, Pliny the Elder declared ammonite a most holy stone because it instilled prophetic dreams. In the Middle Ages ammonites were believed to be dragons' heads and were bound to the left arm for magical protection. The Blackfoot tribe of North America, who called it Buffalo Stone, used it to ward off evil spirits. This stone converts negative energy into a harmoniously flowing spiral. Holding the wisdom of the ancients, it is particularly effective placed on the soma chakra. A powerful karmic cleanser, it releases mental obsessions.

Ammolite represents coming full circle and activates personal empowerment. Stimulating survival instincts and encoding your life path, Ammolite offers structure and clarity, and relieves birth trauma affecting craniosacral flow. Called the Seven Color Prosperity Stone by Feng Shui masters, Ammolite has absorbed cosmic energy over eons and stimulates Qi, life force, through the body. Keep in the home to attract health and prosperity, and in business premises to promote business dealings. As jewelry, it imparts charisma and sensuous beauty.

See also Aragonite (page 190).

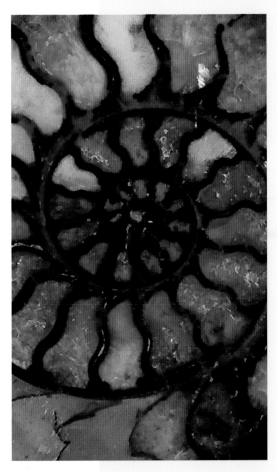

Ammolite section.

Aragonite

Crystal system	Orthorhombic
Chemistry	$CaCO_3$ Calcium carbonate
Hardness	3.5–4
Source	USA (Arizona and New Mexico), UK, Morocco, Namibia, Spain
Chakra	Earth, base
Number	9
Zodiac sign	Capricorn
Beneficial for	Patience, emotional stress, anger, reliability, acceptance, flexibility, tolerance, pain (especially lower back), grounding, wound healing, Reynaud's disease, chills, bones, calcium absorption, disc elasticity, night twitches, muscle spasm, immune system, regulates processes.

Natural Aragonite formation

Aragonite resonates to the Earth Mother and is an excellent earth-healer and grounding stone. Transforming geopathic stress and blocked ley lines, this stone can be placed on a map to heal disturbance in the earth. Centering physical energies and calming oversensitivity, Aragonite deepens connection with the earth, settling "floaty" people comfortably into their body. Combating disease, especially nervous twitching arising out of inner unrest, and warming the extremities, Aragonite distributes energy through the whole body. It stabilizes spiritual development that is occurring too fast. Useful for people who push themselves too hard, Aragonite encourages delegating. Its disciplined energy promotes a pragmatic approach to life. A supportive stone, it gives insight into causes of problems and gently takes you back into childhood or beyond.

Agate

Crystal system	Trigonal
Chemistry	SiO_2 Silicon dioxide
Hardness	6
Source	USA, India, Morocco, Czech Republic, Brazil, Africa
Chakra	Varies according to color and type
Number	7 (varies according to color and type)
Zodiac sign	Gemini (varies according to color and type)
Planet	Mercury
Beneficial for	Emotional trauma, self-confidence, concentration, perception, analytical abilities, aura stabilization, negative-energy transformation, emotional disease, digestive process, gastritis, eyes, stomach, uterus, lymphatic system, pancreas, blood vessels, skin disorders.

Polished Agate

A truth amulet in ancient Rome, or bound to the left arm to ensure bountiful crops, Agate was sometimes engraved with a snake to guard against snakebite. A grounding stone with a powerful multilevel cleansing effect, bringing about emotional, physical, and intellectual balance, Agate stabilizes energy and harmonizes yin and yang. It can bring hidden information to light. Soothing and calming, this stone works slowly but with great strength. Agate facilitates acceptance of your Self and speaking your truth. Overcoming bitterness of the heart, it heals inner anger, fostering courage to start again. Encouraging assimilation of life experiences, Agate facilitates stable spiritual growth.

Brown Spinel

Crystal system	Cubic
Chemistry	$MgAl_2O_4$ Magnesium aluminum oxide
Hardness	7.5–8
Source	Sri Lanka, Myanmar, Canada, USA, Brazil, Pakistan, Sweden (may be synthetic)
Chakra	Earth
Zodiac sign	Cancer, Scorpio
Planet	Pluto
Beneficial for	Muscular and nerve conditions, blood vessels.

Natural Brown Spinel

In addition to carrying the generic properties of Spinel (page 260), Brown Spinel opens the earth chakra and grounds you into physical reality. Cleansing the aura, it opens connections to the physical body.

Boji Stones

Crystal system	Cubic
Chemistry	Varies according to location, contains Limonite or Iron Pyrite
Hardness	5
Source	USA, UK
Chakra	Base, earth, aligns all
Number	1, 9
Zodiac sign	Taurus, Leo, Scorpio, Aquarius
Planet	Mars
Beneficial for	Grounding, plants and crops, emotional and energy blockages, pain, painful memories, tissue regeneration, revitalization, cleansing.

An effective grounding stone after multidimensional spiritual work, Boji Stones return you to earth and into your body, locating you in the present moment. Extremely useful for people who have only a toehold in incarnation, they have a strong protective function. Assisting in translating subtle energy healing into physical well-being, Boji Stones are particularly useful for overcoming blockages. The smooth stones have feminine energy, the protruded ones masculine, and a pair balance male–female energy within the body, aligning the chakras and repairing the aura.

Bojis bring up negative thought patterns and self-defeating behaviors for transformation, going to the cause of psychosomatic disease. Holding a Boji Stone aligns you to your shadow self, bringing up repressed qualities for release and finding the gift in them. Boji Stones stimulate energy flow through the meridian systems. Bringing your attention to mental imprints and hypnotic commands from the past, Boji Stones can be emotionally stabilizing but insist that necessary work is completed.

Natural Boji Stones— "female" (top) and "male" (bottom)

Andradite Garnet

Crystal system	Cubic
Chemistry	$Ca_3Fe_2(SiO_4)_3 + Al$
Hardness	6.5–7
Source	Europe, USA (Arizona and New Mexico), South Africa, Australia
Chakra	Base and heart, purifies and energizes all
Zodiac sign	Virgo, Capricorn
Planet	Mars
Beneficial for	Courage, stamina, and strength; formation of blood; liver; assimilation of calcium; magnesium, and iron; drawing off stress from the body; attracting love; dreaming; blood diseases; regenerating the body; metabolism; spinal and cellular disorders; blood; heart; lungs; regeneration of DNA; assimilation of minerals/vitamins.

In addition to carrying the generic properties of Garnet (page 47), Andradite, named for a mineralogist from Brazil, d'Andrada Silva, is dynamic and flexible, stimulating creativity. Bringing into your relationships what you most need for your development, it dissolves feelings of isolation or alienation and promotes sharing. Andratite realigns the magnetic fields of the body, and cleanses and expands the aura, opening metaphysical vision.

Andradite Garnet on matrix

Bornite (Peacock Ore)

Crystal system	Cubic
Chemistry	Cu_5FeS_4
Hardness	3
Source	USA, Canada, Morocco, Germany, Poland, England, Chile, Australia, Kazakhstan, Czech Republic, France, Norway
Chakra	Third eye, activates and synthesizes all
Number	2, 4
Zodiac sign	Cancer
Beneficial for	Cellular structures, metabolic imbalances, dissolving calcified deposits, overacidity, assimilation of potassium, swelling.

Polished Bornite

Named after Ignaz von Born, an 18th-century mineralogist, Bornite is an excellent tool for rebirthing work. Transforming heavy situations, it brings a freshness and newness to life. Integrating mind, body, emotions, and soul, Bornite teaches you how to negotiate obstacles with least stress, encouraging you to find happiness in the present moment. An excellent protection against negativity, which it transmutes, it identifies the source and filters out that which is no longer relevant. Opening metaphysical abilities, Bornite enhances inner knowing, teaching how to trust the process and information you receive. Assisting with visualization and creating your own reality, it can be programmed to send healing from a distance, and should be worn over the thymus of the patient.

Note: Bornite is a toxic stone and should be used in tumbled form.

Bornite on Silver

Crystal system	Cubic
Chemistry	Cu_5FeS_4
Hardness	3
Source	USA, Canada, Morocco, Germany, Poland, England, Chile, Australia, Kazakhstan, Czech Republic, France, Norway
Chakra	Third eye
Zodiac sign	Cancer
Beneficial for	Cellular structures, metabolic imbalances, dissolving calcified deposits, overacidity, assimilation of potassium, swelling.

Bornite on Silver matrix

Silver is an energizing and stabilizing metal that strengthens the qualities of the stone to which it is attached and focuses the energy appropriately. As silver is a feminine, moon-attuned metal, it can act as a reflective mirror for mystic visions, scrying, or inspiration, heightening perception and intuition. In addition to carrying the generic proprties of Bornite (left), Bornite on Silver reinforces the silver cord that connects the astral body to the physical, ensuring safe return whenever and wherever you journey. It is particularly useful for accessing and reframing the cause of third-eye blockages, especially where these have been deliberately proscribed in the past, and facilitates cellular memory reprogramming and etheric blueprint adjustments.

Bornite on Silver enhances mothering and the nurturing process, and platonic or romantic love.

Bronzite

Crystal system	Orthorhombic
Chemistry	$MgSiO_3$
Hardness	5.5–6
Source	Germany, Finland, India, Sri Lanka, USA
Chakra	Activates and synthesizes all
Number	1
Zodiac sign	Leo
Beneficial for	Harmony, self-assertion, willfulness, stress, chronic exhaustion, masculine energy, pain, overalkalinity, assimilation of iron, cramp, nerves.

Polished Bronzite

Bronzite is marketed as particularly effective against curses. Traditionally, however, iron-bearing crystals such as Bronzite return ill-wishing, curses, or spells back to the source magnified three times over, perpetuating the problem as it "bounces," becoming stronger each time, whereas Black Tourmaline (page 211) neutralizes it. A protective, grounding crystal, helpful in discordant situations where you feel powerless and in the grip of events beyond your control, Bronzite restores composure and assists in keeping a cool head. A "stone of courtesy" that strengthens nonjudgmental discernment, pinpoints your most important choices, and promotes decisive action, Bronzite allows you simply to "be," entering a dynamic state of nonaction, nondoing.

Desert Rose

Crystal system	Monoclinic
Chemistry	$CaSo_4 + 2H_2O$ Calcium sulfate
Hardness	1.5–2
Source	Germany, Morocco, Australia, Tunisia, Saudi Arabia, Middle East, USA, Canada
Chakra	Solar plexus, earth
Beneficial for	Lactation, connective tissue, structure of bones and osteoporosis, oversensitivity to cold or temperature, chronic fatigue, detoxification, judgment, insight, aligning the spinal column, flexibility, epilepsy.

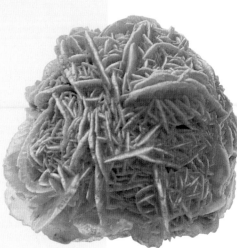

Desert Rose formation

In myth Desert Roses were carved by Native American warriors who returned from the spirit world. The roses were scattered over the earth so that the home of the spirits would be kept sacred, set apart, and the stone helps you dim your light while traveling and is reputed to facilitate clandestine meetings. Carrying the generic properties of Selenite (page 257) or Barite (page 244), Desert Rose releases a self-imposed negative program or belief system. Meditating with this stone transmutes ancient hatred into love, or assists in traveling back to heal the conflict. Helping you to receive as well as to give and enhancing love, it controls emotional outbursts. An excellent healer for the earth, Desert Rose can be used to grid disturbed earth-energy locations. Strengthening affirmations of purpose, it connects to the nourishment and protection of Mother Earth.

Chiastolite (Cross Stone, Andalusite)

Crystal system	Orthorhombic
Chemistry	Al_2SiO_5 Aluminum silicate
Hardness	6.5–7.5
Source	USA, Brazil, China, Spain, Italy, Australia, Chile, Russia
Chakra	Base
Number	3, 4
Zodiac sign	Libra
Beneficial for	Guilt, memory, analytic capability, fever, stanching blood flow, overacidification, rheumatism, gout, lactation, chromosome damage, immune system, paralysis, nerve fortifier.

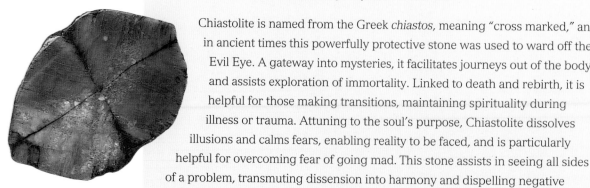

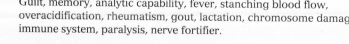

Chiastolite is named from the Greek *chiastos*, meaning "cross marked," and in ancient times this powerfully protective stone was used to ward off the Evil Eye. A gateway into mysteries, it facilitates journeys out of the body and assists exploration of immortality. Linked to death and rebirth, it is helpful for those making transitions, maintaining spirituality during illness or trauma. Attuning to the soul's purpose, Chiastolite dissolves illusions and calms fears, enabling reality to be faced, and is particularly helpful for overcoming fear of going mad. This stone assists in seeing all sides of a problem, transmuting dissension into harmony and dispelling negative thoughts and feelings.

Natural Chiastolite

Staurolite (Fairy Cross)

Crystal system	Monoclinic
Chemistry	$Fe_2Al_{19}Si_4O_{22}(OH)_2$ Ferrous aluminum
Hardness	7–7.5
Source	USA, Russia, France, Austria, Switzerland, Scotland, Namibia, Middle East
Number	5
Zodiac sign	Pisces
Beneficial for	Stopping smoking, addictions, stress, depression, overwork, scattered energy, cellular disorders, growths, assimilation of carbohydrates, depression, fever.

Staurolite in matrix

A talisman for good luck, Staurolite derives from the Greek *stauros*, meaning "cross." Known as the Fairy Cross, it was said to form from tears the fairies shed at Christ's death, and equal-armed crosses depict interpenetration of the spiritual and physical worlds. Giving access to ancient wisdom of the Middle East, Staurolite links to devas and elemental spirits and is excellent for those who garden or till the soul. Staurolite strengthens rituals and is useful in white magic. This stone connects the physical, etheric, and spiritual planes, promoting communication between them. Assisting in recognizing hidden reasons behind addiction to nicotine, it provides grounding for airy people who use nicotine to anchor to earth.

Chrysanthemum Stone

Crystal system	Triclinic
Chemistry	Complex
Hardness	Not established
Source	China, Japan, Canada, USA
Number	3
Zodiac sign	Taurus, Aquarius
Beneficial for	Stability, trust, resentment, animosity, bigotry, ignorance, narrow-mindedness, self-righteousness, jealousy, physical maturation, skin, skeleton, eyes, detoxification, growths.

Facilitating time travel, Chrysanthemum Stone synthesizes change with equilibrium and shows how the two can work together. Facilitating being centered in the present moment, it encourages the Self to bloom. Enhancing the environment with its calm presence, it radiates harmony. Chrysanthemum Stone teaches how to remain childlike, fun-loving, and innocent while on the spiritual path, stimulating self-development. Strengthening character, it encourages showing more love to the world, and brings more love into your life. This stone counteracts superficiality and guards against distractions. With the aid of Chrysanthemum Stone, the bigger picture can be perceived.

Chrysanthemum Stone

Brown Jade

Crystal system	Monoclinic
Chemistry	$Na(AlFe)Si_2O_6$
Hardness	6
Source	USA, China, Italy, Myanmar, Russia, Middle East
Chakra	Base, earth
Zodiac sign	Taurus
Planet	Venus
Beneficial for	Longevity, self-sufficiency, detoxification, filtration, elimination, kidneys, suprarenal glands, cellular and skeletal systems, stitches, fertility, childbirth, hips, spleen, water–salt–acid–alkaline ratio.

In addition to carrying the generic properties of Jade (page 120), Brown Jade is a powerful earthing stone, which assists in adjusting to a new environment, bringing comfort and reliability.

Carved Brown Jade figure

Goethite

Crystal system	Orthorhombic
Chemistry	FeOOH Hydrous iron oxide
Hardness	4–5.5
Source	USA, Germany, England, France, Canada
Chakra	Clears base and aligns all
Number	44
Zodiac sign	Aries
Beneficial for	Weight training, epilepsy, anemia, menorrhagia, ears, nose, throat, alimentary canal, veins, esophagus.

Goethite was named after the German poet Johann Wolfgang von Goethe and resonates to 44, the number of metamorphosis. Facilitating clairaudience, this stone enhances dowsing abilities, attuning to the note of the earth. Increasing powers of divination, Goethite shows your future where helpful for your soul journey. Meditating with Goethite feels like being suspended in a silent point of nonaction and nondoing. This stone also supplies the energy necessary for enjoying the human journey. An excellent communication tool, it combines inspiration with the pragmatic ability to get things done. To encourage the landing of a spaceship, grid an area with Goethite.

Iridescent Rainbow Goethite cuts through dark clouds, especially gloom and despondency, bringing light and hope into your life.

Raw Goethite

Hemimorphite

Crystal system	Orthorhombic
Chemistry	$Zn_4Si_2O_7(OH)_2H_2O$ Hydrated zinc silicate hydroxide
Hardness	5
Source	England, Mexico, USA, Zambia
Number	4
Zodiac sign	Libra
Beneficial for	Social responsibility, reframing the past, emotional communication, realistic goal-setting, emotional angst, convalescence, weight loss, pain relief, blood disorders, heart, cellular structures, ulcerative conditions, burns, genital herpes, warts, restless legs.

Non-crystalline Hemimorphite on matrix

Named from *hemi*, "half," and *morph*, "shape," Hemimorphite takes different shapes, raises the body's vibrations, and facilitates communication with the highest spiritual levels. It brings about self-development in the fastest way possible and teaches personal responsibility for your own happiness or disease, showing how reality is created through the thoughts and attitudes you hold. It assists in recognizing where you fall under outside influences not in accord with your soul-view. Developing inner strength, Hemimorphite manifests your highest potential. A protective stone, particularly against malicious thoughts, in ancient times it was reputedly used to counteract poison.

Crystalline Hemimorphite

Dendritic Chalcedony

Crystal system	Trigonal
Chemistry	SiO_2 Silicon dioxide with inclusions
Hardness	7
Source	USA, Austria, Czech Republic, Slovakia, Iceland, England, Mexico, New Zealand, Turkey, Russia, Brazil, Morocco
Number	9
Zodiac sign	Cancer, Sagittarius
Planet	Moon
Beneficial for	Processing memories, chronic illness, problems associated with smoking, immune system, assimilation of copper, lawsuits, nightmares, negative thoughts, turbulent emotions, cleansing, mineral assimilation, mineral build-up in veins, dementia, senility, physical energy, holistic healing, bones, circulatory system.

In addition to carrying the generic properties of Chalcedony (page 247), Dendritic Calcite brings joy to life, encourages living in the present moment, and supports when facing up to unpleasant matters.

Facilitating a friendly approach to other people, it promotes tolerant interaction without judgment. This stone is useful when you are under attack, as it facilitates calm communication while remaining relaxed, promoting clear and precise thought.

Tumbled Dendritic Chalcedony

Dravide Tourmaline

Crystal system	Trigonal
Chemistry	Complex silicate
Hardness	7–7.5
Source	Sri Lanka, Brazil, Africa, USA, Australia, Afghanistan, Italy, Germany, Madagascar, Tanzania
Chakra	Earth, protects all
Zodiac sign	Aries
Beneficial for	Community spirit, social commitment, creativity, craftwork, dysfunctional family relationships, empathy, intestinal disorders, skin diseases, regeneration, protection, detoxification, spinal adjustments, balancing male–female energy, paranoia, dyslexia, hand-eye coordination, assimilation and translation of coded information, bronchitis, emphysema, pleurisy, pneumonia, energy flow, removal of blockages.

Raw Dravide Tourmaline

An excellent grounding stone, clearing and opening the earth chakra and the grounding cord that holds the physical body in incarnation, Dravide Tourmaline cleanses the aura and aligns and protects the etheric body. In addition to carrying the generic properties of Tourmaline (page 210), this stone is excellent for soul retrieval and for removing entity attachments or demonic forces. Dravide Tourmaline makes you feel comfortable in a large group.

Brown Jasper

Crystal system	Trigonal
Chemistry	SiO_2 Silicon dioxide with impurities
Hardness	7
Source	Worldwide
Chakra	Earth, past life
Zodiac sign	Scorpio
Planet	Saturn
Beneficial for	Night vision, immune system, clearing pollutants and toxins, cleansing organs, skin, giving up smoking, electromagnetic and environmental pollution, radiation, stress, prolonged illness or hospitalization, circulation, digestive and sexual organs, balancing mineral content of the body.

Tumbled Brown Jasper

In addition to carrying the generic properties of Jasper (page 45), Brown Jasper is a powerful cleanser for the physical body, cleansing and repairing the aura and ameliorating the effects of trauma, anesthetics, drugs, or psychic attack. It is effective for removing thought forms. Encouraging ecological awareness, stability and balance, it is particularly effective for alleviating geopathic and environmental stress. Brown Jasper facilitates deep meditation, centering, and grounding, bringing about results that you desire. Facilitating regression to the past, it reveals the karmic causes behind disease. Brown Jasper is particularly useful for people who live in their heads to the detriment of their body.

Mookaite Jasper (Australian Jasper)

Crystal system	Trigonal
Chemistry	SiO_2 Silicon dioxide with impurities
Hardness	7
Source	Australia
Chakra	Earth, solar plexus
Number	5
Beneficial for	Dispelling illusion, versatility, water retention, glandular and immune systems, wounds, purifying blood, stomach, hernia, rupture, electromagnetic and environmental pollution, radiation, stress, prolonged illness or hospitalization, circulation, digestive and sexual organs, balancing mineral content of the body.

Tumbled Mookaite

In addition to carrying the generic properties of Jasper (page 45), protective and strengthening Mookaite acts as a companion for the bereaved or lonely. Meditating with this stone takes you into a calm center to wait out any storm, and can assist in contacting souls on other planes. Balancing inner and outer experiences, Mookaite imparts a desire for new experiences and a deep calm with which to face them, and encourages facing present circumstances with equanimity if change is not possible. This flexible and pragmatic stone points out all possibilities and assists in choosing the right one.

Tiger Iron

Crystal system	Complex
Chemistry	Complex combination
Hardness	7
Source	Australia, South Africa
Chakra	Solar plexus
Number	7
Zodiac sign	Leo
Beneficial for	Vitality, blood, balancing red–white cell count, toxicity, lower limbs, muscles, stress, prolonging sexual pleasure, prolonged illness or hospitalization, brain hemisphere integration, perception, internal conflicts, pride, willfulness, emotional balance, broken bones, timid women, willpower, triple heater meridian, legal situations, iron absorption, Reynaud's disease, leg cramps, spinal alignment, fractures.

Raw Tiger Iron

Extremely helpful for people who take on other people's feelings, or who are deeply exhausted at any level, especially those suffering from emotional or mental burnout or family stress, Tiger Iron assists people who are chemically sensitive and who react to noise pollution. In addition to carrying the generic properties of Jasper (page 45), Hematite (page 222), and Tiger's Eye (page 206), this stone aids change, pointing to a place of refuge when danger threatens and returning evil to its source. Promoting change by opening space to contemplate what is needed, it supplies the energy necessary for action. Tiger Iron's solutions are pragmatic and simple. This is a creative and artistic stone that brings out inherent talents.

Tumbled Tiger Iron

Picture Jasper

Crystal system	Trigonal
Chemistry	SiO_2 Silicon dioxide
Hardness	7
Source	USA, South Africa
Chakra	Base, earth
Number	8
Zodiac sign	Leo
Beneficial for	Guilt, envy, hatred, love, writer's or artist's block, immune system, kidneys, electromagnetic and environmental pollution, radiation, stress, prolonged illness or hospitalization, circulation, digestive and sexual organs, balancing mineral content of the body.

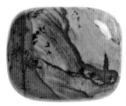

Tumbled Picture Jasper

Said to be Mother Earth speaking to her children, Picture Jasper contains a message from the past. In addition to carrying the generic properties of Jasper (page 45), this stone brings to the surface hidden feelings and thoughts that are normally pushed aside, whether from present or past lives. Once the repression is released, they are seen as lessons along the way. Instilling a sense of proportion and harmony, Picture Jasper brings comfort and alleviates fear. This stone protects women during childbirth.

Polished Picture Jasper

Magnetite (Lodestone)

Crystal system	Cubic
Chemistry	Fe_3O_4 Iron oxide
Hardness	5.5-6.5
Source	USA, Canada, India, Mexico, Romania, Italy, Finland, Austria
Chakra	Connects base and earth, aligns all
Number	4
Zodiac sign	Aries, Virgo, Capricorn, Aquarius
Planet	Mars
Beneficial for	Fear, anger, grief, commitment, loyalty, overattachment, tenacity, telepathy, meditation, visualization, sports injuries, aches and pains in muscles or joints, night cramps, nosebleeds, anti-inflammatory, asthma, blood and circulatory system, skin, hair.

Magnetite

Magnetite is reputed to have been discovered by Magnetis, an ancient Greek shepherd, when his iron-soled sandals stuck to the path and the metal tip of his crook to a large boulder. With its powerful polarity, Magnetite can be used for magnetic therapy on the body's biomagnetic field and meridians, and that of the planet for earth healing, and can assist the flow of earth energy to the base chakras. A strongly grounding stone, Magnetite energizes and sedates as required. This stone attracts love, encouraging a balanced perspective and trust in your own intuitions. Alleviating negative emotions, it draws in positive ones. Magnetite assists in removing yourself from detrimental situations and promotes objectivity, balancing intellect with emotion.

Pietersite

Crystal system	Trigonal
Chemistry	SiO$_2$ Silicon dioxide with impurities
Hardness	7
Source	Namibia
Chakra	Third eye, past life, soma
Number	9
Zodiac sign	Leo
Beneficial for	Exhaustion, nervous disease, stubborn blocks, confusion, stimulating the pituitary gland, balancing the endocrine system, blood pressure, growth, sex, temperature control, headaches, breathing difficulties, lungs, liver, intestines, feet, legs, absorption of nutrients, meridian pathways of the body.

Tumbled Pietersite

Named after its finder, Sid Pieters of South Africa, Pietersite is said to hold "the keys to the kingdom of heaven" and promotes "walking your truth." It reminds you that you are a spiritual being on a human journey, and can be used for a vision quest or shamanic journey. During moving meditations or Tai Chi, it accesses a high state of altered awareness. Said to dispel the illusion of individual separateness, it removes conditioning imposed by other people. Linking you to inner guidance, it tests the veracity of other people's words. In past-life healing, Pietersite processes ancient conflicts and suppressed feelings and removes disease caused by not following one's own truth. It releases you from vows and promises made in other lives that have carried over into the present.

Mahogany Obsidian

Crystal system	Amorphous
Chemistry	SiO$_2$ Silicon dioxide with iron
Hardness	5–5.5
Source	Mexico, volcanic regions
Chakra	Base, sacral, solar plexus
Number	4
Zodiac sign	Scorpio
Planet	Pluto
Beneficial for	Energy blockages, detoxification, pain, circulation, compassion, strength, digestion of anything that is hard to accept, blockages, hardened arteries, arthritis, joint pain, cramp, injuries, bleeding, circulation, enlarged prostate, warming the extremities.

In addition to carrying the generic properties of Obsidian (page 214), Mahogany Obsidian resonates with the earth, grounds and protects, gives strength in times of need, vitalizes purpose, and stimulates multidimensional growth. Strengthening a weak aura, it restores the correct spin to the sacral and solar plexus chakras, balances yin and yang, dark and light, mind and higher consciousness. This is an excellent stone for reclaiming your power.

Natural Mahogany Obsidian

Rutile

Crystal system	Tetragonal
Chemistry	TiO_2 Titanium oxide
Hardness	6–6.5
Source	USA, Africa, Australia, Brazil, Switzerland
Number	4
Zodiac sign	Taurus, Gemini
Beneficial for	Lactation, elasticity of blood vessels, cell regeneration, bronchitis, premature ejaculation, impotence, frigidity, anorgasmia.

Often found included within other crystals, to which it imparts an ethereal vibration, Rutile powerfully amplifies healing properties. It enhances out-of-body journeying, metaphysical protection, and angelic contact. Cleansing and purifying the aura, it brings it into balance with the physical body. Going directly to the root of a problem, Rutile heals psychosomatic disease and pinpoints the karmic causes of chronic illness. This stone creates emotional stability to underpin partnership. See also Rutilated Quartz (below), Rutilated Topaz (page 88), Lavender Quartz (page 174).

Rutilated Quartz with Rutile crystals (also called Golden Quartz)

Rutilated Quartz (Angel's Hair)

Crystal system	Hexagonal
Chemistry	SiO_2 Silicon dioxide with rutile
Hardness	7
Source	Worldwide
Chakra	Harmonizes all, aligns the aura
Zodiac sign	All
Planet	Sun
Beneficial for	Mercury poisoning in nerves, muscles, blood, and intestinal tract; immune system; chronic conditions; impotence; infertility; energy depletion; respiratory tract; bronchitis; thyroid; parasites; cell regeneration; torn tissues; encourages upright posture; lactation; elasticity of blood vessels; cell regeneration; bronchitis; premature ejaculation; impotence; frigidity; anorgasmia.

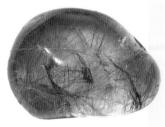

Tumbled Rutilated Quartz

Rutilation creates very powerful vibrational healing as it intensifies energy flow within the Quartz (see page 230 for generic properties) and integrates it within the body. Said to have a perfect balance of cosmic light and to be an illuminator for the soul, Rutilated Quartz breaks down the barriers to spiritual progress, letting go of the past, and promotes forgiveness at all levels. It opens the aura, allowing healing in, and filters negative energy from a patient, supporting emotional release and confrontation with the darker aspects of the psyche. It gives powerful protection against psychic attack. In past-life healing it draws off disease, promotes insights into events in past lives affecting the present, and connects to soul lessons and the plan for the present life. Rutilated Quartz reaches the root of problems and facilitates transitions and a change of direction. Emotionally, Rutilated Quartz soothes dark moods and acts an antidepressant. It relieves fears, phobias, and anxiety, releasing constrictions and countering self-hatred.

Vanadinite

Crystal system	Hexagonal
Chemistry	$Pb_5 (VO_4)_3Cl$ Lead chloro-vanadinate
Hardness	2.75–3
Source	USA, Morocco, Zambia, Mexico
Chakra	Earth, sacral, base
Number	9
Zodiac sign	Virgo
Beneficial for	Circular breathing, chronic exhaustion, bladder problems, endometriosis, fibroids, intrauterine growths, balancing female hormones, menopause, PMS, stabilizing menstrual cycle, asthma, congested lungs.

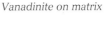

Excellent for people who have problems accepting their physicality, Vanadinite has a strong connection with the earth chakra that grounds the soul into the physical body, assisting in being comfortable in the earth environment. Teaching how to conserve energy, it opens an internal channel within the body to receive an inflooding of universal energy, aligning the chakras. Shutting off mind chatter, Vanadinite facilitates a state of "no mind" or can be used consciously to direct awareness for metaphysical vision and journeying. This stone fills the gap between thought and intellect. Defining goals, it combines rational thought with inner guidance.

Vanadinite on matrix

Note: Vanadinite is toxic; use with care.

Cymophane

Crystal system	Orthorhombic
Chemistry	$BeAl_2O_4$
Hardness	8.5
Source	Russia, Sweden, Sri Lanka, Myanmar, Brazil, Canada, Ghana, Norway, Zimbabwe, China, Australia
Chakra	Opens crown and aligns to solar plexus
Number	6
Zodiac sign	Leo
Beneficial for	Eye disorders, night vision, headaches and facial pain, adrenaline, cholesterol, chest, liver, creativity, strategic planning, compassion, forgiveness, generosity, confidence, self-healing. Wear on the right side of the body.

In addition to carrying the generic properties of Chrysoberyl (page 82), Cymophane stimulates and stabilizes the intellect and supports flexibility of mind. It enhances unconditional love.

Tumbled Cymophane

Sardonyx

Crystal system	Trigonal
Chemistry	SiO_2 Silicon dioxide with impurities
Hardness	7
Source	Brazil, India, Russia, Turkey, Middle East
Chakra	Base, sacral (varies according to color)
Number	3
Zodiac sign	Aries
	Mars
Beneficial for	Tinnitus, lungs, bones, spleen, sensory organs, fluid regulation, cell metabolism, immune system, absorption of nutrients, elimination of waste products.

A protective and detoxifying stone that can be gridded around the house and garden to prevent crime, Sardonyx is a stone of strength and protection that strengthens willpower and character. Invoking the search for a meaningful existence, it promotes integrity and virtuous conduct. Said to bring lasting happiness and stability to marriage and partnership, Sardonyx attracts friends and good fortune. This stone increases stamina, vigor, and self-control, alleviates depression, and overcomes hesitancy. It improves perception and aids absorption and processing of information.

Shiva Lingam

Crystal system	Complex
Chemistry	Complex sandstone
Hardness	1
Source	Narmada River, India (may be artificially created)
Chakra	Base
Zodiac sign	Scorpio
Beneficial for	Infertility, impotence, menstrual cramps.

Natural shaped Shiva Lingam

This shaped stone has been sacred for thousands of years, symbolizing the god Shiva and his union with his consort, Kali. A symbol of sexuality and potent male energy, a Shiva Lingam raises and controls kundalini energy, grounding it into the body, and can be used for sexual healing and to facilitate the union of opposites such as masculine and feminine, or the body and the soul. It severs sexual connections after a relationship is over and removes etheric phallic hooks from the vagina. A stone of insight, it assists in letting go of all that is outgrown. Particularly useful for emotional pain that arises from early childhood, especially sexual abuse, it reinstates trust in male energy. A Shiva Lingam reenergizes the base chakras and opens the way for a new relationship.

Serpentine

Crystal system	Monoclinic
Chemistry	(MgFe)$_3$Si$_2$O$_5$(OH)4 Magnesium iron silicate hydroxide
Hardness	3–4.5
Source	UK, Norway, Russia, Zimbabwe, Italy, USA, Switzerland, Canada
Chakra	Crown, clears all
Number	8
Zodiac sign	Gemini
Planet	Saturn
Beneficial for	Longevity, detoxification, parasite elimination, calcium and magnesium absorption, hypoglycemia, diabetes.

Serpentine was so named because it resembles a serpent's skin and was believed to protect against snake venom and creatures such as spiders, bees, and scorpions. It is excellent for trance work, ritual, and shamanism and is said to be particularly good for Celts. This earthing stone aids meditation and helps you understand the spiritual basis of life. It opens new pathways for the kundalini energy to rise. Serpentine helps you feel more in control of your life, correcting mental and emotional imbalances and focusing healing energy toward problem areas.

Raw Serpentine

Brown Zircon

Crystal system	Tetragonal
Chemistry	ZrSiO$_3$ Zirconium silicate
Hardness	6.5–7.5
Source	Australia, USA, Sri Lanka, Ukraine, Canada (may be heat-treated to intensify color)
Chakra	Earth
Zodiac sign	Sagittarius
Planet	Sun
Beneficial for	Synergy, constancy, jealousy, possessiveness, victimization, homophobia, misogyny, racism, sciatica, cramp, insomnia, depression, bones, muscles, vertigo, liver, menstrual irregularity. *(Zircon may cause dizziness in those who wear pacemakers or are epileptic—if so, remove immediately.)*

In addition to carrying the generic properties of Zircon (page 261), Brown Zircon is excellent for centering and grounding.

Raw Brown Zircon

Tiger's Eye

Crystal system	Trigonal
Chemistry	$NaFe^{+3}(SiO_3)_2$ Silicon dioxide with impurities
Hardness	4–7
Source	USA, Mexico, India, Australia, South Africa
Chakra	Third eye
Number	4
Zodiac sign	Leo, Capricorn
Planet	Sun
Beneficial for	Brain hemisphere integration, perception, internal conflicts, pride, willfulness, emotional balance, yin–yang, fatigue, hemophilia, hepatitis, mononucleosis, depression, eyes, night vision, throat, reproductive organs, constrictions, broken bones.

Polished Tiger's Eye

It is said that Roman soldiers wore an engraved Tiger's Eye to protect them in battle, and it is still used as a protective stone. Combining earth energy with the energies of the sun, it creates a high vibrational state that draws spiritual energies to earth. Tiger's Eye heals mental disease and personality disorders; deals with issues of self-worth, self-criticism, and blocked creativity; and is excellent for people who are spaced out or uncommitted. Facilitating assertion and anchoring change into the physical body, this stone assists in recognizing talents and faults to be overcome and supports an addictive personality in making changes. Facilitating correct use of power, Tiger's Eye supports integrity and assists in accomplishing goals. It differentiates between wishful thinking and what one really needs, and assists in recognizing other people's needs.

Cat's Eye

Tumbled Cat's Eye

Crystal system	Orthorhombic
Chemistry	$BeAl_2O_4$
Hardness	8.5
Source	Russia, Sweden, Sri Lanka, Myanmar, Brazil, Canada, Ghana, Norway, Zimbabwe, China, Australia
Chakra	Opens crown and aligns to solar plexus
Number	6
Zodiac sign	Leo
Planet	Venus
Beneficial for	Eye disorders, night vision, headaches and facial pain, adrenaline, cholesterol, chest, liver, creativity, strategic planning, compassion, forgiveness, generosity, confidence, self-healing. Wear on the right side of the body.

Long believed to have magical properties and to protect against the Evil Eye, the ancient Assyrians believed that Cat's Eye endowed the wearer with invisibility. In addition to carrying the generic properties of Chrysoberyl (page 82), this is a grounding stone that stimulates intuition. Cat's Eye dispels negative energy from the aura and provides general protection. Traditionally, it brings beauty, confidence, happiness, serenity, and good luck.

Wulfenite

Crystal system	Tetragonal
Chemistry	$PbMoO_4$ Lead molybdate
Hardness	3
Source	USA, Mexico, Bohemia, Morocco, Yugoslavia, Zaire, Australia
Chakra	Past life, base, sacral
Number	7
Zodiac sign	Sagittarius
Beneficial for	Uterine healing following childbirth, miscarriage, abortion, sexuality, mortification, cellular memory, rejuvenation, energy preservation.

Named after Franz Xavier Wulfen, an Austrian Jesuit whose interest in creation resulted in him becoming an expert in lead ores, Wulfenite is a powerful past-life healing stone. If you suffered for beliefs connected with magic, Wulfenite heals the experience, making it feel safe again. This stone can be programmed to bring you into contact with soul links. If you have made an agreement with another soul that you will meet, Wulfenite facilitates recognition of the contract. Bonding souls together while the purpose or lesson is carried out, it releases when appropriate. Wulfenite enhances ritual working and journeying, and facilitates regaining magical knowledge from other lives to be put into practice in the present. It assists in accepting less positive aspects of life and prevents despondency from setting in during negative situations. Useful for people who have become unbalanced by focusing only on the positive, repressing negative traits and becoming "sugary sweet," inauthentic, and ungrounded, Wulfenite integrates shadow energies.

Note: Wulfenite is toxic; use with care.

Wulfenite on matrix

Additional brown stones

Almandine Garnet (page 48), Amber (page 79), Apatite (page 133), Aventurine (page 97), Barite (page 244), Brown Fluorite (page 177), Carnelian (page 44), Cinnabar (page 50), Dendritic Agate (page 101), Diopside (page 104), Grossular Garnet (page 41), Idocrase (page 116), Iron Pyrite (page 91), Magnesite (page 252), Moss Agate (page 101), Muscovite (page 31), Ocean Orbicular Jasper (page 118), Peridot (page 120), Prehnite (page 122), Septarian (page 85), Smithsonite (page 138), Stilbite (page 260), Wavellite (page 123), Yellow Topaz (page 87), Zoisite (page 56).

Black, silver, and gray crystals

Black stones are strongly protective because they entrap negative energies, which are then transmuted. They are also excellent detoxifiers. Many silver-gray stones are metallic in origin and were traditionally believed to have alchemical properties of transmutation and invisibility. Black and gray crystals are associated with the planet Saturn, while silver crystals are associated with the moon and with the planet Mercury.

Tourmaline

Crystal system	Trigonal
Chemistry	Complex silicate, content varies according to color
Hardness	7–7.5
Source	Sri Lanka, Brazil, Africa, USA, Australia, Afghanistan, Italy, Germany, Madagascar
Chakra	Earth, protects all
Number	2 (varies according to color)
Zodiac sign	Libra (varies according to color)
Beneficial for	Protection, detoxification, spinal adjustments, balancing male–female energy, paranoia, dyslexia, hand-eye coordination, assimilation and translation of coded information, bronchitis, diabetes, emphysema, pleurisy, pneumonia, energy flow, removal of blockages. Each of the different colors of Tourmaline has its own specific healing ability.

Natural Black Tourmaline

Tourmaline comes from the Singhalese term *turamali*. This stone is piezoelectric, meaning that it generates electricity under pressure, and pyroelectric, generating electricity with heat. The Dutch called Tourmaline *aschentrekker*, "ash remover," as when heated it attracted ashes from a pipe. Tourmaline has a strong affinity with devic energies and is extremely beneficial for plants, keeping pests at bay, and, buried in soil, encourages growth of all crops.

Purifying and transforming dense energy into a lighter vibration, Tourmaline grounds spiritual energy; balances chakras, meridians, and auric bodies; and forms a protective shield. Traditionally used for scrying, it pointed to the culprit or cause in times of trouble, and indicated a "good" direction in which to move.

A powerful mental healer, balancing right and left hemispheres of the brain and transmuting negative thought patterns into positive ones, Tourmaline assists in understanding oneself and others, taking you deep into your inner being, promoting self-confidence, and diminishing fear. Banishing any feeling of victimization, it attracts inspiration, compassion, tolerance, and prosperity.

Close-up of typically striated Black Tourmaline with Mica inclusions.

Black Tourmaline (Schorl)

Crystal system	Trigonal
Chemistry	Complex silicate
Hardness	7–7.5
Source	Sri Lanka, Brazil, Africa, USA, Australia, Afghanistan, Italy, Germany, Madagascar
Chakra	Earth, protects all
Number	3, 4
Zodiac sign	Capricorn
Beneficial for	Negative energies, debilitating disease, immune system, arthritis, pain relief, realigning spinal column, protection, detoxification, spinal adjustments, balancing male–female energy, paranoia, hand-eye coordination, assimilation and translation of coded information, bronchitis, emphysema, pleurisy, pneumonia, energy flow, removal of blockages.

Natural Black Tourmaline

In addition to carrying the generic properties of Tourmaline (left), Black Tourmaline is the most effective blocker of curses, psychic attack, and ill-wishing. It protects against cellphone emanations, electromagnetic disturbance, radiation, and negative energies of all kinds. Wear around your neck or place between yourself and the source of electromagnetics. Place point out from the body, it draws off negative energy and clears blockages. Gridded around the house or open space, it affords protection on all levels. Connecting with the base chakra, Black Tourmaline grounds energy and increases physical vitality, dispersing tension and stress. Clearing negative thoughts, it promotes a laid-back attitude, encouraging objective neutrality with clear, rational thought processes. It also instills a positive attitude no matter what the circumstances and stimulates altruism and practical creativity.

Tourmaline Wand

Crystal system	Trigonal
Chemistry	Complex silicate
Hardness	7–7.5
Source	Sri Lanka, Brazil, Africa, USA, Australia, Afghanistan, Italy, Germany, Madagascar
Chakra	Earth, protects all
Number	2 (varies according to color)
Zodiac sign	Libra (varies according to color)
Beneficial for	Protection, detoxification, spinal adjustments, balancing male–female energy, paranoia, dyslexia, hand-eye coordination, assimilation and translation of coded information, bronchitis, diabetes, emphysema, pleurisy, pneumonia, energy flow, removal of blockages.

Useful healing tools, natural or shaped Tourmaline wands (see Tourmaline, left, and Wands, page 279) clear the aura, remove blockages, disperse negative energy, and point to solutions for specific problems. Excellent for balancing and connecting the chakras, at a physical level they rebalance the energy meridians. Each color of Tourmaline wand has specific properties (see appropriate entry).

Jet

Crystal system	Amorphous
Chemistry	Oxygenated hydrocarbon
Hardness	0.5–2.5
Source	Worldwide, especially USA
Chakra	Base, heart
Number	8
Zodiac sign	Capricorn
Planet	Saturn
Beneficial for	Mood swings, depression, migraine, epilepsy, colds, glandular and lymphatic swellings, stomach pain, menstrual cramps.

Electrically charged when rubbed, Jet has been looked on as a magical talisman against "entities of darkness" since the Stone Age and is said to become part of the body of the wearer. In ancient Greece, worshippers of Cybele wore Jet to seek her favors, and in Britain fishermen's wives burned it to ensure their husbands' protection. It is said that those who are attracted to this stone are "old souls" with long experience of incarnation on earth. Jet promotes taking control of life, transmutes negative energy and alleviates unreasonable fears, guards against violence and illness, and gives protection during spiritual journeying. To stabilize finances and protect businesses, place in a cashbox or the wealth corner. Jet cleanses the base chakra and stimulates kundalini and, placed at the chest, directs kundalini toward the crown chakra.

Raw Jet

Polished Jet

Black Spinel

Crystal system	Cubic
Chemistry	$MgAl_2O_4$ Magnesium aluminum oxide
Hardness	7.5–8
Source	Sri Lanka, Myanmar, Canada, USA, Brazil, Pakistan, Sweden (may be synthetic)
Chakra	Base, earth
Zodiac sign	Taurus
Planet	Pluto
Beneficial for	Muscular and nerve conditions, blood vessels.

In addition to carrying the generic properties of Spinel (page 260), Black Spinel is protective and grounds energy to balance rising kundalini. It offers insights into material problems and gives the stamina to continue.

Black Spinel

Nebula Stone

Crystal system	Complex
Chemistry	Complex combination
Hardness	6–7
Source	USA
Chakra	All
Number	2
Zodiac sign	Scorpio, Pisces
Beneficial for	Profound healing at the cellular level, macular degeneration, herpes, bronchitis, skin, convalescence, emotional body, self-pity, anxiety, realistic goals, emotional trauma, grief, stamina, nervous and immune systems, dehydration, brain, thyroid, liver, gallbladder, adrenal glands, self-esteem, integrity, sensitivity, focusing goals, muscles and muscle pain, bones, metabolic system. As an elixir it softens the skin.

Tumbled Nebula Stone

Composed of Aegirine (see page 102 for generic properties), potassium feldspar, Quartz (page 230), and Epidote (page 114), Nebula Stone is said to have unique metaphysical properties. The light vibration of Quartz is transferred into the physical body, enlightening the cells and activating their consciousness, raising overall awareness and bringing remembrance of the soul's roots. The feldspar constituent assists in letting go of the past and moving confidently into the future, at the same time understanding underlying feelings. Gazing into a Nebula Stone takes you outward into infinity and inward into the smallest particle of being until, ultimately, the two become one. This stone accesses the Akashic Record and facilitates aura readings. A stone of nonduality and oneness, it increases self-awareness and self-love.

Black Sapphire

Crystal system	Hexagonal
Chemistry	Al_2O_3 Aluminum oxide
Hardness	9
Source	Myanmar, Czech Republic, Brazil, Kenya, India, Australia, Sri Lanka, Canada, Thailand, Madagascar
Chakra	Earth, past life
Zodiac sign	Sagittarius
Planet	Moon, Saturn
Beneficial for	Serenity, peace of mind, concentration, multidimensional cellular healing, overactive body systems, glands.

In addition to carrying the generic properties of Sapphire (page 160), protective and centering Black Sapphire imparts confidence in your own intuition. Wearing this stone heightens employment prospects and assists in retaining a job.

Faceted Black Sapphires

Obsidian

Crystal system	Amorphous
Chemistry	SiO$_2$ Silicon dioxide with impurities
Hardness	5–5.5
Source	Mexico, volcanic regions
Number	1
Zodiac sign	Sagittarius
Planet	Saturn
Beneficial for	Compassion, strength, digestion of anything that is hard to accept, detoxification, blockages, hardened arteries, arthritis, joint pain, cramp, injuries, pain, bleeding, circulation, enlarged prostate, warming the extremities.

The Aztecs fashioned flat sheets of Obsidian into scrying mirrors, and ancient peoples created arrowheads and axes with magical properties. Having no crystalline structure, Obsidian has no boundaries or limitations, working extremely fast with great power. Obsidian's greatest gift is insight into the cause of disease. Mercilessly exposing flaws, weaknesses, blockages, and disempowering conditions, nothing can be hidden. Impelling growth, it lends solid support but needs careful handling and is best used under the guidance of a qualified therapist. Providing deep soul healing, Obsidian goes back to past lives to heal festering emotions or trauma carried forward into the present, bringing depth and clarity to emotions.

A strongly protective stone, Obsidian forms a shield against negativity, providing a grounding cord from the base chakra to the center of the earth. It absorbs negative energies from the environment and blocks psychic attack and negative spiritual influences. Obsidian brings clarity to the mind and clears confusion and constricting beliefs but makes it absolutely clear what lies behind mental distress or disease.

An Obsidian ball is excellent for scrying and divination but requires tact in expressing what is seen.

Raw Obsidian

Note: If Obsidian works too powerfully, remove immediately and use Selenite and Rose Quartz to regain equilibrium.

Black Obsidian

Crystal system	Amorphous
Chemistry	SiO_2 Silicon dioxide with impurities
Hardness	5–5.5
Source	Mexico, volcanic regions
Number	3
Zodiac sign	Sagittarius
Planet	Saturn
Beneficial for	Strength, digestion of anything that is hard to accept, detoxification, blockages, hardened arteries, arthritis, joint pain, cramp, injuries, pain, bleeding, enlarged prostate.

Raw Obsidian

In addition to carrying the generic properties of Obsidian (left), this shamanic stone removes disorder from the body and powerfully draws off negativity and repels curses. Grounding the soul and spiritual forces into the physical plane, Black Obsidian brings them under the direction of the conscious will. Black Obsidian forces facing up to one's true Self, taking you deep into the subconscious mind, magnifying negative energies so that they can be fully experienced and released. This healing effect can work on the ancestral and family line. Reversing previous misuse of power, Black Obsidian addresses power issues on all levels.

Obsidian Wand

Crystal system	Amorphous
Chemistry	SiO_2 Silicon dioxide with impurities
Hardness	5–5.5
Source	Mexico, volcanic regions
Number	1
Zodiac sign	Sagittarius
Planet	Saturn
Beneficial for	Strength, digestion of anything that is hard to accept, detoxification, blockages, hardened arteries, arthritis, joint pain, cramp, injuries, pain, bleeding, circulation, enlarged prostate.

Useful where there are negative energies within the emotional body that require removal and the person is ready for these to surface, an Obsidian wand (see Wands, page 279) facilitates release and protects the aura, connecting to the earth. Obsidian wands can be used for diagnosis and location of blockages. (Each color of Obsidian has its own attributes.)

Obsidian wand

Snowflake Obsidian

Crystal system	Amorphous with complex crystals
Chemistry	SiO_2 Silicon dioxide with impurities (feldspar)
Hardness	5–5.5
Source	Mexico, volcanic regions
Chakra	Sacral
Number	8
Zodiac sign	Virgo
Planet	Saturn
Beneficial for	Releasing "wrong thinking," stressful mental patterns, fear, veins, skeleton, circulation, wound healing, compassion, strength, detoxification, blockages, hardened arteries, arthritis, joint pain, cramp, injuries, pain, bleeding, circulation, warming the extremities.

In addition to carrying the generic properties of Obsidian (page 214), Snowflake Obsidian is a stone of purity, providing balance for body, mind, and spirit. It calms and soothes, making you receptive before bringing to your attention ingrained patterns of behavior and then gently releasing emotional blockages. With the assistance of Snowflake Obsidian, isolation and loneliness become empowering. This stone teaches how to surrender in meditation. Teaching you to value mistakes as well as successes, it shows the gift in experiences and promotes dispassion and inner centering.

Tumbled Snowflake Obsidian

Apache Tear

Crystal system	Amorphous
Chemistry	SiO_2 Silicon dioxide with impurities
Hardness	5–5.5
Source	Mexico, volcanic regions
Chakra	As protection, spleen for women, base for men; cleanses earth
Number	6
Zodiac sign	Aries
Planet	Saturn
Beneficial for	Spontaneity, forgiveness, snakebite, detoxification, assimilation of vitamins C and D, muscle spasm.

Traditionally said to be the tears Native American women shed for their men, Apache Tear heals grief, providing insight into the source of distress and promoting forgiveness. In addition to carrying the generic properties of Obsidian (page 214), this stone gently brings up emotional negativity for transmutation and is excellent for absorbing negative energy and protecting the aura. This stone stimulates analytical capabilities and removes self-limitations.

Natural water-polished Apache Tear

Black Kyanite

Crystal system	Triclinic
Chemistry	Al_2SiO_5 Aluminum silicate
Hardness	5.5–7
Source	USA, Brazil, Switzerland, Austria, Italy, India
Chakra	Aligns all
Number	4
Zodiac sign	Aries, Taurus, Libra
Beneficial for	Reprogramming cellular memory, environmental detoxification, mental cleansing, urogenital and reproductive system, muscles, throat, parathyroid, metaphysical abilities, logical and linear thought, victimhood, frustration, anger, stress, resignation, pain, dexterity, muscular disorders, fevers, thyroid and parathyroid, adrenal glands, brain, blood pressure, infections, excess weight, cerebellum, motor responses, yin–yang balance, larynx, hoarseness, motor nerves.

In addition to the generic properties of Kyanite (page 152), Black Kyanite is a powerful healing stone, said to keep the physical cells connected to the overall divine blueprint in order to maintain optimum health. Assisting in fully incarnating into earth life and moving back into the between-life state to access knowledge of the current life plan and into other lives where necessary, Black Kyanite has been used to access potential future lives to view the results of multiple choices made in the present so that the most constructive future can be created. With its strong links to the earth, it supports environmentalism and links to those who are assisting with the evolution of the earth.

Black Kyanite fan

Tektite

Crystal system	Amorphous
Chemistry	Extraterrestrial
Hardness	Variable
Source	Middle and Far East, Philippines, Polynesia, USA, India, Russia
Chakra	All, corrects spin
Number	9
Zodiac sign	Aries, Cancer
Beneficial for	Fevers, capillaries, circulation, psychic surgery.

A meteorite from outer space, traditionally Tektite has been worn as a fertility talisman. It can reveal past lives and those lived on other planets or planes. Said to encourage extraterrestrial communication and spiritual growth through absorption of higher knowledge, Tektite helps let go of undesirable experiences, remembering the lessons learned. It takes you deep into the heart of a matter, promoting insight into the true cause and necessary action. This stone strengthens the biomagnetic envelope around the body and balances male–female energies within the personality.

See also Moldavite (page 121).

Natural Tektite

Basanite (Black Jasper)

Crystal system	Trigonal
Chemistry	SiO_2 Silicon dioxide with impurities
Hardness	7
Source	Worldwide
Chakra	Earth
Zodiac sign	Scorpio, Capricorn
Beneficial for	Electromagnetic and environmental pollution, radiation, stress, prolonged illness or hospitalization, circulation, digestive and sexual organs, balancing mineral content of the body.

In addition to carrying the generic properties of Jasper (page 45), Black Jasper is a useful scrying stone that takes you deep into an altered state of consciousness and brings about prophetic dreams and visions. It can call up your power animal and has strong links to the Black Panther shamanic line.

Polished Basanite

Hawk's Eye

Crystal system	Trigonal
Chemistry	$NaFe^{+3} (SiO_3)_2$ Silicon dioxide with impurities
Hardness	4–7
Source	USA, Mexico, India, Australia, South Africa
Chakra	Base, third eye
Number	4
Zodiac sign	Leo, Capricorn
Planet	Sun
Beneficial for	Revealing psychosomatic reasons behind a frozen shoulder or stiff neck, circulatory system, bowels, legs, brain hemisphere integration, perception, internal conflicts, pride, willfulness, yin–yang, fatigue, night vision, constrictions.

Placed in the wealth corner of a house or room, Hawk's Eye attracts prosperity. In addition to carrying the generic properties of Tiger's Eye (page 206), this stone assists vision and insight, and increases metaphysical abilities such as clairvoyance. Gently surfacing locked-in emotions and disease from present or past lives, Hawk's Eye dissolves restrictive and negative thought patterns and ingrained behavior. Bringing issues into perspective, it ameliorates pessimism and mitigates the desire to blame others for problems of your own making. Hawk's Eye grounds energy and heals earth energy.

Tumbled Hawk's Eye

Onyx

Crystal system	Trigonal
Chemistry	SiO_2 Silicon dioxide with carbon and iron
Hardness	7
Source	Italy, Mexico, USA, Russia, Brazil, South Africa
Number	6
Zodiac sign	Leo
Planet	Mars, Saturn
Beneficial for	Making wise decisions, self-confidence, centering, vigor, hearing, steadfastness, stamina, grief, overwhelming fears, quelling sexual desire, balancing yin and yang, teeth, bones, bone marrow, blood disorders, feet.

Tumbled Onyx

In ancient times Onyx was believed to have a demon imprisoned within that would awaken at night, sowing discord, especially between lovers. Nowadays, strength-giving Onyx is a protective stone for dark nights and lonely places. Taking you forward to view the future, it facilitates being master of your destiny. A stone of separation that banishes old habits, Onyx is useful when a relationship needs stabilizing or when it has passed its sell-by date and needs releasing. Assisting in keeping your own counsel, Onyx holds memories of what happens to the wearer and can be used for psychometry. Effective in past-life work for healing old injuries and physical trauma affecting the present life, it anchors the flighty into a stable way of life and imparts self-control.

Black Actinolite

Crystal system	Monoclinic
Chemistry	$Ca_2 (MgFe)_5 Si_8 O_{22} (OH)_2$ Calcium magnesium iron silicate hydroxide
Hardness	5.5–6
Source	USA, Brazil, Russia, China, New Zealand, Canada, Taiwan
Chakra	Base
Number	4, 9
Zodiac sign	Scorpio
Beneficial for	Asbestos-related cancers, the immune system, liver, kidneys.

Natural Black Actinolite

In addition to carrying the generic properties of Actinolite (page 104), Black Actinolite can be programmed to remove gently all that is outworn and outgrown, opening the way for new energies to manifest. It is an excellent stone for shielding yourself against your own negative thoughts.

Black Opal

Crystal system	Amorphous
Chemistry	$SiO_2 \cdot nH_2O$ Hydrated silica with impurities
Hardness	5.5–6.5
Source	Australia, Brazil, USA, Tanzania, Iceland, Mexico, Peru, UK, Canada, Honduras, Slovakia
Chakra	Earth
Zodiac sign	Cancer, Libra, Scorpio, Pisces
Beneficial for	Self-worth, strengthening the will to live, intuition, fear, loyalty, spontaneity.

Polished Black Opal

In addition to carrying the generic properties of Opal (page 254), Black Opal is highly prized as a power stone for ritual magic.

Nuummite

Crystal system	Orthorhombic
Chemistry	$(Mg,Fe)_7(Si_8O_{22})(OH,F)_2(Mg,Fe)_5(Al_2O_{22})(OH,F_2)$
Hardness	6
Source	Greenland
Chakra	Past life, soma, opens and integrates all
Number	3
Zodiac sign	Sagittarius
Planet	Pluto
Beneficial for	Change, intuition, insomnia, stress, degenerative disease, tissue regeneration, strengthening triple heater meridian, Parkinson's, limbic brain, headache, insulin regulation, eyes, brain, kidneys, nerves.

Said to be the oldest mineral on earth, Nuummite is the sorcerer's stone. Strengthening the auric shield, it assists in traveling with stealth and sureness. The magic within this powerful stone needs to be used with right intention. Assisting in recognizing past-life contacts and highlighting karmic debts stemming from misuse of power, Nuummite reminds you not to get entangled again. Drawing karmic debris out of the physical and emotional bodies, it quickly restores energy and power. Severing entanglements that stem from previous manipulation or ritual working, it removes difficulties that arise from another person's misguided sense of needing to protect you. Nuummite teaches respect, encouraging you to fulfill only obligations and promises relevant to your life today. This stone aligns the aura with the physical body, and removes mental implants from an extraterrestrial source. Use set in silver.

Polished Nuummite

Black Calcite

Crystal system	Hexagonal
Chemistry	$CaCO_3$ Calcium carbonate
Hardness	3
Source	USA, UK, Belgium, Czech Republic, Slovakia, Peru, Iceland, Romania, Brazil
Chakra	Past life, base, earth
Zodiac sign	Cancer
Beneficial for	Study, motivation, laziness, organs of elimination, calcium uptake in bones, dissolving calcification, skeleton, joints, intestinal conditions.

In addition to carrying the generic properties of Calcite (page 245), Black Calcite is a record-keeper stone that assists in regaining memories so that the past can be released. Encouraging the soul to return to the body after trauma or stress, it alleviates black depression, and is a useful companion during a dark night of the soul.

Natural Black Calcite

Merlinite (Psilomelane)

Crystal system	Hexagonal
Chemistry	SiO_2 Silicon dioxide with impurities
Hardness	7
Source	USA (New Mexico)
Chakra	Past life, soma, higher heart
Number	6
Zodiac sign	Gemini
Planet	Sun, Moon
Beneficial for	Past-life healing, harmony, balancing yin–yang and masculine and feminine energies, conscious and subconscious, intellect and intuition, respiratory system, circulatory system, intestines, heart.

A combination of Quartz (see page 230 for generic properites) and Psilomelane, Merlinite is attuned to the four elements of earth, air, fire, and water and holds the wisdom of shamans, alchemists, magician-priests, and workers of magic. Offering glimpses of the future, this stone supports during shamanic practices or magical ritual, bringing about a successful conclusion. Its dual coloring balances complementarities and blends spiritual and earthly vibrations, accessing multidimensions. A powerful energy cleanser, Merlinite reprograms ingrained patterns of behavior in the mental and emotional etheric blueprints. Reaching into the past, it facilitates reading the Akashic Record, and is excellent for past-life healing. Merlinite can bring magic and luck into your life. Psilomelane is an energy-saving stone that slows down processes and assists in coming to terms with negative experiences.

Polished Merlinite

Hematite

Crystal system	Hexagonal
Chemistry	Fe_2O_3 Iron oxide
Hardness	5.5–6.5
Source	USA, Canada, Italy, Brazil, Switzerland, Sweden, Venezuela, England
Chakra	Earth, base, past life
Number	9
Zodiac sign	Aquarius, Aries
Planet	Saturn
Beneficial for	Timid women, self-esteem, willpower, triple heater meridian, study of mathematics and technical subjects, legal situations, compulsions, addictions, overeating, smoking, overindulgence, stress, hysteria, inflammation, courage, hemorrhage, menstrual flooding, drawing heat from the body, formation of red blood cells, regulating blood, iron absorption, circulatory problems, Reynaud's disease, anemia, kidneys, regenerating tissue, leg cramps, nervous disorders, insomnia, spinal alignment, fractures.

Tumbled Hematite

Said to protect a soldier going into battle, Hematite enhances personal magnetism. It can heal the anger and hurt felt by those who were warriors in previous lives, supporting those who face a karmic battle in the present life. Harmonizing mind, body, and spirit, this effective grounding stone removes excess energy and separates your emotions from those of other people. Worn on the right in right-handed people, it shuts down metaphysical awareness. On the left, it allows metaphysical faculties to remain open. During out-of-body journeying, Hematite protects the soul and guides it back into the body. Strongly yang, it balances meridians, redresses yin imbalances, dissolves negativity, and protects the aura.

Enhancing survival ability, this is an excellent stone for accessing the subconscious mind, drawing attention to unfulfilled desires that drive your life. Assisting in coming to terms with mistakes as learning experiences, it helps face the shadow side of your personality. An excellent booster for the memory, Hematite should not be used where inflammation is present, or for long periods of time.

Unpolished Hematite

Specular Hematite

Crystal system	Hexagonal
Chemistry	Fe_2O_3 Iron oxide
Hardness	5.5–6.5
Source	USA, Canada, Italy, Brazil, Switzerland, Sweden, Venezuela, England
Chakra	Earth, crown
Zodiac sign	Aquarius
Planet	Saturn
Beneficial for	Hemoglobin, anemia, blood disorders. Specular Hematite works best beyond the physical level.

In addition to carrying the generic properties of Hematite (left), Specular Hematite assists in manifesting your own unique spirit here on earth and identifies where your particular talents can best be used. Grounding high-frequency spiritual energies into everyday reality, it shifts the physical vibration of the subtle and physical bodies. This stone counteracts electromagnetic energies and is a useful stone to place by a computer.

Polished Specular Hematite

Galena

Crystal system	Cubic
Chemistry	PbS Lead sulfide
Hardness	2.6
Source	USA, Russia, UK
Number	22
Zodiac sign	Capricorn
Planet	Saturn
Beneficial for	Detoxification, multidimensional cellular healing, inflammation and eruptions, fatty deposits, circulation, veins, joints, assimilation of selenium and zinc, hair.

A "stone of harmony," Galena creates balance on all levels and harmonizes the physical, etheric, and spiritual planes. Facilitating holistic healing, it is excellent for doctors, homeopaths, and herbalists and encourages further investigation and trials. A grounding stone that anchors the soul into incarnation, it assists in centering in oneself. Galena opens up the mind, expanding ideas and dissolving self-limiting mental assumptions from the past.

Note: Galena is a very toxic stone; use with care.

Raw Galena

Molybdenite

Crystal system	Hexagonal
Chemistry	MoS_2 Molybdenum sulfide
Hardness	1–1.5
Source	USA, England, Canada, Sweden, Russia, Australia
Chakra	Third eye
Number	7
Zodiac sign	Scorpio
Beneficial for	Jaw pain, teeth, circulation, oxygenation, immune system.

The name Molybdenite comes from the Greek word *molybdos*, meaning "lead." Known as the dreamer's stone, it integrates the everyday self with the higher self and facilitates spiritual expansion. If you need a healing dream, place Molybdenite under your pillow. Repairing and replenishing the subtle bodies, this stone operates exceptionally well at a mental level. It has a powerful electrical charge that continually recharges and rebalances the body when in its field. Molybdenite eliminates mercury toxicity from the body, and harmonizes mercury fillings to a more beneficial vibration. It is reputed to facilitate intergalactic contact.

Note: Molybdenite is a toxic stone; use with care.

Molybdenite on Quartz matrix

Pyrolusite

Crystal system	Tetragonal
Chemistry	MnO_2 Manganese oxide
Hardness	6–6.5
Source	USA, Germany, Ukraine, South Africa, Brazil, India, UK
Number	7
Zodiac sign	Leo
Beneficial for	Confidence, optimism, determination, bronchitis, metabolism, blood vessels, sexuality, eyesight.

Derived from the Greek for "fire wash," Pyrolusite was used in glass-making to remove iron staining. With the ability to restructure energies, this stone heals energetic disturbances and transmutes disease in all the bodies. Repelling negative energy and dispelling psychic interference, it prevents undue mental influence, dissolves emotional manipulation, and provides a barrier to the attentions of the lower astral worlds. Enabling you to stay true to your own beliefs, this tenacious stone gets to the bottom of problems and facilitates transformation. Offering support during deep emotional healing or bodywork, it releases disease and blockages in the emotional body, and stabilizes relationships.

Raw Pyrolusite on matrix

Stibnite

Crystal system	Orthorhombic
Chemistry	Sb_2S_3 Antimony sulfide
Hardness	2
Source	Japan, Romania, USA, China
Number	8
Zodiac sign	Scorpio, Capricorn
Planet	Saturn
Beneficial for	Astral travel, rigidity, esophagus, stomach.

Named from *stibi*, the Greek word for "antimony," Stibnite was used to separate gold and is excellent for separating out the pure from the dross, and for releasing entity possession or negative energy. In meditation, it provides protection and forms an energetic shield. Helping you see the gold in your center, it illuminates the gift in difficult experiences. Eliminating "tentacles" from clingy relationships, especially after physical separation, it helps tie-cutting and past-life releases and is particularly useful in situations where you find it difficult to say no to a former partner. Stibnite carries the energy of the wolf and can be used to attract and journey with this shamanic power animal.

Note: Stibnite is a toxic stone; use with care.

Natural Stibnite wand

Silver Sheen Obsidian

Crystal system	Amorphous
Chemistry	SiO_2 Silicon dioxide with impurities
Hardness	5–5.5
Source	Mexico, volcanic regions
Chakra	Third eye
Number	2
Zodiac sign	Sagittarius
Planet	Saturn
Beneficial for	Compassion. Works best beyond the physical levels.

In addition to carrying the generic properties of Obsidian (page 214), Silver Sheen Obsidian, a mirror of inner being, enhances meditation and is perfect for scrying. During journeys out of the body, it connects the astral body with the physical and draws the soul back. Silver Sheen Obsidian brings advantages throughout life and imparts patience and perseverance.

Polished Silver Sheen Obsidian

Gray-banded and Botswana Agate

Crystal system	Trigonal
Chemistry	SiO$_2$ Silicon dioxide
Hardness	6
Source	USA, India, Morocco, Czech Republic, Brazil, Africa
Chakra	Crown
Zodiac sign	Scorpio
Planet	Mercury
Beneficial for	Releasing emotional repression, detoxification, sensuality, sexuality, fertility, artistic expression, depression, the brain, assimilating oxygen, emotional trauma, self-confidence, concentration, perception, analytical abilities, aura stabilization, negative-energy transformation.

Polished Gray-banded Agate

Carrying the generic properties of Agate (page 190), Gray-banded and Botswana Agate are very similar in banded appearance and effect, harmonizing the physical body with the subtle bodies, removing dualities, and maintaining well-being. Placed on the third eye, Gray-banded Agate quickly cuts mental cords to a guru, partner, parent, or mentor who retains manipulative control over another soul in the present life, replenishing energy lost in such situations. Protecting the aura, its bands take you traveling into multidimensional realities. If you are easily hurt, it teaches you to look to solutions rather than problems. Giving the broader picture, it assists you to explore unknown territory and your own creativity while at the same time paying attention to detail. Botswana Agate can be programmed to protect you and your family, encouraging a protective love that is objective and nonsmothering. It is said that Gray-banded Agate repels spiders, and it may cause a pleasant giddiness. Botswana Agate is excellent for anyone connected with fire or smoke, especially smokers and those who want to quit.

Polished Botswana Agate

Pumice

Crystal system	Noncrystalline
Chemistry	Not known
Hardness	1
Source	Worldwide
Chakra	Higher heart, solar plexus
Beneficial for	Colonic irrigation, detoxification.

Although not a crystal, Pumice is a powerful healer, releasing pain held in the heart and gut, and long-standing emotional wounds. Assisting toxin release during colonic hydrotherapy, it also removes negative energy from the therapist. Pumice helps defensive people who appear to be abrasive because of the pain they carry, but who actually feel vulnerable inside. Promoting trust and acceptance, this stone gently assists in letting go of protective barriers, letting other people in, and encouraging intimacy on all levels.

Natural sea-worn Pumice

Labradorite (Spectrolite)

Crystal system	Triclinic
Chemistry	$(CaNa)(SiAl)_4O_8$
Hardness	5–6
Source	Italy, Greenland, Finland, Russia, Canada, Scandinavia
Chakra	Third eye, crown, higher crown, soma
Number	6, 7
Zodiac sign	Leo, Scorpio, Sagittarius
Beneficial for	Witness during radionic treatment, aligning physical and etheric bodies, PMS, removing warts (tape and leave in place), vitality, originality, patience, eyes, brain, stress, regulating metabolism, colds, gout, rheumatism, hormones, blood pressure.

Natural Labradorite

A stone of transformation, Labradorite prepares body and soul for the ascension process. This highly mystical and protective stone raises consciousness and deflects unwanted energies from the aura, preventing energy leakage. Holding esoteric knowledge, it takes you into another world or into other lives. This crystal helps banish fears and insecurities and the psychic debris from previous disappointments, strengthening trust in the universe. Labradorite removes other people's projections, including thought forms hooked into the aura. With Labradorite, analysis and rationality are balanced with inner sight. Labradorite is a useful companion through change, imparting strength and perseverance.

Tumbled Labradorite

Polished Labradorite

Additional black and grey stones

Black: *Andradite Garnet (page 192), Cassiterite (page 139), Dendritic Agate (page 101), Diopside (page 104), Garnet (page 47), Hemimorphite (page 197), Magnetite (page 200), Melanite Garnet (page 50), Opal (page 254), Phenacite (page 256), Sardonyx (page 204), Vivianite (page 116), Wavellite (page 123).* **Gray:** *Anhydrite (page 243), Apatite (page 133), Barite (page 244), Black Chalcedony (page 247), Cerussite (page 247), Chiastolite (page 194), Chrysanthemum Stone (page 195), Cinnabar (page 50), Diopside (page 104), Iolite (page 150), Larimar (page 153), Magnesite (page 252), Muscovite (page 31), Onyx (page 219), Petalite (page 255), Smithsonite (page 138), Thulite (page 36), Variscite (page 122), Vivianite (page 116), Zircon (page 261).*

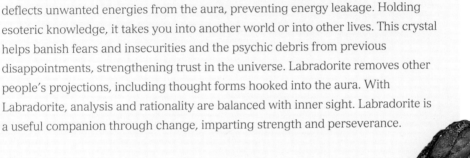

White and colorless crystals

White and colorless stones carry the vibration of pure light, linking to the highest realms of being, and resonate with the higher crown chakra and with the moon. Powerful energizers, they purify and heal the biomagnetic sheath and radiate energy out into the environment.

Quartz

Crystal system	Hexagonal
Chemistry	SiO_2 Silicon dioxide
Hardness	7
Source	Worldwide
Chakra	Harmonizes all, aligns the aura (see different types)
Number	4
Zodiac sign	All
Planet	Sun, Moon
Beneficial for	Energy enhancement, multidimensional cellular memory healing, efficient receptor for programming, enhancing muscle testing, cleansing and enhancing the organs, protecting against radiation, immune system, bringing the body into balance, soothing burns. A master healer for any condition.

Quartz barnacle and bridge cluster

Artificially shaped double-terminated Quartz

Although the Greeks called Quartz *krystallos*, meaning "ice," the name may be Germanic in origin. Prized for millennia as a worker of magic and a potent shamanic tool, Native Americans call it the brain cells of Grandmother Earth. Containing every color, Clear Quartz works on multidimensional levels of being. Generating electromagnetism and dispelling static electricity, it is an extremely powerful healing and energy amplifier. Absorbing, storing, releasing, and regulating energy, a Quartz crystal, when held, doubles your biomagnetic field, and acupuncture needles coated in Quartz increase efficacy by 10 percent. Working at a vibrational level attuned to specific requirements of the user, Quartz takes energy to the most perfect state possible, before the disease set in, acting as a deep soul cleanser, and connects the physical dimension with the mind.

Working like a cosmic computer, Quartz stores information and has the ability to dissolve karmic seeds. It enhances metaphysical abilities and attunes to spiritual purpose.

This stone is found in many shapes and formations, all of which share generic properties but also have specific, and unique, properties. Quartz points and formations have deeply significant shapes according to how fast they formed (pages 272–273).

Close-up of a Quartz cluster that is part of a much larger multidimensional formation.

Quartz Wand

Crystal system	Hexagonal
Chemistry	SiO_2 Silicon dioxide
Hardness	7
Source	Worldwide
Chakra	Harmonizes all, aligns the aura
Zodiac sign	All
Planet	Sun, Moon
Beneficial for	Multidimensional cellular memory healing, efficient receptor for programming, cleansing and enhancing the organs, immune system, bringing the body into balance, energy enhancement. A master healer for any condition.

In addition to carrying the generic properties of Quartz (left) and Wands (page 279), a long, Clear Quartz wand, natural or shaped, emits a positive and negative electrical charge. Strongly amplifying energy, it focuses this where it is needed, or draws it off as appropriate. A Quartz wand reaches the underlying cause of disease and transforms this. It indicates, and treats, areas of blockage or weakness in the physical body or the aura.

Shaped Quartz wand

Laser Quartz

Crystal system	Hexagonal
Chemistry	SiO_2 Silicon dioxide
Hardness	7
Source	Worldwide
Chakra	Harmonizes all, aligns the aura (see different types)
Zodiac sign	All
Planet	Sun, Moon
Beneficial for	Multidimensional cellular memory healing, efficient receptor for programming, energy enhancement, cleansing and enhancing the organs, immune system, bringing the body into balance, psychic surgery. A master healer for any condition.

Naturally formed Laser Quartz is a powerful healing tool that needs purity of intent. In addition to carrying the generic properties of Quartz (left) and Points (page 277), this stone focuses, concentrates, and accelerates energy into a tight beam that is suitable for psychic surgery, stimulating acupuncture points, and reaching tiny structures deep within the body, such as the pineal or pituitary gland, or performing precision work. Detaching entities or attachments and ties to other people, Laser Quartz cuts away negativity, inappropriate attitudes, outmoded thought patterns, and energy blockages, sealing the place where it has been.

Laser Quartz

Candle Quartz

Crystal system	Hexagonal
Chemistry	SiO_2 Silicon dioxide
Hardness	7
Source	Worldwide
Chakra	Heart, soma, cleanses aura
Planet	Moon
Beneficial for	Psychosomatic disease, converting the energy of carbohydrates and nutrients, regulating insulin, headaches.

Looking like melting wax, Candle Quartz is said to be a light-bringer for the planet and those who have incarnated to help the earth change vibration. In addition to carrying the generic properties of Quartz (page 230), it can be used as a scrying stone or for personal illumination. Highlighting soul purpose and focusing the life path, it assists in putting ancient knowledge into practice and brings a guardian angel closer. Making you feel good about yourself and your body, it is useful for those who find physical incarnation difficult. Dissipating feelings of oppression and despair, Candle Quartz creates tranquillity and confidence. Instilling clarity and assisting in looking within to find your truth, Candle Quartz is helpful in understanding how the physical body is damaged by emotional or mental distress, and for healing the heart. A large Candle Quartz can be programmed to attract spiritual abundance.

Natural Candle Quartz, twinflame formation

Cathedral Quartz

Crystal system	Hexagonal
Chemistry	SiO_2 Silicon dioxide
Hardness	7
Source	South America
Chakra	Past life, crown, higher crown
Beneficial for	Exceptional pain relief, rapid healing for minor conditions, energy enhancement, multidimensional cellular memory healing, efficient receptor for programming.

Containing the wisdom of the ages, Cathedral Quartz is a Light Library that gives access to all that has occurred on earth, and is particularly good for working with groups. Many Cathedral Quartzes are extremely large, but even a small piece will give you the information you need. This crystal appears to be composed of several convoluted or separate points, but these are in fact all part of the main crystal. Meditating with Cathedral Quartz aids attunement to the universal mind and assists the evolution of consciousness by raising thought to a higher vibration. In addition to carrying the generic properties of Quartz (page 230), it links into other crystals, amplifying their effects, and acts as a receptor and transmitter for group thought which is raised to a higher vibration. It can be programmed to bring about a better world. Place over the site of pain or disease for rapid relief.

Natural Cathedral Quartz

Elestial Quartz

Crystal system	Hexagonal
Chemistry	SiO_2 Silicon dioxide
Hardness	7
Source	Worldwide
Chakra	Crown, past life, soma, bridges the flow of energy between all
Planet	Moon
Beneficial for	Multidimensional cellular healing, regeneration, restructuring, confusion, spiritual evolution, self-healing, restoring brain cells after drug or alcohol abuse, master healing, energy enhancement, cleansing and enhancing the organs, bringing the body into balance.

Elestial Quartz may contain an inner "skeleton" that can take you into other lives to understand your karma or deep into your Self to give an insight into the spiritual processes at work. In addition to carrying the generic properties of Quartz (page 230), this stone facilitates deep karmic release and brings about core soul-healing and trust in the universe. A stone of change and transformation, rapidly stimulating spiritual and personal evolution and excellent for attuning to the knowledge at the heart of the universe and within one's own soul, Elestial Quartz sets you on your life path. This stone connects to the divine and higher spiritual planes and opens spiritual gifts. A catalyst, it removes blockages and fear, balancing polarities and opening the way to necessary change—which may come about abruptly and unexpectedly. Sustaining and comforting, Elestial Quartz overcomes emotional burdens and can generate enormous healing and clearing energy.

Note: Elestial Quartz is a high-vibration stone.

Clear Elestial Quartz, natural formation

Fenster Quartz

Crystal system	Hexagonal
Chemistry	SiO_2 Silicon dioxide
Hardness	7
Source	Worldwide
Chakra	Soma, past life, harmonizes all, aligns the aura
Zodiac sign	All
Planet	Sun, Moon
Beneficial for	Multidimensional cellular memory healing, cleansing and enhancing the organs.

Fenster Quartz has natural etched triangle formations within the planes of the crystal. These planes can be traversed as an inner landscape and stimulate clairvoyance. In addition to carrying the generic properties of Quartz (page 230), Fenster Quartz heals dysfunctional patterns and outgrown emotions and is excellent for sending healing light and for any energy work that requires a high vibration. It can throw light on the past-life causes of addiction and remove them.

Note: Fenster Quartz is a high-vibration stone.

Fenster Quartz

Faden Quartz

Crystal system	Hexagonal
Chemistry	SiO_2 Silicon dioxide
Hardness	7
Source	Worldwide
Chakra	All, especially crown, soma, past life
Zodiac sign	All
Planet	Moon, Pluto
Beneficial for	Breaks and fractures, stability at all levels, removing cysts and encrustations, back pain, inner alignment.

Named from the German *faden*, after the thread or growth line found within, Faden Quartz may have been created by seismic activity breaking the crystal, which then healed. The resulting thread may hang in a fluid or gaseous chamber within the crystal. It represents the "silver cord" that attaches the subtle body to the physical during out-of-body experiences, and this stone provides protection during such journeys.

In addition to carrying the generic properties of Quartz (page 230), Faden Quartz is helpful during past-life regression, especially when previous lives are viewed from the between-life perspective to provide an overview of soul lessons and root causes of disease, and links to the higher self when seeking answers of all kinds. This positive stone forms chains of connection, and its energy powerfully enhances self-healing and personal growth. Intense internal conflict or trauma is healed by this stone. A "gap bridger," it is useful when working with three or more people, as it harmonizes and attunes group energies, particularly if the intention is to heal something "broken" or to overcome disharmony or conflict. In distance healing it maintains the connection between healer and patient. An excellent stone for communication, it encourages integration of fragmented soul parts and stabilizes emotional instability, bringing insightful growth. This stone has been used to grid areas of unstable earth or physical energy.

Faden Quartz with characteristic "thread"

Sichuan Quartz

Crystal system	Hexagonal
Chemistry	SiO_2 Silicon dioxide with impurities
Hardness	7
Source	China
Chakra	All, especially past life, soma, connects third eye and crown
Zodiac sign	Virgo
Beneficial for	Energy meridians, cellular memory, eating disorders, breaking dependent or codependent relationships, centering in one's Self, energy enhancement.

Double-terminated Black Spot Sichuan Quartz

In addition to carrying the generic properties of Quartz (page 230), Tibetan Quartz (below), and Herkimer Diamond (page 241), Sichuan Quartz has an extremely high vibration and rapidly opens psychic and inner vision. This rareified and yet grounded Quartz has a centered energy that passes rapidly into the body and the personal self, harmonizing the subtle bodies with the physical. Bridging energy gaps along the chakra line, it creates deep healing of the aura and etheric blueprint from which the present physical body devolved. Accessing the Akashic Record to put you in touch with ancient Chinese wisdom, it highlights the past-life reasons for disease or karmic lessons being dealt with in the present life and is beneficial and insightful if held by a healer or past-life therapist while working with a client.

Note: Sichuan Quartz is a high-vibration stone.

Tibetan Black Spot Quartz

Crystal system	Hexagonal
Chemistry	SiO_2 Silicon dioxide with inclusions
Hardness	7
Source	Tibet
Chakra	Harmonizes all, aligns the aura
Zodiac sign	Scorpio
Planet	Sun, Moon
Beneficial for	Energy meridians, eating disorders, breaking of dependent or codependent relationships, centering in one's Self, energy enhancement.

Tibetan Black Spot Quartz

Tibetan Quartz occurs in single and double terminations and may have "black spot" inclusions within it. Carrying the generic properties of Quartz (page 230) and the resonance of Tibet and ancient esoteric knowledge, it accesses the Akashic Record and is extremely useful for ascertaining past-life reasons for disease or the karmic lessons being dealt with in the present life. Beneficial if held by a healer or past-life therapist while working with a client, Tibetan Black Spot Quartz has a strongly centered energy that passes into the body and the personal self, bringing about deep healing of the aura and etheric blueprint and creating multidimensional cellular regeneration.

Tourmalinated Quartz

Crystal system	Complex
Chemistry	Complex combination
Hardness	7
Source	Worldwide
Chakra	Protects and cleanses all, especially base and earth
Zodiac sign	Scorpio
Beneficial for	Energy enhancement; detrimental environmental influences; shadow energies; self-sabotage; problem-solving; harmonizing meridians, aura, and chakras; master healing for any condition; multidimensional cellular memory healing; efficient receptor for programming; protecting against radiation; energy flow.

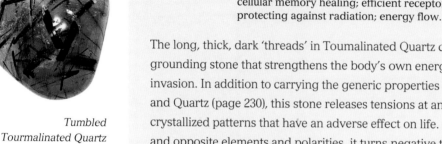

Tumbled Tourmalinated Quartz

The long, thick, dark 'threads' in Tourmalinated Quartz create an effective grounding stone that strengthens the body's own energy field against external invasion. In addition to carrying the generic properties of Tourmaline (page 210) and Quartz (page 230), this stone releases tensions at any level and dissolves crystallized patterns that have an adverse effect on life. Harmonizing disparate and opposite elements and polarities, it turns negative thoughts and energies into positive ones. Tourmalinated Quartz facilitates out-of-body experiences and provides protection while traveling.

Shift Crystal

Crystal system	Hexagonal
Chemistry	SiO_2 Silicon dioxide with impurities
Hardness	7
Source	Worldwide
Chakra	Transforms and harmonizes all, aligns the aura
Zodiac sign	All
Planet	Sun, Moon
Beneficial for	Multidimensional cellular healing, instant change, efficient receptor for programming.

Formed around Calcite that then dissolved to leave a complex, fascinating Quartz landscape (see page 230 for generic properties of Quartz), and thought by some to be created at the edge of tectonic plates, a Shift Crystal does exactly what the name suggests: it rapidly moves you into a new space, and accelerates your spiritual growth. It is the perfect stone to take into meditation or to place under your pillow at night, and you need to be ready to accept whatever it offers. There is no going back with a Shift Crystal, and its effects can be dramatic, particularly as it brings about multidimensional cellular memory healing and can bring hidden matters to the surface for resolution.

Note: Shift Crystal is a high-vibration stone.

Natural formation Shift Crystal

Spirit Quartz

Crystal system	Hexagonal
Chemistry	SiO_2 Silicon dioxide with impurities
Hardness	7
Source	Magaliesberg, South Africa
Chakra	Crown, higher crown, cleanses all (depends on type)
Zodiac sign	Depends on type
Beneficial for	Ascension, rebirthing, self-forgiveness, patience, purifying and stimulating the auric bodies, insightful dreams, reframing the past, blending male and female, yin and yang, healing discord, astral projection, detoxification, obsessive behavior, fertility, skin eruptions, energy enhancement.

In addition to carrying the generic properties of Quartz (page 230) and Drusy Quartz (page 63), Spirit Quartz carries universal love. The covering radiates high-vibration energy, while the core tightly focuses healing. Facilitating smooth transfer between beta and alpha brain waves, it induces deep trance states. Spirit Quartz heals the etheric blueprint and pinpoints significant karmic connections and the gift or karmic justice in situations. After death, Spirit Quartz guides the soul through the different levels of the afterlife to those who are waiting to welcome it home and comforts those left behind. It takes you to meet the spirits of your ancestors and those of the planet, and can be programmed for ancestral healing. Useful for those who give service to others, it facilitates groups and provides insights into community or family discord. Spirit Quartz can be used as a wand to remove negative or diseased energy from the physical or subtle bodies. It cleanses other stones and transfers their energy in a healing layout, or stabilizes earth energies.

Note: Spirit Quartz is a high-vibration crystal.

Fairy Quartz

Crystal system	Hexagonal
Chemistry	SiO_2 Silicon dioxide with impurities
Hardness	7
Source	South Africa
Chakra	Past life, solar plexus, soma
Planet	Sun, Moon
Beneficial for	Detoxifying tissues, pain, nightmares.

A less ethereal stone than Spirit Quartz, the crystals being less prominent and its vibrations more earthy, Fairy Quartz links into the Faery kingdom and the devas. In addition to carrying the generic properties of Quartz (page 230), this stone helps you unravel your family myths and the ancestral or cultural stories in which you are locked. It soothes the environment, removes emotional pain, and calms children after nightmares.

Spirit Quartz

Fairy Quartz

Sugar Blade Quartz

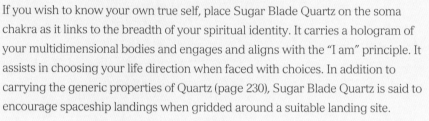
Sugar Blade Quartz

Crystal system	Hexagonal
Chemistry	SiO_2 Silicon dioxide
Hardness	7
Source	South Africa
Chakra	Soma
Zodiac sign	All
Planet	Sun, Moon
Beneficial for	Works best at the nonphysical level.

If you wish to know your own true self, place Sugar Blade Quartz on the soma chakra as it links to the breadth of your spiritual identity. It carries a hologram of your multidimensional bodies and engages and aligns with the "I am" principle. It assists in choosing your life direction when faced with choices. In addition to carrying the generic properties of Quartz (page 230), Sugar Blade Quartz is said to encourage spaceship landings when gridded around a suitable landing site.

Starseed Quartz

Starseed Quartz

Crystal system	Hexagonal
Chemistry	SiO_2 Silicon dioxide
Hardness	7
Source	Worldwide
Chakra	Soma, past life, heart
Beneficial for	Starseed Quartz works at subtle levels

Starseed Quartz can take you to a state of pure form and exceptional clarity. It connects and realigns to the blueprint that informs the etheric blueprint. Reputed to be the perfect crystal for interstellar communication, it assists in traveling the dimensions. It puts you in touch with ancient Lemuria and shows which star you are associated with. Used with Sugar Blade Quartz, it activates the unmanifest, bringing heart and soul into unity and highlighting your purpose in incarnating.

Hematite-included Quartz

Hematite-included Quartz

Crystal system	Complex combination
Chemistry	Complex combination
Hardness	7
Source	Worldwide
Chakra	Solar plexus, base
Beneficial for	Circulation, energizing the blood, energy enhancement, cleansing and enhancing the organs, triple heater meridian, addictions, inflammation, courage, hemorrhage.

In addition to carrying the generic properties of Quartz (page 230) and Hematite (page 222), this is an excellent energizing stone that invigorates, cheers, and rejuvenates. Hematite-included Quartz is particularly useful when you feel at a very low ebb and without hope, as it will restore optimism and faith in the future.

Snow Quartz (Milk Quartz, Quartzite)

Crystal system	Hexagonal
Chemistry	SiO_2 Silicon dioxide
Hardness	7
Source	Worldwide
Chakra	Soma, solar plexus
Zodiac sign	Cancer
Planet	Moon
Beneficial for	Snow Quartz works best at the emotional and subtle levels.

Snow Quartz

Slower and gentler than Clear Quartz (page 230), Snow Quartz assists with letting go of overwhelming responsibilities and limitations and supports you while you are learning lessons. Overcoming martyrdom and victimhood, it is perfect for people who feel put upon while needing to be needed. Enhancing tact and cooperation, it helps you think before you speak. In meditation, it links to deep inner wisdom.

Phantom Quartz

Crystal system	Hexagonal
Chemistry	SiO_2 Silicon dioxide with inclusions
Hardness	7
Source	Worldwide
Chakra	Varies according to color
Zodiac sign	Varies according to color
Planet	Sun, Moon
Beneficial for	Old patterns, hearing disorders, clairaudience, multidimensional healing, efficient receptor for programming, cleansing and enhancing the organs.

Named from the Latin *phantasma*, Phantoms are ghostly crystals encompassed within another, usually but not necessarily Quartz (page 230). They form when a crystal stops growing, mineral dust falls on it, and then the crystal begins to grow again, the mineral inclusion determining the color. Symbolizing universal awareness and the many lifetimes of the soul, this crystal is helpful in making transitions, especially to the next life. Taking you traveling through many dimensions, or into your innermost being, multilayered Phantom strips away the layers to reveal your core. Activating healing abilities and stimulating healing for the planet, a Phantom facilitates accessing the Akashic Record and recovering repressed memories. Taking you into the between-lives state to discover the plan for the current lifetime and to assess the next step, a Phantom accesses information for healing the physical body through the etheric blueprint, and can rearrange detrimental landscape patterns and remove entities. This stone reconciles you to your shadow.

Note: Many Phantoms are high-vibration stones.

Phantom pyramids in Quartz

White Phantom Quartz

Crystal system	Hexagonal
Chemistry	SiO_2 Silicon dioxide
Hardness	7
Source	Worldwide
Chakra	Past life, soma, third eye, harmonizes all, aligns the aura
Planet	Sun, Moon
Beneficial for	Old patterns, hearing disorders, clairaudience, multidimensional healing.

In addition to carrying the generic properties of Phantoms (page 239) and Quartz (page 230), a White Phantom Quartz considerably expands the ability to transmit light and information between the higher realms and the earth, opening the recipient to receive healing across immense distances, particularly when multilayered. It can be used for psychic surgery and to remove layers of past-life karma, opening the way for the karma of grace to operate.

White Phantom Quartz

Desirite

Crystal system	Hexagonal
Chemistry	SiO_2 Silicon dioxide with inclusions
Hardness	7
Source	One mine in South Africa
Chakra	Solar plexus, third eye, heart, sacral, harmonizes all, aligns the aura
Number	44
Zodiac sign	All
Beneficial for	Getting out of old patterns, hearing disorders, clairaudience, multidimensional healing. Works best at the subtle levels.

Rare and newly discovered, Desirite has been dubbed the "as above so below" stone, reflecting the fact that it is both physical and spiritual. In addition to carrying the generic properties of Quartz (page 230), Phantoms (page 239), and Orange Phantoms (page 68), this strongly grounding stone takes you to a very high vibration, each level being accessed successively, the first linking to Native America and Lemuria. Rubbing your thumb up the crystal takes you into profound meditative states, the phantoms acting like elevator stops. Excellent for angel and Ascended Master work, it accesses past lives far back in the history of the planet. As Desirite resonates to the master number 44, it leads into metamorphosis and transmutation on all levels and a recognition of the interweaving of the divine with the spiritual. Desirite is a subtle stone that does not work well as part of a healing layout; it is best used alone or to align and rebalance after a healing session.

Note: Desirite is a high-vibration stone.

Desirite slice

Star Hollandite Quartz

Crystal system	Hexagonal
Chemistry	SiO_2 Silicon dioxide with Goethite inclusions
Hardness	7
Source	Worldwide
Chakra	Third eye, crown, higher crown
Beneficial for	Detoxification, energy enhancement.

Stimulating contact with the stars, star lore, or universal wisdom, Star Quartz brings a depth to meditation that takes you into the oneness of all things. In addition to carrying the generic properties of Quartz (page 230) and Goethite (page 196), this stone assists rational thought and helps disperse tension and anxiety. Drawing off negative energy at the physical and mental levels, it brings about a state of calm acceptance and watchfulness.

Natural Star Hollandite formation

Herkimer Diamond

Small Herkimer Diamond

Crystal system	Trigonal
Chemistry	SiO_2 Silicon dioxide
Hardness	7
Source	USA, Mexico, Spain, Tanzania, India, China
Chakra	Earth, third eye, purifies all
Number	3
Zodiac sign	Sagittarius
Beneficial for	Inner vision, telepathy, stress, detoxification, soul healing, multidimensional cellular healing, protection against radioactivity and disease caused by contact, insomnia from geopathic stress or electromagnetic pollution, corrects DNA, cellular disorders, metabolic imbalances, recall of past-life injuries and disease that affect the present, influenza, throat, bronchitis.

Facilitating soul retrieval and core soul healing, Herkimer Diamond creates a powerful soul shield when journeying or undertaking spiritual work and is a powerful attunement crystal, especially an exceptionally clear stone. It stimulates metaphysical abilities, linking into guidance from higher dimensions, and promotes dream recall. Accessing past-life information so that you recognize blockages or resistance to your spiritual growth, Herkimer gently releases and transforms, bringing your soul's purpose to the fore and activating the light body. Attuning healer and patient, with a crystal memory into which information can be poured for later retrieval, it can be programmed for other people to draw on. Herkimer Diamond is one of the strongest crystals for clearing electromagnetic pollution or radioactivity. Blocking geopathic stress, it is excellent gridded around a house or bed, for which the larger stones should be used. Position between you and the source of electromagnetic smog.

Note: Herkimer Diamond is a high-vibration stone.

Large Herkimer Diamond

Apophyllite

Crystal system	Tetragonal
Chemistry	$KCa_4 (Si_4O_1O)(F)$ $8H_2O$ Hydrous calcium potassium (fluoro) silicate
Hardness	4.5–5
Source	India, USA, Mexico, UK, Australia, Brazil, Czech Republic, Italy
Chakra	Third eye, crown and higher crown
Number	4
Zodiac sign	Gemini, Libra
Beneficial for	Stress reduction, anxiety, worry, fears, respiratory system, asthma, allergies, regeneration of mucous membranes, skin, eyes.

Derived from the Greek *apo*, meaning "off," and *phyllon*, "leaf," Apophyllite flakes when heated. Excellent for stimulating metaphysical abilities, especially scrying and past-life work, its high water content makes it a powerful vibrational transmitter and efficient conductor of energy. A carrier of the Akashic Record, during out-of-body journeys Apophyllite keeps a strong connection with the physical body, anchoring the soul comfortably in incarnation. A stone of truth, promoting introspection and correction of imbalances, Apophyllite abandons pretense and breaks down reserve, bringing recognition of one's true Self. Releasing mental blocks and negative thought patterns, Apophyllite imbues universal love into analysis so that mind is attuned to spirit. Releasing suppressed emotions, it calms apprehension and tolerates uncertainty. Especially helpful in healing the spirit, Apophyllite is the perfect Reiki stone, taking the patient into deeper receptiveness and moving the healer's ego aside so that transmission of healing energy is purer. It is an excellent stone for working with devas, fairies, and the plant kingdom.

Natural Apophyllite cluster

Apophyllite Pyramid

Crystal system	Tetragonal
Chemistry	$KCa_4 (Si_4O_1O)(F)$ $8H_2O$ Hydrous calcium potassium (fluoro) silicate
Hardness	4.5–5
Source	India, USA, Mexico, UK, Australia, Brazil, Czech Republic, Italy
Chakra	Third eye, crown, higher crown, soma
Number	4
Zodiac sign	Gemini, Libra
Beneficial for	Stress reduction, anxiety, worry, fears, respiratory system, asthma, allergies, regeneration of mucous membranes, skin, eyes.

Apophyllite pyramid

In addition to carrying the generic properties of Apophyllite (above), an Apophyllite pyramid amplifies and tightly focuses energy through its point, drawing off negative energy and replacing it with pure light. Place on the third eye when channeling or meditating or the soma chakra to link third eye, crown, and higher crown chakras.

Note: Apophyllite pyramids are high-vibration stones.

Anhydrite

Crystal system	Orthorhombic
Chemistry	$CaSO_4$ Calcium sulfate
Hardness	3–3.5
Source	USA, Brazil, China, Spain, Italy, Australia
Number	5
Zodiac sign	Cancer, Pisces, Scorpio
Beneficial for	Eloquence, self-expression, headaches, throat problems, fluid retention, swellings, cellular memory healing.

Named from the Greek *anhydrous*, "without water," Anhydrite is useful for people who have difficulty being in incarnation and long for the "postdeath" state. Offering support and strength on the earth plane, it assists acceptance of the physical body as a transient vessel for the soul. Helping face with equanimity what tomorrow may bring, this stone teaches acceptance of all that life has brought, releasing any hankering for the past, and is useful for past-life healing. It shows the gift in all that has been.

Natural Anhydrite

Azeztulite

Crystal system	Hexagonal
Chemistry	SiO_2 with impurities
Hardness	7
Source	USA (North Carolina—mined out), England, Canada
Chakra	Third eye, crown, higher crown, soma
Number	1
Zodiac sign	All
Beneficial for	Chronic conditions, revitalizing purpose and will, cancer, cellular disorders, inflammation. Azeztulite's major healing work is at the spiritual vibration, working on chakra connections to higher reality and facilitating a multidimensional vibrational shift.

A rare light-bearing crystal and a form of Quartz (page 230), Azeztulite has an extremely pure vibration that never requires cleansing and is always energized. Attuned to the highest frequencies that it transfers to the earth to aid spiritual evolution, if you are ready, it expands your consciousness, promotes physical ascension, and assists in giving out a positive vibration to benefit others. The vibrational shift it induces is powerful and can create unpleasant side effects until fully assimilated, and denser forms of Azeztulite are now available that work more slowly. Old patterns need to be dissolved and emotional cleansing completed before undertaking this shift. The opaque form has a denser vibration and is a useful intermediary to working with the transparent crystal. Azeztulite facilitates meditation, instantly inducing a state of "no mind" and creating a protective sheath around the physical body. It stimulates the kundalini to rise up the spine.

Note: Azeztulite is a high-vibration stone.

Opaque Azeztulite

Barite

Crystal system	Orthorhombic
Chemistry	$BaSo_4$ Barium sulfate
Hardness	3–3.5
Source	USA, UK, Germany
Chakra	Throat
Number	1
Zodiac sign	Aquarius
Beneficial for	Oversensitivity to cold or temperature change, confusion, memory, shyness, chronic fatigue, detoxification, vision, overcoming addictions, sore throat, calming the stomach.

Natural Barite

Barite derives from the Greek *barys*, meaning "heavy," and was reputedly used by Native Americans to travel from the physical to the spiritual worlds. Stimulating dreaming and dream recall and encouraging the pursuit of dreams, this stone assists in communicating your intuitive vision and heightens your ability to organize and express thought. Strongly motivating, Barite assists people whose energies are scattered or exhausted by the processes of life to recoup energy and focus. A powerful transformer, it can bring about a catharsis and is best used under the supervision of a crystal therapist. Barite strengthens your boundaries and enhances your ability to stand alone. If you have been at the beck and call of others, or conformed to their ideals instead of your own, Barite sets you free. It is beneficial for friendships and insight into your relationships.

See also Celestobarite (page 62), Celestite (page 149) and Desert Rose (page 194).

Clevelandite

Crystal system	Triclinic
Chemistry	$NaAlSi_3O_8$
Hardness	6–6.5
Source	Pakistan
Number	4
Zodiac sign	Libra
Beneficial for	Puberty, menopause, cell membranes, cardiovascular disorders, joints, strokes.

A stone of initiation, Clevelandite links the three phases of the goddess—maiden, mother, and crone—and brings about rebirth. Excellent if you want to bring about a profound life change, Clevelandite helps you focus on exactly what change you need and shows you the gifts and tools you have at your disposal, helping you move forward into the future with equanimity and providing a safe passage for your journey. Clevelandite also assists in turning difficult circumstances into positive, life-affirming situations and can release deeply held emotional fears of abandonment, rejection, and betrayal or the consequences of such experiences.

Clevelandite "wave" formation

Calcite

Crystal system	Hexagonal
Chemistry	$CaCO_3$ Calcium carbonate
Hardness	3
Source	USA, UK, Belgium, Czech Republic, Slovakia, Peru, Iceland, Romania, Brazil
Chakra	Varies according to color
Number	8
Zodiac sign	Cancer
Beneficial for	Study, motivation, laziness, revitalization, emotional stress, organs of elimination, calcium uptake in bones, dissolving calcification, skeleton, joints, intestinal conditions, skin, blood clotting, tissue healing, immune system, growth in small children, ulcers, warts, suppurating wounds.

The name Calcite comes from the Greek *chalx*, meaning "lime." A doubly refractive stone, it splits light entering the stone in two, so that anything viewed through the stone appears double. Many of the artefacts of ancient Egypt were created from Calcite. This stone is a powerful amplifier and cleanser of energy that facilitates higher awareness and metaphysical abilities. Connecting emotions with intellect, it facilitates emotional intelligence and has a positive effect, especially where someone has lost hope. A good mental healer, Calcite calms the mind, teaches discernment and analysis, stimulates insights, and boosts memory.

Shaped Clear Calcite

Natural Clear Calcite

Clear Calcite

Crystal system	Hexagonal
Chemistry	$CaCO_3$ Calcium carbonate
Hardness	3
Source	USA, UK, Belgium, Czech Republic, Slovakia, Peru, Iceland, Romania, Brazil
Chakra	Soma, third eye, cleanses and aligns all
Zodiac sign	Cancer
Planet	Moon
Beneficial for	Study, motivation, laziness, revitalization, emotional stress, organs of elimination, calcium uptake in bones, dissolving calcification, skeleton, joints, intestinal conditions, skin, tissue healing, immune system, growth in small children, ulcers, warts, suppurating wounds.

A "cure-all," especially as an elixir, Clear Calcite brings the gift of deep soul healing and revitalization of the aura. A powerful detoxifier, physically it acts as an antiseptic and at subtle levels it cleanses and aligns all the chakras. In addition to carrying the generic properties of Calcite (above), this stone opens the inner and outer eyes. A clear Calcite with rainbows brings about major change, as it is a stone of new beginnings.

Shaped Clear Calcite

Iceland Spar (Optical Calcite)

Crystal system	Hexagonal
Chemistry	$CaCO_3$ Calcium carbonate
Hardness	3
Source	USA, UK, Belgium, Czech Republic, Slovakia, Peru, Iceland, Romania, Brazil
Chakra	Third eye
Zodiac sign	Cancer
Beneficial for	Cleansing the aura, migraine, eyes, study, motivation, revitalization, emotional stress, organs of elimination, dissolving calcification, skeleton, joints, intestinal conditions, skin, blood clotting, tissue healing, immune system, growth in small children, ulcers, warts, suppurating wounds.

Iceland Spar (see also page 245) amplifies images and assists in seeing reality in a new way. It elucidates the hidden meaning behind words, increases perception, and reminds you that you are a spiritual being on a human journey.

Iceland Spar

Rhomboid Calcite

Crystal system	Hexagonal
Chemistry	$CaCO_3$ Calcium carbonate
Hardness	3
Source	USA, UK, Belgium, Czech Republic, Slovakia, Peru, Iceland, Romania, Brazil
Chakra	Third eye, past life
Zodiac sign	Cancer
Beneficial for	Mental healing, study, motivation, laziness, revitalization, emotional stress, organs of elimination, calcium uptake in bones, dissolving calcification, skeleton, joints, intestinal conditions, skin, blood clotting, tissue healing, immune system, growth in small children, ulcers, warts, suppurating wounds, bringing mental stillness, closing off mind chatter.

Rhomboid Calcite (see also page 245) is a powerful healer of the past.

Natural Rhomboid Calcite

Clear Kunzite

Crystal system	Monoclinic
Chemistry	$LiAl(SiO_2)_2$ (contains lithium)
Hardness	6.5–7
Source	USA, Madagascar, Brazil, Myanmar, Afghanistan
Chakra	Past life, third eye, heart
Zodiac sign	Taurus, Leo, Scorpio
Planet	Venus, Pluto
Beneficial for	Combining intellect, intuition, and inspiration; humility; service; tolerance; self-expression; creativity; stress-related anxiety; bipolar disorder; psychiatric disorders and depression; introspection; immune system; witness for radionic practitioners; anesthetic; circulatory system; heart muscle; neuralgia; epilepsy; joint pain.

Clear Kunzite (see also page 30) aligns the spiritual and physical bodies and repairs the etheric blueprint. It assists in soul retrieval work and in emotional healing, facilitating the journey back to the site of the soul loss. It can be used as a receptacle for the soul part until it is reintegrated into the body.

Clear Kunzite

Cerussite

Crystal system	Orthorhombic
Chemistry	PbCO₃ Lead carbonate
Hardness	3–3.5
Source	Germany, Zambia, Colorado, New Mexico, California, Australia, Namibia
Number	2
Zodiac sign	Virgo
Beneficial for	Jet lag, homesickness, vitality, creativity, integrity, personal responsibility, involuntary movements, Parkinson's, Tourette's syndrome, muscles, bones, insomnia, nightmares. As an elixir: pest control, houseplants.

*Record-keeper
Cerussite on matrix*

Named from the Latin *cerussa*, meaning "white lead," Cerussite may form as a star-shaped crystal or record-keeper (page 273) attuned to higher wisdom and karmic purpose. It facilitates exploring extraterrestrial past lives. Explaining why you came to earth, the lessons and tasks, it highlights gifts you bring to aid evolution, and the people you have met before. It assists in letting go of the past and is a useful grounding stone for feeling comfortable in the environment and adjusting to other cultures. If you need to make compromises, Cerussite aids and imparts the ability to listen attentively. It balances right- and left-brain hemispheres, excellent for the arts.

Note: Cerussite is a toxic stone; use with care.

Chalcedony

Crystal system	Trigonal
Chemistry	SiO₂ Silicon dioxide
Hardness	7
Source	USA, Austria, Czech Republic, Slovakia, Iceland, England, Mexico, New Zealand, Turkey, Russia, Brazil, Morocco
Chakra	Cleanses and aligns all
Number	9
Zodiac sign	Cancer, Sagittarius
Planet	Moon
Beneficial for	Generosity, hostility, lawsuits, nightmares, fear of the dark, hysteria, depression, negative thoughts, turbulent emotions, cleansing, open sores, maternal instinct, lactation, mineral assimilation, mineral build-up in veins, dementia, senility, physical energy, holistic healing, gallbladder, eyes, bones, spleen, blood, circulatory system.

Chalcedony geode

Named for the Greek city Chalcedon, in ancient times chalices carved from Chalcedony and lined with silver were believed to prevent poisoning, and this protective stone guards against accidents and assists in remaining safe during political upheaval. In the 16th century it was prescribed to banish illusions and fantasies. This stone brings mind, body, emotions, and spirit into harmony. A powerful cleanser, it absorbs negative energy and dissipates it to prevent onward transmission. Chalcedony promotes brotherhood and enhances group stability and can be used to assist telepathy. Removing self-doubt and facilitating constructive inward reflection, it creates an open and enthusiastic persona.

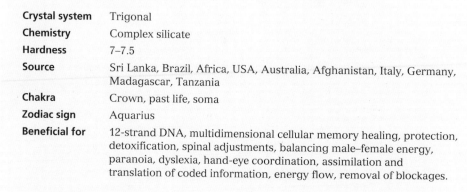

Achroite (Colorless Tourmaline)

Crystal system	Trigonal
Chemistry	Complex silicate
Hardness	7–7.5
Source	Sri Lanka, Brazil, Africa, USA, Australia, Afghanistan, Italy, Germany, Madagascar, Tanzania
Chakra	Crown, past life, soma
Zodiac sign	Aquarius
Beneficial for	12-strand DNA, multidimensional cellular memory healing, protection, detoxification, spinal adjustments, balancing male–female energy, paranoia, dyslexia, hand-eye coordination, assimilation and translation of coded information, energy flow, removal of blockages.

Aligning the meridians of the physical and etheric bodies, Achroite clears and protects the aura. In addition to carrying the generic properties of Tourmaline (page 210), this is a useful stone for healing deep soul damage and for activating the karma of grace. It assists in contact with high spiritual beings and facilitates channeling and automatic writing.

Faceted Achroite

Diamond

Crystal system	Cubic
Chemistry	$C_{11}+(Al,Ca,Cr,Fe,Mg,Mn,Si,Sr,Ti)$ Carbon with impurities
Hardness	10
Source	Africa, Australia, Brazil, India, Russia, USA
Chakra	Activates the crown chakra, linking to divine light
Number	33
Zodiac sign	Aries
Beneficial for	Enlightenment, clarity of mind, imagination, inventiveness, constancy, commitment, fidelity, fearlessness, invincibility, fortitude, mental pain, glaucoma, clears sight, brain, allergies, chronic conditions, metabolism, geopathic stress.

Faceted Diamond

A symbol of purity and love since ancient Greece and said to enhance the love of a husband for his wife, Diamond bonds relationships. One of the Ayurvedic healing gems, these stones were believed to have fallen from the sky after a battle between two dragons. Diamond has perfect cleavage in four directions and was traditionally used to counteract poisons. An amplifier of energy, Diamond never needs recharging and is very effective used with other crystals for healing, as it enhances their power, but can increase negative energy as well as positive. The merciless light of Diamond pinpoints anything that requires transformation. Healing "holes" in the aura and cleansing anything shrouding your inner light, it encourages the soul light to shine and facilitates spiritual evolution. Diamond has been a symbol of wealth for thousands of years and is one of the stones of manifestation, attracting abundance.

Raw Diamond

Elbaite (Multicolored Tourmaline)

Crystal system	Trigonal
Chemistry	Complex silicate
Hardness	7–7.5
Source	Sri Lanka, Brazil, Africa, USA, Australia, Afghanistan, Italy, Germany, Madagascar
Chakra	Crown and higher crown
Number	8
Zodiac sign	Gemini
Beneficial for	Imagery, dreams, creativity and enhanced imagination, immune system, metabolism, protection, detoxification, spinal adjustments, balancing male–female energy, paranoia, dyslexia, hand-eye coordination, assimilation and translation of coded information, energy flow, removal of blockages.

Natural Elbaite

In addition to carrying the generic properties of Tourmaline (page 210), Elbaite contains all colors and, as a result, it brings the mind, body, spirit, and soul into wholeness, providing a gateway into the inner being and facilitating accessing the higher spiritual realms.

Agrellite

Crystal system	Triclinic
Chemistry	$NaCa_2(Si_4O_1O)F$
Hardness	5.5
Source	Canada
Chakra	Third eye
Number	44
Zodiac sign	Aquarius
Beneficial for	Immune system, bruises, infections, chemotherapy, overalkalinity.

Agrellite is an extremely effective stone for bringing hidden matters to the surface, including things repressed deep within your psyche that block soul growth. It helps you face your own inner saboteur and access untapped potential. Agrellite shows where you have been controlling others and encourages self-respect and independence.

This stone detects blockages within the physical body or aura with a distinctive energetic response, although other crystals may be required to heal the condition. Agrellite enhances distance healing and makes a patient more receptive to radionic treatment.

Natural Agrellite formation

Halite

Crystal system	Cubic
Chemistry	NaCl Sodium chloride
Hardness	2
Source	USA, France, Germany
Chakra	Crown (varies according to color)
Number	1
Zodiac sign	Cancer, Pisces
Beneficial for	Anxiety, detoxification, metabolism, water retention, intestinal problems, bipolar disorders, respiratory disorders, skin.

A stone of purification and evolution on the physical and spiritual planes, Halite is a dissolvable salt and symbolizes spiritual discernment. Protecting against negative energies, entity attachment, or psychic attack, Halite dissolves old behavior patterns, negative thoughts, and emotions. It draws out impurities at all levels and creates balance. Overcoming feelings of abandonment or rejection, this stone promotes well-being and increases goodwill. Halite stimulates the meridians of the body and can be used to enhance acupuncture or acupressure.

Natural Halite

Dalmatian Stone (Aplite)

Crystal system	Monoclinic
Chemistry	Complex combination
Hardness	5–7.5
Source	Mexico
Number	9
Zodiac sign	Gemini
Beneficial for	Animals, balancing yin–yang, mood elevation, nightmares, athletes, fidelity, cartilage, nerves and reflexes, sprains.

A protective influence, Dalmatian Stone is said to sound a warning when danger is near. Helping you get out of your head and into your body, grounding and centering Dalmatian Stone physicalizes the soul, assisting in coming joyfully into incarnation. Harmonizing your emotions, it maintains composure and helps avoid overanalysis. Dalmatian Stone helps you to move forward in life, but at the same time it allows you to reflect on potential actions and plan with care. A fortifying stone, it stimulates your sense of fun and is an excellent pick-me-up. This stone transmutes negative energy and outgrown patterns.

Tumbled Dalmatian Stone

Moonstone

Crystal system	Monoclinic
Chemistry	$K(AlSi_3O_8)+Na,Fe,Ba$
Hardness	6
Source	India, Sri Lanka, Australia
Chakra	Soma, third eye, solar plexus
Number	4
Zodiac sign	Cancer, Libra, Scorpio
Planet	Moon
Beneficial for	Hyperactive children, deep emotional healing, disorders of upper digestive tract related to emotional stress, anxiety, female reproductive cycle, menstrual-related disease and tension, conception, pregnancy, childbirth, breastfeeding, PMS, digestive and reproductive systems, pineal gland, hormonal balance, fluid imbalances, the biorhythmic clock, shock, assimilation of nutrients, detoxification, fluid retention, degenerative conditions, skin, hair, eyes, fleshy organs, insomnia, sleepwalking.

Polished Moonstone

Natural Moonstone

Said to protect sailors at sea and travelers on water, Moonstone is more potent during a waxing moon and less so during the waning. This is the stone to use if you seek to embody the goddess. Activating intuition, care has to be taken that it does not induce illusions or an overwhelming emotional or psychic feeling. Like the moon, the stone is reflective and reminds you that everything is part of a cycle of change. Lessening a tendency to overreact emotionally, Moonstone can also amplify emotions in sensitive people at full moon, especially those picked up from other people. This stone encourages lucid dreaming, especially at full moon, and has traditionally been used to enhance metaphysical abilities and to develop clairvoyance. A stone of new beginnings, Moonstone is filled with receptive, passive, feminine energy. It balances male–female energies and assists men who want to get in touch with their feminine side. It is the perfect antidote for the excessively macho man—or aggressive female. Opening the mind to sudden and irrational impulses, serendipity, and synchronicity, placed on the solar plexus it draws out old emotional patterning.

Rainbow Moonstone

Crystal system	Monoclinic
Chemistry	$K(AlSi_3O_8)+Na,Fe,Ba$
Hardness	6
Source	India, Sri Lanka, Australia
Chakra	All
Number	77
Zodiac sign	Cancer
Planet	Moon
Beneficial for	Internal organs, eyes, arteries and veins.

Polished Rainbow Moonstone

In addition to carrying the generic properties of Moonstone (above), Rainbow Moonstone houses a spiritual being that carries the vibration of light and spiritual healing for the whole of humanity, reminding you that you are part of an ongoing, ever-unfolding "cycle of cycles." Linking you to your overall lives-plan as well as the current life plan, it helps you see the unseen, read symbols and synchronicities intuitively, and open yourself to spiritual gifts.

Tumbled Rainbow Moonstone

Magnesite

Crystal system	Hexagonal
Chemistry	$MgCo_3$ Magnesium carbonate
Hardness	3.5–4.5
Source	Russia, USA, Austria, Italy, China, Brazil
Chakra	Third eye, heart
Number	3
Zodiac sign	Aries
Beneficial for	Emotional stress; intolerance; irritability; magnesium absorption; detoxification; body odor; harmonizing brain hemispheres; antispasmodic; muscle relaxant; menstrual, stomach, intestinal, and vascular cramps; gallbladder and kidney stones; bone and teeth disorders; epilepsy; headaches; migraine; slowing blood clotting; fat metabolism; cholesterol; arteriosclerosis; angina; heart disease; body temperature; fevers; chills.

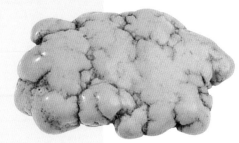

Brain-form Magnesite

Tumbled Magnesite

Named from the Latin *magneus carneus,* or "flesh magnet," Magnesite practices unconditional love in situations where relationships with other people are difficult because of behavior or addictions. This stone assists standing in your own center, placidly accepting the other person without requiring them to change or being affected by their difficulties. Magnesite also helps you love yourself—necessary before you can accept love from others. This stone surfaces self-deceit, helping you recognize unconscious thoughts and feelings and inducing a positive attitude to life. Magnesite shows egotistical people how to take a back seat and teaches how to listen attentively to others. The brainlike form has a powerful effect on the mind and all forms bring a calming effect to the emotions.

Okenite

Crystal system	Triclinic
Chemistry	$CaH_2Si_2O_6 \; H_2O$ Zeolite
Hardness	4.5–5
Source	India, Iceland, Greenland, Chile, USA
Number	7
Zodiac sign	Virgo, Sagittarius
Beneficial for	Blood flow, lactation, circulation in the upper body, fever, nervous disorders, skin eruptions.

A stone of karmic grace, Okenite teaches that everything is part of the cycle of learning the soul's lessons and, evolving from that knowledge, nothing has to be endured forever. Bringing deep self-forgiveness, it assists in completing karmic cycles and eases karmic guilt. When you have done all you can, you can step out of a situation without incurring further karmic debt. Okenite clears obstacles from your path and promotes the stamina to finish your life tasks. As a stone of truth, it instills integrity and protects from the harshness that can arise when others speak their truth. Okenite releases old patterns and brings in more appropriate beliefs. It is helpful for anyone suffering from prudishness, especially where this is linked to past-life vows of chastity.

Okenite on matrix

Menalite

Crystal system	Unknown
Chemistry	Unknown
Hardness	9
Source	USA, Africa, Australia
Chakra	Sacral
Number	6
Zodiac sign	Cancer, Libra, Scorpio, Pisces
Beneficial for	Fertility, menopause, menstruation, lactation.

Natural Menalite formation

Chalky white Menalites resemble power animals or ancient fertility goddesses and are not dissimilar to flint in their core. This nurturing stone provides a powerful link to the Earth Mother, taking you back into her womb and reconnecting to wise femininity and to the power of the priestess. It is the perfect stone for the rites of the passage that mark out the transitions of womanhood. This deeply shamanic stone has been used for eons to journey to other realms and to remember your soul.

Natural Menalite formation

Novaculite

Crystal system	Trigonal
Chemistry	SiO_2 Silicon dioxide
Hardness	6–7
Source	USA
Chakra	Crown and higher crown; opens, energizes, and aligns all
Number	5
Zodiac sign	Scorpio
Beneficial for	Etheric body, obtaining a new perspective, depression, obsessive disorders, warts, moles, chills, cellular structure, elasticity, healthy skin, multidimensional healing.

Extremely fine microcrystalline Quartz, Novaculite is named from the Latin *novacula*, meaning "razor," and this stone was used over 3,000 years ago to make spear points and arrow tips. Traditionally a whetstone to sharpen metals, it hones the soul and the psyche. Helpful in finding the gift in any situation no matter how dire, Novaculite has an extremely high energy that facilitates angelic contact and spiritual journeying. The ultimate cord-cutting tool, gliding through blockages and problems, it can be used at the chakras or on the etheric body for psychic surgery. An excellent conductor of electromagnetic energy, Novaculite amends the etheric blueprint. Helpful to those who sell services to others, it brings buyer and seller together and enhances personal magnetism. It is reputed to boost interstellar contact and decipher ancient languages.

Novaculite flake

Note: Novaculite is a high-vibration stone. Be careful when you handle it, as it is extremely sharp.

Opal

Crystal system	Amorphous
Chemistry	$SiO_2 \, nH_2O$ Hydrated silica with impurities
Hardness	5.5–6.5
Source	Australia, Brazil, USA, Tanzania, Iceland, Mexico, Peru, UK, Canada, Honduras, Slovakia
Chakra	Varies according to color
Number	8
Zodiac sign	Cancer, Libra, Scorpio, Pisces
Beneficial for	Self-worth, strengthening the will to live, intuition, fear, loyalty, spontaneity, female hormones, menopause, Parkinson's, infections, fevers, memory, purifying blood and kidneys, regulating insulin, childbirth, PMS, eyes, ears, earth healing.

Opal enhances cosmic consciousness and induces metaphysical and mystical visions. When programmed, Opal makes you "invisible" and is useful when venturing into dangerous places, including shamanic work where stealth is required. Absorbent and reflective, it picks up thoughts and feelings, amplifies them, and returns them. A karmic stone, it teaches that what you put out comes back. This stone brings characteristics to the surface for transformation. A seductive stone, Opal has always been associated with love and passion, desire and eroticism, but you need to be centered before using Opal to explore or induce feelings or to have other stones standing by to aid integration. Opal heals the earth's energy field, repairing depletions and reenergizing and stabilizing the grid.

Polished Opal

Clear Topaz

Crystal system	Orthorhombic
Chemistry	$Al_2 (SiO_4)(F, OH)_2$ Aluminum hydroxyl fluoro
Hardness	8
Source	USA, Russia, Mexico, India, Australia, South Africa, Sri Lanka, Pakistan, Myanmar, Germany
Chakra	Crown, higher crown, past life, soma
Zodiac sign	Sagittarius
Planet	Sun, Jupiter
Beneficial for	Astuteness, problem-solving, honesty, forgiveness, self-realization, emotional support, manifesting health, digestion, anorexia, sense of taste, nerves, metabolism, skin, vision.

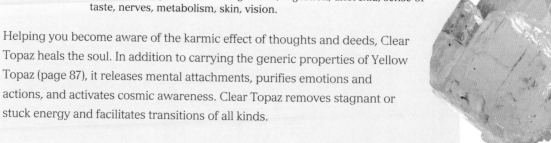

Helping you become aware of the karmic effect of thoughts and deeds, Clear Topaz heals the soul. In addition to carrying the generic properties of Yellow Topaz (page 87), it releases mental attachments, purifies emotions and actions, and activates cosmic awareness. Clear Topaz removes stagnant or stuck energy and facilitates transitions of all kinds.

Tumbled Clear Topaz

Natural Clear Topaz

Goshenite (Clear Beryl)

Crystal system	Hexagonal
Chemistry	$Be_3Al_2Si_6O_{18}$
Hardness	7.5–8
Source	USA, Brazil, China, Ireland, Switzerland, Australia, Czech Republic, France, Norway
Chakra	Crown, past life, soma
Number	3
Zodiac sign	Libra
Planet	Moon
Beneficial for	Nausea, eyesight, pain, courage, stress, overanalysis, elimination, pulmonary and circulatory systems, sedation, resistance to toxins and pollutants, liver, heart, stomach, spine, concussion, throat infections.

Raw Goshenite

In addition to carrying the generic properties of Beryl (page 81), Goshenite is useful in past-life healing or regression. It highlights pain or karma repeating in the present life and facilitates clearing the pattern. Instilling composure and a sense of being in control whatever the circumstances, it counteracts outside influences, particularly where these are manipulating your life. If you need to become more focused, Goshenite increases your efficiency. It brings the same focused energy to learning situations.

Petalite

Crystal system	Monoclinic
Chemistry	$LiAlSi_4O_1O$
Hardness	6–6.5
Source	Brazil, Madagascar, Namibia
Chakra	Higher crown, throat, soma, third eye
Number	7
Zodiac sign	Leo
Beneficial for	Stress relief, stabilizing the pulse, depression, endocrine system, triple heater meridian, AIDS, cancer, cells, eyes, lungs, muscular spasm, intestines. Works best at subtle levels.

Raw Petalite

Named from the Greek for "leaf," Petalite is sometimes known as the Angel Stone because it enhances angelic connection. A shamanic stone that opens cosmic consciousness, it provides a safe environment for spiritual contact or a vision quest and facilitates spiritual purification, taking you to a dimension from which causes can be ascertained and transmuted. Particularly useful for ancestral and family healing, it reaches back to a time before the dysfunction arose and releases negative karma. Clearing entities from the aura or the mental body, Petalite is extremely helpful during tie-cutting, as it brings the higher selves of each person into the process and overcomes manipulation at any level. This stone enhances the environment and neutralizes black magic.

Note: Petalite is a high-vibration stone.

Natural Phenacite

Phenacite

Crystal system	Trigonal
Chemistry	Be_2SiO_4
Hardness	7.5–8
Source	Madagascar, Russia, Zimbabwe, USA (Colorado), Brazil
Chakra	Crown and higher crown
Number	9
Zodiac sign	Gemini
Beneficial for	Multidimensional healing. Works beyond the physical plane.

An extremely powerful activator for the crown and higher crown chakras, Phenacite produces a "fountain effect" in which golden energy pours in from the highest realms of being. It assists in understanding the deepest meaning of a dream *as it is occurring*. It takes you to the core of a problem and can assist in traveling back to before it occurred, in this or any other life, to reframe the whole experience and move forward as though it had never happened. With one of the highest crystal vibrations yet discovered, Phenacite connects personal consciousness to a supra-frequency and contacts the angelic realms and the Ascended Masters. It resonates with the etheric body, activates the light body, and facilitates the ascension process. This crystal heals the soul. With different properties depending on its source and color, Madagascan Phenacite is interdimensional and intergalactic, while that from Brazil often has its own "crystal guardian." Phenacite works at a subtle level, purifying the body and clearing energy pathways. Downloading information from the Akashic Record via the etheric blueprint, it activates healing from the etheric body to the physical and brings about multidimensional cellular healing. Phenacite has the power to amplify the energy of other healing crystals.

Note: Phenacite is a high-vibration stone.

Clear Phenacite

Crystal system	Trigonal
Chemistry	Be_2SiO_4
Hardness	7.5–8
Source	Madagascar, Russia, Zimbabwe, USA (Colorado), Brazil
Chakra	Crown, higher crown
Number	9
Zodiac sign	Gemini
Beneficial for	Multidimensional healing. Works beyond the physical level.

In addition to carrying the generic properties of Phenacite (above), Clear Phenacite assists in interdimensional travel and facilitates accessing vibratory spiritual states that would not normally be reached from earth. It activates memories of earlier spiritual initiations and teaches that "like attracts like," urging you to raise your vibrations, purify your thoughts, and put out only positive energy. The spirit of this stone is profoundly joyful and teaches that life, and spiritual evolution, should be fun.

Note: Phenacite is a high-vibration stone.

Clear Phenacite

White Jade

Crystal system	Monoclinic
Chemistry	$Na(AlFe)Si_2O_6$
Hardness	6
Source	USA, China, Italy, Myanmar, Russia, Middle East
Chakra	Third eye, crown
Zodiac sign	Gemini
Planet	Venus
Beneficial for	Longevity, self-sufficiency, detoxification, filtration, elimination, cellular and skeletal systems, stitches, hips, water–salt–acid–alkaline ratio.

In addition to carrying the generic properties of Jade (page 120), White Jade directs energy in the most constructive way possible. It filters distractions to achieve optimum results, and assists in decision-making as it accesses all relevant information. It is a very pure stone.

Selenite

Crystal system	Monoclinic
Chemistry	$CaSo4_{-2}$ (H_2O) Hydrated calcium sulfate
Hardness	2
Source	England, USA, Mexico, Russia, Austria, Greece, Poland, Germany, France, Sicily
Chakra	Higher crown
Number	8
Zodiac sign	Taurus
Planet	Moon
Beneficial for	Judgment, insight, aligning the spinal column, flexibility, epilepsy, mercury poisoning from dental amalgam, free radicals, breastfeeding. Its finest healing occurs at the energetic levels.

The name Selenite derives from the Greek moon goddess, Selene, and means "moonlike glow." With a very fine vibration, Selenite induces clarity of mind and accesses angelic consciousness. This crystal anchors the light body in the earth vibration. The purest translucent white Selenite has an ethereal quality and is said to inhabit the space between light and matter.

An ancient stone, it is one of the most powerful crystals for the new vibration on earth and can be used for scrying, to see the future or to ascertain what has occurred in the past. A powerful disperser and stabilizer for erratic emotions, it brings about a conscious understanding of what is taking place at the subconscious level. Selenite creates a protective grid around a house, and a large piece placed in the house ensures a peaceful atmosphere.

Note: Selenite is a high-vibration stone.

Shaped Selenite pillar with key "gateway"

Angel's Wing (Fishtail Selenite)

Crystal system	Monoclinic
Chemistry	$CaSO_{4\text{-}2}$ (H_2O) Hydrated calcium sulfate
Hardness	2
Source	England, USA, Mexico, Russia, Austria, Greece, Poland, Germany, France, Sicily
Chakra	Higher crown
Zodiac sign	Pisces
Planet	Moon
Beneficial for	Nerve healing, repairing 12-strand DNA, core soul healing, insight, aligning the spinal column, flexibility, epilepsy, mercury poisoning from dental amalgam, free radicals, breastfeeding. Its finest healing occurs at the energetic levels.

Natural Angel's Wing

In addition to carrying the generic properties of Selenite (page 257), Angel's Wing facilitates angelic contact and is extremely calming, stabilizing emotions and defusing tension.

Note: Angel's Wing is a high-vibration stone.

Selenite Wand

Crystal system	Monoclinic
Chemistry	$CaSO_{4\text{-}2}$ (H_2O) Hydrated calcium sulfate
Hardness	2
Source	England, USA, Mexico, Russia, Austria, Greece, Poland, Germany, France, Sicily
Chakra	Higher crown
Zodiac sign	Taurus and Pisces
Planet	Moon
Beneficial for	Aligning the spinal column, flexibility, epilepsy, mercury poisoning from dental amalgam, free radicals. Its finest healing occurs at the energetic levels.

In addition to carrying the generic properties of Wands (page 279) and Selenite (page 257), Selenite wands have a very pure vibration and detach entities or thought forms from the aura and prevent anything external from influencing the mind. Long and delicate natural Selenite wands are sometimes attached to another crystal to form a powerful healing tool that resonates at a high frequency and imparts deep wisdom and ancient knowledge.

Note: Selenite wands are high-vibration stones.

Natural Selenite wand

Selenite Scepter

Crystal system	Monoclinic
Chemistry	$CaSo_{4}\text{-}_{2}(H_{2}O)$ Hydrated calcium sulfate
Hardness	2
Source	Usually manufactured and shaped, occasionally natural in England
Chakra	Higher crown
Zodiac sign	Taurus
Planet	Moon
Beneficial for	Judgment, insight, aligning the spinal column, flexibility, epilepsy, mercury poisoning from dental amalgam, free radicals. Its finest healing occurs at the energetic levels.

This is a rare and difficult-to-find scepter. In addition to carrying the generic properties of Scepters (page 273) and Selenite (page 257), a Selenite scepter can be used to cut out diseased or damaged parts of the etheric blueprint that carry the imprint of past-life wounds from the physical or emotional level and which have impinged on the present-life body.

Note: Selenite scepters are high-vibration stones.

Natural Selenite Scepter

Selenite Phantom

Crystal system	Monoclinic
Chemistry	$CaSo_{4}\text{-}_{2}(H_{2}O)$ Hydrated calcium sulfate with inclusions
Hardness	2
Source	England, USA, Mexico, Russia, Austria, Greece, Poland, Germany, France, Sicily
Chakra	Past life, higher crown, soma, solar plexus
Zodiac sign	Taurus
Planet	Moon
Beneficial for	Spinal column alignment, joint flexibility, insight, flexibility, epilepsy, mercury poisoning from dental amalgam, free radicals, breastfeeding, old patterns, hearing disorders, clairaudience, multidimensional healing, multidimensional cellular memory healing, efficient receptor for programming, cleansing and enhancing the organs, bringing the body into balance. Its finest healing occurs at the energetic levels.

Carrying the generic properties of Selenite (page 257) and acting in a similar manner to other Phantoms (page 239), this rare formation strips away all that has been overlaid on the soul core and, when working at the highest spiritual vibration, Selenite Phantom can connect to the true spiritual Self and its overall evolutionary purpose. Selenite Phantom clears mental and spiritual confusion and removes karmic entanglements. The point cuts through karmic debris, especially when used as a wand to draw it off, and emotional disease and the insights gained can be grounded and earthed into the physical body with the wider end of the Phantom.

Note: Selenite Phantom is a high-vibration stone.

Selenite Phantom

Spinel

Crystal system	Cubic
Chemistry	$MgAl_2O_4$ Magnesium aluminum oxide
Hardness	7.5–8
Source	Sri Lanka, Myanmar, Canada, USA, Brazil, Pakistan, Sweden (may be synthetic)
Chakra	Varies according to color, colorless higher crown
Number	3 (varies according to color), colorless 7
Zodiac sign	Aries, Sagittarius (varies according to color)
Planet	Pluto
Beneficial for	Muscular and nerve conditions, blood vessels.

Derived from the Latin *spina*, meaning "thorn," Spinel opens the chakras and facilitates movement of kundalini energy up the spine. This stone offers energy renewal, encouragement in difficult circumstances, and rejuvenation. Enhancing positive aspects of the personality, it facilitates achieving and accepting success with humility.

Stilbite

Crystal system	Monoclinic
Chemistry	$Ca(A_{12}Si_7O_{18}$ y H_2O $NaCa_4)$ $(Al_9Si_{27})O_{72}$ $3O- H_2O$ Zeolite
Hardness	3.5–4.0
Source	India, Iceland, Russia, USA, Brazil
Number	33
Zodiac sign	Aries
Beneficial for	Detoxification, brain disorders, ligaments, laryngitis, loss of taste, pigmentation in the skin.

From the Greek *stilbein*, meaning "to shine," Stilbite contains information about the soul and its component parts and is of assistance in deep soul healing. A highly creative stone that opens the intuition and carries a loving and supportive vibration in any endeavor, Stilbite facilitates multidimensional metaphysical working. Grounding spiritual energy, it manifests intuitive thought and assists spiritual journeying. The stone gives guidance and direction throughout the journey, no matter where the destination may lie. At its highest vibration, it facilitates traveling into the upper spiritual realms, bringing back the conscious memory of one's experiences there. Stilbite crystal clusters can be used as a scrying tool. Traditionally, Stilbite was used to counteract poisons.

Natural Stilbite formation

Zeolite

Crystal system	Monoclinic
Chemistry	Hydrous silicate
Hardness	Varied
Source	UK, Australia, India, Brazil, Czech Republic, Italy, USA
Chakra	All
Zodiac sign	All
Beneficial for	Agriculture, gardening, Reiki, detoxification, goiter, addictions, bloating.

Zeolite cluster

The generic name for a group of crystals with powerful detoxification properties, Zeolite creates a protective filter for the crown chakra and acts as a gatekeeper during spiritual work or brings a blown chakra back online. Enhancing the environment, it absorbs toxins and odors. Buried in the ground, this stone benefits agriculture and gardening. A Reiki stone that assists attunement to the energies and symbols, Zeolite enhances the response to the healing.

See also Apophyllite (page 242), Heulandite (page 38), Larimar (page 153), Okenite (page 252), Prehnite (page 122), Stilbite (page 260).

Zircon

Crystal system	Tetragonal
Chemistry	$ZrSiO_3$ Zirconium silicate
Hardness	6.5–7.5
Source	Australia, USA, Sri Lanka, Ukraine, Canada (may be heat-treated to intensify color)
Chakra	Varies according to color; unites base, solar plexus, and heart
Number	4
Zodiac sign	Sagittarius
Planet	Sun
Beneficial for	Synergy, constancy, jealousy, possessiveness, victimization, homophobia, misogyny, racism, sciatica, cramp, insomnia, depression, bones, muscles, vertigo, liver. (*Zircon may cause dizziness in those who wear pacemakers or are epileptic—if so, remove immediately.*)

The name Zircon comes from *zargun*, a Persian word meaning "gold-colored," but some colors are heat-amended. Traditionally it was used to protect against robbery, lightning, bodily harm, and disease. Known as a Stone of Virtue, Zircon was said to test for celibacy. Promoting unconditional love and assisting in letting go of previous partners, Zircon harmonizes the spiritual nature together with the environment and brings all the systems of the physical and subtle bodies into alignment. Overcoming prejudice, Zircon teaches the brotherhood of humanity and clears the effects of discrimination from the emotional body. A stone of union, it instills stamina and tenacity of purpose. This stone enhances clear thinking and separates the significant from the insignificant. Cubic Zircon (the man-made form) has considerably diluted powers.

Combination stones

Combination stones, as might be expected, bring together the qualities of the component crystals, but the whole is greater than its parts. It is as though the stone moves to a higher vibration and becomes more effective. The larger, decorative stones are particularly useful as environmental enhancers, and smaller pieces make excellent healing stones.

Red Feldspar with Phenacite

Crystal system	Complex combination
Chemistry	Complex combination
Hardness	Variable
Source	Madagascar, Russia, Zimbabwe, USA (Colorado), Brazil
Chakra	Crown, higher crown
Number	9
Zodiac sign	Gemini
Beneficial for	Multidimensional healing. Works beyond the physical plane.

Tumbled Red Feldspar with Phenacite

In addition to carrying the generic properties of Phenacite (page 256), Red Feldspar with Phenacite is a powerfully spiritual stone and the key to changing your reality. Heightening self-awareness and the ability to love yourself unconditionally, it firmly grounds spiritual insight into the earth plane to be expressed through your physical body. The spirit of this stone is light and fun, and reminds you that spiritual evolution and life on earth do not have to be taken too seriously; it can be a joyful journey. Red Feldspar with Phenacite can accompany you back into a dream, pointing out the deeper implications as you go and reworking the dream to bring about a fruitful outcome. The Feldspar constituent of this stone is extremely useful in letting go of the past, especially of ingrained mental and spiritual patterns from past lives, enabling the Phenacite to open the way to a much more dynamic and exciting way of being.

Note: Red Feldspar with Phenacite is a high-vibration stone.

Black Tourmaline with Lepidolite

Crystal system	Complex combination
Chemistry	Complex combination
Hardness	Variable
Source	Worldwide
Beneficial for	Debilitating disease, immune system, dyslexia, arthritis, pain relief, realigning spinal column, protection, detoxification, spinal adjustments, balancing male–female energy, paranoia, dyslexia, hand-eye coordination, assimilation and translation of coded information, energy flow, removal of blockages, addictions, emotional or mental dependency, bipolar disorders, nightmares, obsessive thoughts, restructuring DNA, detoxification of skin and connective tissue, illnesses caused by sick-building syndrome, computer stress.

Black Tourmaline with Lepidolite in matrix

In addition to carrying the generic properties of Black Tourmaline (page 211) and Lepidolite (page 181), Tourmaline with Lepidolite is excellent for releasing addictions and for understanding the underlying reasons. Accepting the denial that has inevitably gone on, it helps to live life without the spurious support of the addictive substance or behavior, replacing it with the love and protection of universal energies. This stone gives powerful self-healing potential.

Black Tourmaline Rod in Quartz

Crystal system Complex combination

Chemistry Complex combination

Hardness Variable

Source Worldwide

Chakra Third eye, solar plexus

Beneficial for Energy enhancement, multidimensional cellular memory healing, efficient receptor for programming, enhancing muscle testing, cleansing and enhancing the organs, protecting against radiation, protection, detoxification, removal of blockages.

Quartz (see page 230 for generic properties) containing chunky rods of Black Tourmaline (page 211) is extremely effective for neutralizing psychic attack, as it strengthens the person on the receiving end and enhances well-being. Placed in the environment to guard against terrorist attack, it can also heal the after-effects of such an attack. This stone has the ability to integrate the shadow into the whole personality and to move beyond duality.

Black Tourmaline rod in Quartz

Black Tourmaline with Mica

Crystal system Complex combination

Chemistry Complex combination

Hardness Variable

Source Worldwide

Chakra Throat

Beneficial for Debilitating disease, immune system, protection, detoxification, spinal adjustments, balancing male–female energy, paranoia, dyslexia, hand-eye coordination, assimilation and translation of coded information, energy flow, removal of blockages, illnesses caused by sick-building syndrome, computer stress.

In addition to carrying the generic properties of Black Tourmaline (page 211), Lepidolite (page 181), and Muscovite (page 31), Black Tourmaline with Mica gently returns ill-wishing to its source, subtly transformed so the perpetrator no longer puts out negative thoughts. This combination is particularly effective at nullifying electromagnetic smog and is excellent for absorbing computer emanations.

Black Tourmaline with Mica

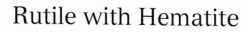

Rutile with Hematite

Crystal system	Complex combination
Chemistry	Complex combination
Hardness	Variable
Source	Africa, Australia
Chakra	Past life, soma
Beneficial for	Works at a nonphysical level.

Rutile (see page 202 for generic properties) with Hematite (page 222) brings together cleansing properties with grounding and protection. This powerfully regenerative stone assists with reconciliation and the bringing together of opposites of every kind. Whatever needs balancing in your life can be helped by this stone, and it can assist you with deep karmic and soul cleansing and repair, giving insight into psychosomatic disease.

Note: Rutile with Hematite is a high-vibration stone.

Rutile with Hematite

Ruby in Zoisite (Anyolite)

Crystal system	Complex combination
Chemistry	Complex combination
Hardness	Variable
Source	India
Chakra	Crown
Zodiac sign	Aquarius
Planet	Uranus
Beneficial for	Recovery from extended stress or chronic illness, physical vitality, fertility, testicles, ovaries, overacidity, insomnia, heart, restricted blood flow, heart, circulatory system.

Ruby (see page 55 for generic properties) in Zoisite (page 56) powerfully amplifies the biomagnetic field around the body and strengthens the life force. Assisting communication with the spirit world and inducing trance, it creates an altered state of consciousness and facilitates multidimensional cellular healing. Accessing soul memory and spiritual learning, it is extremely helpful in core soul healing and past-life work. This stone promotes individuality while at the same time retaining interconnectedness with the rest of humanity.

Raw Ruby in Zoisite

Malachite with Chrysocolla

Crystal system	Complex combination
Chemistry	Complex combination
Hardness	Variable
Source	USA, Australia, Zaire, France, Russia, Germany, Chile, New Mexico, Romania, Zambia, Congo, Middle East, UK, Mexico, Peru, Zaire
Chakra	Third eye, solar plexus
Beneficial for	Personal power, creativity, self-awareness, confidence, motivation. Works best at a subtle level.

Raw Malachite with Chrysocolla

Symbolizing wholeness and peace, the combination of Malachite (see page 96 for generic properties) with Chrysocolla (page 137) may manifest as a gemmy crystal with a very high healing vibration. Placed on an area of imbalance, it gently restores equilibrium. To restore balance to mind, body, and emotions, place one on the third eye and another on the solar plexus.

Note: Malachite with Chrysocolla is a high-vibration stone.

Tumbled Malachite with Chrysocolla

Azurite with Malachite

Crystal system	Complex combination
Chemistry	Complec combination
Hardness	Variable
Source	USA, Australia, Italy, Zaire, France, Russia, Germany, Chile, Romania, Zambia, Congo, Middle East, Peru
Chakra	Third eye, crown, higher crown
Zodiac sign	Scorpio, Sagittarius
Planet	Venus
Beneficial for	Healing crisis, the mind and mental processes, phobias, detoxification, transformation, psychosexual problems, inhibitions, rebirthing, DNA, cellular structure, immune system. If palpitations occur, remove immediately.

A powerful conductor of energy, the combination of Azurite (see page 142 for generic properties) and Malachite (page 96) unlocks spiritual vision, strengthens the ability to visualize, and opens the third eye. At an emotional level it brings deep healing, cleansing ancient blocks, miasms, or thought patterns. It overcomes muscle cramps and fortifies and detoxifies the liver.

Tumbled Azurite with Malachite

Glossary

Akashic Record
Storehouse existing beyond time and space with information on all that has occurred, and will occur, in the universe.

Amorphous
With no particular shape to confine it, energy flows rapidly through amorphous crystals. They are strong-acting and instant in their effect.

Ancestral line
The means by which family patterns and beliefs are inherited from previous generations.

Angelic realm
The energetic level where angels are said to be found.

Ascended Masters
Highly evolved spiritual beings, who may or may not previously have been incarnated, who guide the spiritual evolution of the earth.

Ascension process
The means by which people on earth seek to raise their spiritual and physical vibrations.

Astral travel
The soul is able to leave the physical body behind and travel to distant locations. Also known as out-of-body experience or soul journeying.

Attached entities
Spirit forms attached to the aura of a living person.

Aura
The biomagnetic sheath or etheric body around the body, comprising the emotional, mental, and spiritual subtle bodies.

Ball (sphere)
A spherical crystal emits energy in all directions equally. A window to the past or future, it moves energy through time and provides a glimpse of what is to come, or what has been.

Between-lives state
In esoteric thought, the vibratory state in which the soul resides between incarnations.

Cellular memory
Cells carry a memory of past-life or ancestral attitudes, trauma, and patterns that have become deeply ingrained as ongoing negative programs, such as mortification of the flesh or poverty consciousness, which create disease or are replayed in the present in slightly different forms.

Chakra
An energy linkage point between the physical and subtle bodies, seen by a clairvoyant eye as a whirling pool of energy. Malfunction can lead to physical, emotional, mental, or spiritual disease or disturbance.
- Earth: Between the feet, linkage point to the earth.
- Base: At the perineum, one of the sexual and creative centers.
- Sacral: Just below the navel, the other sexual and creative center.
- Solar plexus: The emotional center.
- Spleen: Under the left armpit, potential site of energy leakage.
- Heart: Over the physical heart, the love center.
- Higher heart: Over the thymus, center of immunity.
- Throat: Over the physical throat, center of truth.
- Past life: Just behind the ears, stores past-life information.
- Third eye: Midway between the eyebrows and the hairline. Center of spiritual sight and insight.
- Soma: At the hairline above the third eye, center of spiritual identity and consciousness activation.
- Crown: At the top of the head, the spiritual connection point.
- Higher crown: Above the crown, linkage points for spirit.

Channeling
The process whereby information is passed from a soul not in incarnation to or through an incarnate being.

Christ consciousness
The state in which all life forms of the universe are linked in universal love and awareness, the highest manifestation of divine energy.

Clairaudience
Hearing with the metaphysical ear rather than the physical one; hearing what is inaudible to physical hearing.

Cluster

Small, or large, crystals that radiate out from a base pulse energy to the surrounding environment. Clusters also absorb detrimental energy. This formation can be programmed and left in place to cleanse a room or act for a specific purpose.

Companion crystal

Two crystals entwined and partly growing in each other, or a small crystal that grows out of the main crystal, form a nurturing companion that provides enormous support, particularly during difficult times. They can help to better understand a relationship and to recognize how one partner can best support the other.

Cosmic consciousness

A very high state of awareness in which the subject is part of nonphysical universal energy.

Devas

Nature spirits, believed in esoteric thinking to rule over trees, rivers, mountains, etc.

Diamond window

A true diamond window facet shape is large and connected to the apex and the base, but even small diamond windows balance the spiritual and material worlds. A diamond face facilitates clarity of mind and multidimensional access. Diamond window reflects causes of disease.

Disease

The state that results from physical imbalances, blocked feelings, suppressed emotions, and negative thinking which, if not reversed, will lead to illness.

Double termination

Points at both ends radiate or absorb energy, channeling it in two directions at once. A double termination integrates spirit and matter, provides a bridge between two energy points, and breaks through blockages. Absorbing negative energy and dissolving old patterns, it assists in overcoming addictions and can integrate previously blocked parts of the Self. On the third eye, a double termination enhances telepathy.

Drusy

A minute crystal coating over a base.

Earth healing

Rectifying the distortion of the earth's energy field caused by pollution and the destruction of its resources.

Egg-shaped

Egg-shaped crystals confine and shape energy and can be used to detect and rebalance blockages in the body. If the egg has a pointed end it is a useful reflexology or acupressure tool.

Electromagnetic smog

A subtle but detectable electromagnetic field given off by power lines and electrical equipment that can have an adverse effect on sensitive people.

Emotional blueprint

A subtle energy field carrying the imprint of past- and present-life emotional experiences and attitudes, which influences the present life and may cause psychosomatic disease.

Energy implant

Thoughts or negative emotions implanted in the subtle body by outside sources.

Enhydro

A water bubble in a crystal, named from the Greek for "water," as they contain bubbles of liquid that are millions of years old. Enhydros symbolize the collective unconscious that underlies and unites everything, and can be used for deep emotional healing and transmutation.

Entity

Discarnate spirit who hangs around on a plane close to earth and may attach to an incarnate being.

Entity removal

Detaching an entity and dispatching it to the appropriate post-death place.

Etheric blueprint

The subtle program from which a physical body is constructed. It carries imprints of past-life disease or injury from which present life illness or disability can result.

Etheric body

The subtle biomagnetic sheath surrounding the physical body.

Gateway

A cup-shaped depression that is large enough to hold liquid provides a gateway to past, present, and future and other dimensions. An excellent stone for preparing a gem elixir. If the gateway is sufficiently large, another crystal can be set within it.

Generator

Six faces meeting equally in a sharp point generate energy and focus healing energy. A generator cluster radiates long points in all directions, each of which can be programmed for a specific purpose.

Geode

A hollow sphere with many crystals pointing inward, a geode holds and amplifies energy, diffusing the effect slowly, and softening the energy but not neutralizing it. Geodes are useful for protection and aid spiritual growth. They are beneficial for addictive or overindulgent personas.

Geopathic stress

Earth stress created by energy disturbance from underground water, power lines, and ley lines.

Grids/gridding

Placing crystals around a building, person, or place for energy enhancement or protection.

Grounding

Creating a strong connection between one's soul, physical body, and the earth.

House clearing

Removing entities and negative energies from a house.

Implants

Energies or devices implanted by aliens. Implants may also be thoughts, blockages, or scars created by an outside source in the present or a previous life.

Indigo children

Children who are, allegedly, born with a higher vibration than those already on earth. These children often have extreme difficulty adjusting to the present earth vibration.

Inner child

The part of the personality that remains childlike (but not necessarily childish) and innocent, or that may be the repository of abuse and trauma that requires healing.

Inner levels

The levels of being that encompass intuition, metaphysical awareness, emotions, feelings, the subconscious mind, and subtle energies.

Journeying

Traveling out of body through the spiritual or other worlds.

Karma of grace

When sufficient work has been done, the karma can be released and no longer operates.

Karmic

Experiences or lessons arising from or appertaining to a past incarnation. Debts, beliefs, and emotions such as guilt can be carried over into the present life and create disease.

Key crystal

A key crystal has an indentation in one of its sides that narrows as it penetrates the crystal and provides a doorway to unlock parts of the Self that are normally kept hidden. It is an excellent tool for letting go of anything that holds the soul back and for tie-cutting.

Kundalini

An inner, subtle spiritual and sexual energy that resides at the base of the spine but can be stimulated to rise to the crown chakra.

Layered

Platelike crystals work multidimensionally as they spread energy out in layers and get to the bottom of things.

Lemuria

In esoteric thought, a very early civilization predating Atlantis.

Life-path crystal

A long, thin Clear Quartz crystal with one or more absolutely smooth sides leads you to your spiritual destiny, accessing your life purpose and teaching how to go with the flow and follow your bliss. This stone teaches you to be led by what your soul wants, not your ego.

Long point

Focusing energy in a straight line, a long point is often mimicked in manufactured crystal wands. It rapidly transmits energy if pointed toward the body, or draws it off if turned away.

Manifestation crystal

A manifestation crystal has one or more small crystals totally enclosed by a larger crystal and, when properly programmed, manifests your desires.

Mental influences

The effect of other people's thoughts and opinions on your mind.

Meridian

A subtle energy channel that runs close to the surface of the skin, or the planet, that contains acupuncture points.

Metaphysical abilities

Abilities such as clairvoyance, telepathy, healing.

Metaphysical vampirism

A person's ability to draw off or "feed on" the energy of others.

Miasm

The subtle imprint of an infectious disease or traumatic event from the past that has been passed down through a family or place.

Mortification practices

Many monastic orders or religious people undertook practices such as scourging or wearing a hair shirt that were designed to mortify the flesh, ego, or spirit and subdue passions and desires. Such practices can lead to or attract psychological mortification or humiliation by yourself or others in the present life.

Multidimensional healing

Healing that occurs at multiple levels, including but not limited to the physical, cellular, neurological, psychic, emotional, mental, ancestral, karmic, spiritual and higher spiritual, planetary and stellar, terrestrial and extraterrestrial levels, which can travel along a time line and work on the etheric blueprint of the body, earth, or universe to create total balance and wholeness.

Muscle testing

A method of using the body's response to test for efficacy.

Negative emotional programming

"Oughts" and "shoulds" and emotions such as guilt that have been instilled, often in childhood or other lives, remain in the subconscious mind and influence present behavior, sabotaging effects to evolve until released.

NLP (neurolinguistic programming)

A system for reprogramming the mind and behavior based on hypnotherapy techniques.

Occlusion or inclusion

A mineral deposit within or upon a crystal.

Planetary grid

The subtle and invisible earth energy lines that cover the planet rather like a spider web.

Pleochroic crystal

A crystal appearing to have two or more colors from different angles or light.

Points

Crystal points meet in a sharp termination and are often used in healing. Placed away from the body, a point draws energy off. Pointed inward, it channels energy to the body.

Projection

Disliking in others characteristics we cannot accept are actually part of ourselves.

Psychic attack

Malevolent thoughts or feelings toward another person, whether consciously or unconsciously directed, that create disease and disruption in that person's life.

Psychic vampirism

A person's ability to draw off or "feed on" the energy of others.

Psychopomp

A Greek word for the conductor of a soul through the process of death and into the other world. A psychopomp may be a living person or a spiritual being.

Pyramid

Four sides on a base meeting at a point create a pyramid, but the base may be squared off if the crystal is natural rather than artificially shaped. Naturally occurring pyramid-shaped crystals, such as Apophyllite, amplify and then tightly focus energy through the apex and program well. Pyramids can also be used to draw off negative energies and blockages from the chakras, replenishing energy.

Qi

The life force that energizes the physical and subtle bodies.

Radionic

A method of diagnosis and treatment from a distance.

Reframing

Returning to see a past event in a different, more positive light, so that the situation it is creating in the present life can be healed.

Reiki

A natural hands-on method of healing.

Scry

To discern images in a crystal relating to past, present, or future events.

Self

The Self encompasses both the incarnated personal self and the nonincarnated higher self (the highest vibration of the overall Self). The higher self can influence and communicate with the personal self. Self is also part of the soul.

Self-healed

A self-healed crystal has many small terminations where it has been broken from its base and laid down fresh crystals. This wounded healer facilitates self-healing, teaching how to become whole again no matter how damaged and wounded one may have been.

Sheet crystal

A flat sheet of Quartz, usually between long points, is sheet Quartz. Providing a window into other dimensions, facilitating communication, accessing the Akashic Record, sheet Quartz contacts relevant past lives and enhances visualization.

Silver cord

In esoteric thought, the linkage between the physical and etheric body that goes from the third eye of the physical body to the back of the head of the etheric body.

Soul

The vehicle for carrying the eternal spirit. Soul parts are part of the soul not presently in incarnation, which can include but are not limited to soul fragments that split off (see also Soul retrieval).

Soul group

A cluster of souls who have traveled together throughout time, all or some of whom are in incarnation.

Soul links

The connections between members of a soul group.

Soulmate

A soulmate appears to be an ideal "other half," a soul partner with whom there is rapport on all levels. However, many soulmate connections carry karma to be dealt with, or difficult soul lessons. Soulmate relationships may not be intended to last a lifetime, nor are they necessarily between sexual partners.

Soul retrieval

Trauma, shock, or abuse, and even extreme joy, can cause a part of the soul energy to leave and remain stuck. A soul retrieval practitioner or shaman retrieves the soul part from wherever it may be, bringing it back to the present life body.

Spiral crystal

A spiral has a distinct twist down its axis that draws universal energy into the body. Beneficial for maintaining balance at any level, it clears energy blockages and entities and raises kundalini.

Spirit guides

Discarnate beings who work from the between-lives state to provide assistance to those on the earth.

Spirit releasement

Souls can become trapped close to the earth; spirit releasement sends them home.

Square

Consolidating energy within its form, a square is useful for anchoring intention and for grounding. Naturally occurring square crystals such as Fluorite draw off negative energy and transform it.

Star children

Evolved beings from other planetary systems who have incarnated on the earth to help its spiritual evolution.

Subtle bodies

The layers of the biomagnetic sheath: the subtle energetic bodies that surround the physical body.

Subtle energy field

The invisible but detectable energy field that surrounds all living beings.

Tabby (tabular)

Energy flows quickly through a long, flat Tabby crystal configuration, as it offers little resistance.

Thought forms

Forms created by strong positive or negative thoughts that exist on etheric or spiritual levels, affecting mental functions.

Triple heater meridian

One of the meridians concerned with temperature control.

Twinflame

A soulmate without karma attached. The person with whom you are meant to be in the present life for unconditional mutual support, evolution, and love. Spiritual twinflames have often been together in many previous lives.

"Vogel-type" wand

Vogel and Vogel-type wands have a precise vibratory signature. Specially crafted, indented facets with specific angles create an efficient healing tool with a high, pure vibration. Powers and properties of Vogels vary with the number of faces. The broader end is "female" and attracts pranic energy, which is amplified as it spirals through the facets. The thinner "male" point transmits energy in a strongly focused laserlike beam. Vogels connect chakras, removing entities and negativity. They detect and rectify energy blockages and strongly cohere the energy fields around and within the body, but are best used after appropriate training.

Wands

Most wands are artificially shaped, but naturally formed, long-pointed crystals such as Laser Quartz or Tourmaline rods make excellent healing tools. Traditional tools of shamans, healers, and metaphysicians and the magic wands of myth and legend, wands have the ability to focus energy tightly through their tip, and the healing effect is enhanced when programmed with intent. When pulling stagnant or diseased energy out of the body or the aura, gently rotate and lift away and out. Cleanse the wand before using it to heal and seal the resultant "hole."

Wealth corner

The farthest back-left corner from the front door.

Yin and yang

The complementary positive and negative forces that hold the universe in place.

Index

Bibliography

Hall, Judy, New Crystals and Healing Stones (Godsfield Press, London, 2006)

Hall, Judy, The Crystal Bible (Godsfield Press, London, 2003)

Hall, Judy, Crystal Healing (Godsfield Press, London, 2005)

Hall, Judy, Crystal Prescriptions (O Books, Alresford, 2005)

Hall, Judy, The Illustrated Guide to Crystals (Godsfield Press, London, 2000)

Hall, Judy, Crystal Users Handbook (Godsfield Press, London, 2002)

Hall, Judy, The Art of Psychic Protection (Samuel Weiser, Maine, 1997)

Marion, Joseph B. Indium: New Mineral Discovery of the 21st Century (Pioneers Publishers, 2003)

Melody, Love Is In The Earth (Earth Love Publishing House, Colorado, 1995 with supplements A-Z)

The Thomas Warren Museum of Fluorescence (http://sterlinghill.org/warren/aboutfluorescence.htm)

Raven, Hazel, Heal yourself with Crystals (Godsfield Press, London, 2005)

Acknowledgments

Author acknowledgments

I would like to acknowledge the pioneering work of Melody, it is always such a joy to me when my findings accord with hers. I would like to thank Sue and Simon Lilly for their friendship and support. The staff of Earthworks, Poole (www.earthworksuk.com), Clive at Earth Design in Beaminster, David Spiller of Natural Wonders in Swanage and Debbie of Art and Soul in Petersfield have been extremely helpful in sourcing crystals and in sharing their own knowledge of the stones. Dawn, Jo, Teresa and Jacki were immensely helpful and great fun to be with when exploring the new crystals. Tina Biles (www.crystalmaster.co.uk) was generous in her introduction to Desirite and its properties and sourcing other stones, and John (www.exquisitecrystals.com) brought a new vibration into my life with his gift of Flame Aura Spirit Quartz. Participants on my workshops have also contributed greatly to my knowledge and I send them love and blessings. Komilla Sutton was extremely helpful with her knowledge of Vedic gems. Finally, I could not work with crystals and much else besides without Crystal Clear and Clear Light, the ultimate cleansing tools, for which I thank David Eastoe (estoe@yahoo.com).

Publisher's acknowledgments

Thank you to Earthworks (www.earthworksuk.com), Tina and Jon of Crystal Master (www.crystalmaster.co.uk), Gary of Avalon Crystals (www.avaloncrystals.co.uk) and Marcus McCallum (www.marcusmccallum.com) for generously lending us their crystals and stones for photography.

Picture acknowledgments

Photography: © Octopus Publishing Group Ltd/Andy Komorowski. Other photography: Corbis UK Ltd/Robert Holmes 12. Octopus Publishing Group Ltd 5 top, 22 top left, 22 bottom right, 22 bottom left, 23 top, 26 top, 30 top, 31 top, 32 top left, 33 bottom right, 36 bottom left, 45 bottom, 46 bottom, 50, 59 top left, 59 center right, 59 bottom, 60 top left, 79 top right, 80 right, 82 top left, 84 left, 89 top right, 90 top, 96 bottom right, 97 top, 97 bottom, 98 top, 120 top right, 120 bottom right, 123 left, 130 top, 133 top right, 134 top left, 137 top, 138 left, 143 bottom, 145 left, 147 top, 151 top right, 153 left, 155 bottom right, 157 top right, 159 bottom right, 162 center right, 164 center right, 172 right, 173, 175 left, 176 top left, 181 center left, 183 left, 183 right, 186 bottom right, 190 left, 191 right, 198 right, 201 bottom, 203 top, 204 top, 205 right, 207, 212 left, 214, 215 top, 215 bottom, 216 right, 231 right, 241 left, 246 center right, 247 bottom, 248 top left, 251 top left, 255 bottom, 256 left, 256 right, 258 right, 261; /Walter Gardiner 231 left; /Mike Hemsley 13 center right, 35 top, 37 bottom, 39 bottom, 47 center right, 54 bottom left, 56, 60 center right, 61 bottom right, 61 bottom left, 76 bottom, 81 top, 84 right, 92 bottom right, 107 bottom, 115 bottom, 116 left, 122 right, 124 right, 127 top, 132 left, 142 top left, 156 left, 158 left, 164 top left, 164 bottom left, 174 left, 175 right, 180 left, 181 top right, 194 top, 199 left, 199 top right, 201 top, 203 bottom, 213 top, 217 bottom, 221 top, 221 bottom, 222 left, 230 right, 235 bottom, 242 left, 243 left, 243 right, 247 top, 252 left, 252 top right, 252 bottom right, 260, 262 left, 268 left, 270 right, 271 left, 271 bottom right, 272 center right, 272 bottom right, 272 bottom left, 273 top left, 273 top right, 273 center right, 273 bottom right; /Mike Prior 17 left, 17 right, 18 top, 162 top left, 168 left, 186 top right; /Guy Ryecart 3 picture 9, 3 picture 3, 13 picture 3, 26 bottom, 28 top, 28 bottom, 31 bottom, 40 top left, 44 top, 45 top, 47 top left, 49 top right, 51 bottom, 55 center right, 58 top right, 59 top, 63 bottom, 64 top, 66 top, 67 bottom, 72 top left, 72 top right, 72 bottom right, 80 left, 81 center left, 81 bottom, 82 bottom right, 86 center left, 86 bottom right, 87 bottom, 88 bottom right, 91 top right, 91 center right, 96 top right, 99 top right, 100 left, 101 left, 101 right, 103, 105 left, 111, 112 left, 117 left, 117 top right, 117 center right, 118 bottom right, 120 top left, 120 bottom left, 121 top, 121 bottom, 122 left, 125 right, 126 right, 127 bottom, 133 bottom right, 134 bottom left, 136 bottom right, 137 bottom, 138 right, 139 left, 142 right, 148 bottom right, 149 top, 151 left, 151 bottom right, 155 bottom left, 157 bottom right, 159 left, 160 left, 160 right, 163 right, 177 left, 179 bottom right, 182 left, 194 bottom, 195 bottom, 199 center right, 200 center right, 202 left, 206 left, 206 right, 210 left, 211, 212 top right, 213 bottom, 216 left, 218 left, 219 top, 222 right, 223 left, 224 right, 227 bottom right, 230 top left, 236 left, 241 bottom, 242 right, 248 bottom left, 257, 269 left, 269 right, 271 top right, 273 center left; /Walter Gardiner Photography 22 top right, 134 bottom right. Tema Hecht 16 bottom right.

Executive Editor Sandra Rigby
Managing Editor Clare Churly
Executive Art Editor Sally Bond
Designer Patrick McLeavey
Picture Library Manager Jennifer Veall
Production Manager Louise Hall